Elizabeth Pomada

FUN PLACES
to Go with
Children in

Northern California
8th EDITION

CHRONICLE BOOKS
SAN FRANCISCO

Library of Congress Cataloging-in-Publication Data:
Pomada, Elizabeth.
    Fun places to go with children in Northern California / by Elizabeth Pomada. – 8th ed.
        p.   cm.
    Includes index.
    ISBN 0-8118-1514-5 (pb)
    1. California, Northern–Guidebooks.   2. Family recreation–California, Northern–Guidebooks.   I. Title.
    F867.5.P658   1997
    917.94–dc21   96-50133
                                                              CIP
Printed in the United States of America.

Cover design: Martine Trélaün
Cover photograph: Elizabeth McCullough/Photonica
Book design: Karen Smidth
Composition: Words & Deeds

Distributed in Canada by Raincoast Books
8680 Cambie Street
Vancouver, B.C. V6P 6M9

10 9 8 7 6 5 4 3 2 1

Chronicle Books
85 Second Street
San Francisco, CA 94105

Web Site: www.chronbooks.com

Contents

Needless to say, this book was not done by just one person. I must say "thank you" to Lauren and Jennifer, Elizabeth and Deborah, Diana and Marc, Eric and Chris, Cindy and Christopher, and Alan, our "test" children. But most of all, thank you to my pal, editor, chauffeur, idea man, hero, and the biggest child of them all—M.F.L.   *E.P.*

After living in New York City for 30 years, Elizabeth Pomada moved to San Francisco. She learned about Northern California by traveling over 4,000 miles of it to write *Fun Places to Go with Children in Northern California*. Her other books include *California Publicity Outlets*, now published as *Metro California Media*. She and her partner, Michael Larsen, have created the Painted Ladies® series: *Painted Ladies: San Francisco's Resplendent Victorians*; *Daughters of Painted Ladies: America's Resplendent Victorians*; *How to Create Your Own Painted Lady*; *Painted Ladies Revisited: San Francisco's Painted Ladies Inside and Out*; *The Painted Ladies' Guide to Victorian California*; *America's Painted Ladies: The Ultimate Guide to Our Resplendent Victorians*; and the *Painted Ladies Calendars*. Michael and Elizabeth also run the oldest literary agency in San Francisco.

A Word Before You Go

HERE, BIGGER AND I HOPE better than ever, is the eighth edition of *Fun Places to Go with Children in Northern California*. The countryside is as gorgeous and varied as ever, and it was a pleasure exploring again, both to check on places already in the book and to find new discoveries to share with you.

Maybe it's just provincial pride, but Michael, my husband, and I think that the ocean, rivers, trees, sunshine, mountains—all of the breathtaking beauty and richness that Northern California has been blessed with—make it one of the most beautiful areas on earth. More remarkable still is that so much of it has been protected or left in its natural state for us to marvel at.

We were pleased to find that the interest in preserving the state's colorful historical heritage continues to gain momentum. More museums and historic houses than ever dot the landscape. We believe that if you and your children can learn something and have fun at the same time, then the good time is worth twice as much. Most of the places listed here are enjoyable no matter how old you are.

For this edition of *Fun Places*, we've added a recommended age range for each attraction. These are included as my opinion of the optimal age range for each place; you'll find them in bold in the listings.

Practically all of the locations in *Fun Places* have wheelchair access— indicated with a "W" at the end of the entries—and almost all of the attractions with educational value present special tours for schools and other groups. Just call to arrange your tour.

Most of the nonprofit institutions have gift shops, the sales from which help to sustain museums and nature centers. If you are pleased with what you see, these shops are one way of showing your support. Often a nonprofit will not charge for entrance, but a small donation will be gratefully accepted. If you see a "Donation" listing instead of a fee for a particular site, please support them with a contribution, if you can.

Most of the nonprofit attractions are staffed largely by volunteers. If you live in the area, another way of showing your support and making new friends is helping out. Some places even have volunteer programs for children, which will be learning experiences for the kids and might even lead to a career.

The goal of *Fun Places* is to include every attraction and special event in Northern California that youngsters and the young at heart will enjoy. Since the book concentrates on *places to visit* rather than things to do, playgrounds and activities such as bowling, skateboarding, skiing, skating, shooting pool, and miniature golf generally aren't included. So if a waterslide or balloon site is mentioned in one area, and that sounds like a good idea to you, check the local Yellow Pages to see if there's one nearby. One adventure may lead to another.

I hope that you will help to make the next edition even better. Please write to me at 1029 Jones Street, San Francisco 94109, or call me at (415) 673-0939 if you find an attraction that should be included, or if you think of a way to make *Fun Places* more helpful to parents and teachers. I'd like to create a dialogue around *Fun Places*, so it will continue to improve. This edition has benefited from the many people who have contacted us.

To make the next edition even better, I'll be happy to send an autographed copy of the new edition to the first person to suggest a new place or one we have overlooked for future publications.

If you have any unusual experiences, good or bad, at one of the places in this book, I'd like to know about them. Also, if your children or students write anything memorable about the places they visit, I would like to see it—and perhaps quote them in the next edition. We've included comments from youngsters when it's seemed appropriate. After all, a book for children should have input from children!

The book is arranged with downtown San Francisco as a starting point, with you traveling out from there, first in nearby neighborhoods, then out around San Francisco by county and region.

Prices go up and schedules change, especially in winter and on holidays, so if you're going far, call for up-to-the-minute information and driving and lodging tips. Most places are closed on Thanksgiving, Christmas, and New Year's Day. Local chambers of commerce, tourist offices, and the American Automobile Association will also help you plan your trip. And don't forget to stock the car with drinks, travel snacks and games, books and books on tape, tissues, wet wipes, and a lot of good humor. While driving, we also like to play alphabet, cow count, and license plate state spotting.

I hope that you will enjoy *Fun Places* and the places it inspires you to visit. Bon voyage!

Northern California's Top 11 Places

1. Monterey Aquarium
2. San Francisco Exploratorium
3. Yosemite National Park
4. Oakland Museum
5. Marine World Africa USA, Vallejo
6. Santa Cruz Boardwalk
7. Lawrence Hall of Science, Berkeley
8. San Francisco Zoo
9. California State Railroad Museum, Old Sacramento
10. Point Reyes National Seashore
11. Ardenwood Historic Farm, Fremont

To which I add my personal favorites:
1. John Muir House, Martinez
2. Columbia State Historic Park
3. San Juan Bautista State Historic Park
4. Rosicrucian Museum, San Jose
5. Jack London State Historic Park, Glen Ellen
6. Lachryma Montis, General Vallejo's Home, Sonoma State Historic Park
7. San Francisco Historic Ships at Hyde Street Pier

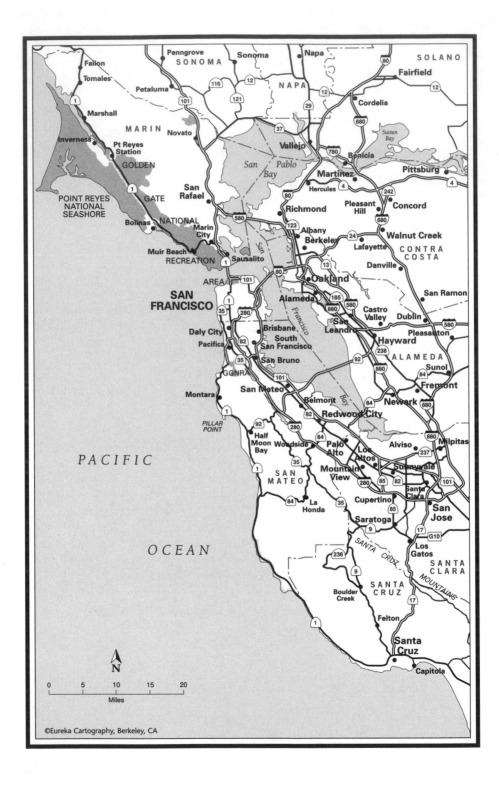

San Francisco and the Bay Area

San Francisco

San Francisco has been called a peninsula bounded on three sides by water and on one side by reality. What makes the City special? It's both large and small. At about 750,000 people, it's small for a major city. Yet it has the amenities of any great city: opera, ballet, theater, a symphony, shopping galore, and restaurants that will please any palate.

San Francisco is a unique blend of elements:

- a beautiful natural setting
- cool, fair weather
- a history that makes up in color what it lacks in length
- a rich multicultural heritage that makes the City hospitable to new people, ideas, and lifestyles
- old and new architecture, with the greatest, most beautiful collection of redwood Victorians in the world (The famous "postcard row" of Painted Ladies standing in front of a view of downtown's skyscrapers is on Alamo Square, Steiner and Hayes Streets.)
- a collection of distinct neighborhoods worthy of wandering and exploration
- a world-class mixture of education, business, culture, and religion that attracts visitors and immigrants from all over the world
- a size small enough to walk around in yet large enough to provide kids of all ages with plenty of things to see and do.

Consider transportation. You can see San Francisco by foot, bicycle, moped, car, taxi, bus (single or double decker), cable car (regular or motorized), trolley car, subway, helicopter, ferry, sailboat, and even by blimp!

Riding the cable car up and down hills can be more fun than Disneyland.

Hungry? San Francisco provides an excellent opportunity to expand your children's enjoyment of the world's cuisines. The first ten blocks of Clement Street in the Richmond District offer the most cosmopolitan concentration of delectable food we know of anywhere. Here, you can feast on Chinese food (including dim sum dumplings as well as Cantonese, Mandarin, Shanghai, Hakka and Hunan cooking), Japanese, Italian, Indonesian, French, Russian, Persian, Vietnamese, Irish, Thai, and health food, barbecue and other American food.

San Francisco suffers from the same problems as any metropolis, but the City's size, human-scale architecture (outside of our mini-Manhattan downtown), and sunny weather give urban blights a more benign quality.

The City has a remarkable capacity for self-renewal. Although still largely populated by the poor and the nefarious, the Tenderloin is being revitalized by Vietnamese immigrants. Kids are playing in the streets, and new stores and restaurants have sprouted up, adding another neighborhood to the City's rich ethnic mix.

Much of the best of what the City has to offer is free. More than one-third of the attractions in this chapter are free. San Francisco is a walker's paradise. Just strolling around Golden Gate Park or the City's neighborhoods—Chinatown, Japantown, the Mission, the Haight, Noe Valley, Clement Street, Union Street, or anywhere on the waterfront from Land's End to the Embarcadero—on a sunny, breezy day is delightful.

For views, try the free ride on the outside elevator to the Crown Room at the top of the Fairmont Hotel, one of the best free rides in the world. Or stop by Coit Tower on the top of Telegraph Hill. The observation platform at the top is 210 feet high (open daily, 9–4:30. $3). Take the 39 bus to the top of Telegraph Hill (673-6864 for information) to avoid parking problems.

San Francisco's newest "view" destination is the SF SkyDeck Observation Platform (41st floor, Embarcadero One Building at Battery between Clay and Sacramento. 800-733-6318. Wed.–Fri., 5–10; Sat. & Sun., 10–10. Adults, $4; seniors & students, $3.50; ages 5–12, $3) with a 360-degree view. The indoor and outdoor viewing platforms also offer multimedia presentations on the history and culture of San Francisco.

Upon climbing the nearby Greenwich Street steps and discovering a flock of green parrots escaped from North Beach homes, 14-year-old Sam, honoring novelist Ray Bradbury, wrote:

"And then I saw them, perching
on the telephone wires above my head.
Green they were, and red-faced."

Take the family on a "Hollywood Tour"—walking down Lombard Street, "The Crookedest Street in the World"; "flying" down Jones between Union and Filbert, or Filbert between Hyde and Leavenworth, pretending to be in the car chase in *The Rock;* driving to the southeast corner of Broadway and Pierce Streets to see "Mrs. Doubtfire's" house; and ending at Land's End under the Golden Gate Bridge where Kim Novak jumped in *Vertigo.*

Unless you hit one of the City's few hot days, the temperature is usually in the low 60s. So the layered look, which enables you to peel off a jacket or sweater if it gets toasty, is always appropriate.

The pink section in the Sunday *Chronicle,* the entertainment pages, will fill you in on special events that are taking place while you are in town.

Whether you live in the City or are just visiting, whether you are young or just young at heart, whether you want cultural enrichment or just plain fun, San Francisco is one of the best places in the world to spend a week or a lifetime. So, as they say these days: "Go for it!"

❥ International Children's Art Museum

World Trade Center (Ferry Building), Suite 103, San Francisco 94111
(415) 772-9977. Mon.–Fri., 11–5. Free. **Ages 5 & up.** *W.*

What started with the idea of children around the world communicating through art and letters has evolved into a collection of over 5,000 works. The schoolchildren exchange packets based on a theme, such as "Sports & Games," "Fairytales of My Country," "The Global Family," or "Inventions, Inventors, & Imagination." The gallery then mounts an exhibit on that theme. Children from over 100 countries are represented.

❥ Golden Gate Ferry to Larkspur or Sausalito

San Francisco Ferry Terminal, San Francisco 94111. Behind the Ferry Building at the foot of Market Street. (415) 923-2000. Telecommunication Device for the Deaf, TDD: (415) 257-4554. Ferries run daily to/from Larkspur and Sausalito in Marin County. Call for up-to-date fares and schedules. Bicycles OK. One-way weekday fares to Larkspur: adults, $2.50; ages 6–12, $1.90; seniors & disabled, $1.25. One-way fares to Sausalito and one-way weekend & holiday fares to Larkspur: adults, $4.25; ages 6–12, $3.20; seniors & disabled, $2.10. Weekdays: kids 5 and under ride free, two per adult. Weekends & holidays: kids 12 and under ride free, two per adult.

The Golden Gate Ferry leaves its slip at the foot of Market Street, passes Alcatraz Island, and docks across the bay. The snack bar serves coffee and snacks, and whether it's sunny or foggy, the views are wonderful. Take a camera.

❥ Jewish Museum of San Francisco

121 Steuart Street, off Mission, San Francisco 94103. (415) 543-8880. Sun., 11–6; Mon.–Wed., 12–6; Thurs., 12–8. Adults, $5; seniors and those under 12, $2.50. First Monday of the month, free. Gift shop. **Ages 5 & up.** *W.*

This museum features exhibitions of historical artifacts and art that focus on Jewish tradition and culture. Explore questions and issues regarding traditional American Jewish identities on guided tours for kindergarten through high school. Kids love seeing the art done by other children on earlier visits.

⇶ San Francisco Museum of Modern Art

151 Third Street, at Mission, San Francisco 94103. (415) 357-4000/ TDD: (415) 357-4154. Fri.–Tues., 11–6; Thurs. 11–9. Museum Store: daily, 10:30–6:30; Thurs. until 9:30 p.m. Caffe Museo: Tues.–Sun., 10–6; Thurs. until 9. Adults, $7; seniors & students, $3.50; children under 13 w/adult, free. First Tuesday of each month, free for all. http://www.sfmoma.org. **Ages 10 & up.** *W.*

SFMOMA offers constantly changing exhibits of paintings, sculpture, works of art on paper, and photography. The permanent collection includes works by Matisse, Jackson Pollock, Franz Kline, San Franciscans Wayne Thiebaud and Clyfford Still, and an in-your-face sculpture self-portrait by Robert Arneson, "California Artist." There are many who feel that children are best able to view modern art, because they're open to everything, with no preconceived ideas about what art should be. We are inclined to agree. There is a small interactive CD-ROM computer section for school groups and kids of all ages. Educational programs include "Making Sense of Modern Art."

SFMOMA is the centerpiece of the **Yerba Buena Gardens,** an urban park with theaters, restaurants, cafes, gardens, and galleries including the **Center for the Arts,** where themed exhibits change every three months (701 Mission Street. 415-978-2727. Tues–Sun., 11–6; until 8 on the first Thurs. of the month—admission free after 6. Seniors free on Thurs., 11–3. Adults $4; students and seniors, $2; kids free).

⇶ California Historical Society

678 Mission, near Third Street, San Francisco 94105. (415) 357-1848. Tues.–Sat., 11–5. Adults, $3; seniors & students, $1; under 6, free. Bookstore. **Ages 8 & up.** *W.*

The California Historical Society's museum/gallery has opened in the historic Hundley Hardware Building. The first exhibit, "Happy Valley to South of the Slot: Transitions in a San Francisco Neighborhood," celebrated the history of the museum's new neighborhood, now part of the Yerba Buena Gardens area. My nephew and I loved the exhibits on the City's firefighters, the lithographs of San Francisco when people still lived in tents, and the pictures of Kate Douglas Wiggin, the author of *Rebecca of Sunnybrook Farm,* who started the first kindergarten in California. Yearly exhibits will be "love letters" to sections of, or areas of interest in,

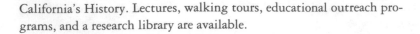

California's History. Lectures, walking tours, educational outreach programs, and a research library are available.

➤ Society of California Pioneers

300 Fourth Street, near Mission, San Francisco 94103. (415) 957-1849.
Ages 8 & up. *Scheduled to open in Summer 1997. W.*

Although the exhibits were still in the process of being designed and assembled at this writing, we were assured that there will be a Children's History Gallery designed to enhance the fourth-grade California history curriculum, along with videos, interactive exhibits, toys, musical instruments, clothes and tools from California's Hispanic and Gold Rush periods.

Also scheduled to open is the **Children's Center** (on top of Moscone Convention Center South). The Complex will include a 10,000-square-foot child care center, a 25,000-square-foot "Children's Place," an activities and cultural center with interactive learning centers, a theater, multimedia lobby, store, workshop, a one-and-a-half-acre garden with interactive creative and play opportunities, a huge skating rink, a 12-lane bowling center, and the newly restored Old Playland carousel.

➤ Cartoon Art Museum

814 Mission Street, San Francisco 94103. (415) CAR-TOON. Wed.–Fri., 11–5; Sat., 10–5; Sun., 1–5, and by appt. Adults, $4; students & seniors, $3; children, $2. Parties. **Ages 6 & up.** *W.*

Original art from cartoon strips, ads, comic books, sports and editorial cartoons, and greeting cards is treated as fine art in the only museum west of the Mississippi dedicated to Cartoon Art. Here visitors will see work by Charles Schultz, Gahan Wilson, Jim Davis, R. Crumb, Art Spiegelman, and dozens of other favorite cartoonists from the past and present. Film and video cartoons are shown as well. The children's museum and interactive CD-ROM gallery with Power Mac stations will attract kids of all ages. The museum also offers Educational Outreach programs that stimulate creativity, literacy, and self-expression through the use of cartoons and comics.

➤ World of Oil

555 Market Street, San Francisco 94105. (415) 894-6697. Mon.–Fri., 8:30–4:30. Group tours by appt. Free. **Ages 7 & up.** *W.*

If you've ever wondered how oil is found, produced, transformed into thousands of products, and used for energy, heat, and lubrication, this is the place to come.

Tapes, films, an energy quiz, and interactive displays show junior scientists how oil was obtained and used in the past. Photos, drilling and rigging tools, and models of offshore wells are eye-openers. Three life-size dioramas show the role oil has played in American life. The first service station and the 1910 kitchen have a nostalgic appeal.

❖ Federal Reserve Bank

101 Market Street, San Francisco 94105. (415) 974-3252. Mon.–Fri., 9–4. Tours by reservation for those in 8th grade and older. Free. **Ages 12 & up.**

The World of Economics, a classy, block-long permanent exhibit in the lobby of the Federal Reserve Bank, teaches all about money and the economy. Press a button to see how money is created; watch a videotape to understand supply and demand. A computer game allows you to be a pretend mogul. Another computer helps you design your own monetary policy. The Economic Time Line mural introduces you to economic theorists such as Karl Marx and Adam Smith.

❖ The Jungle

555 Ninth Street, between Brannan & Bryant, above Toys 'R' Us, San Francisco. (415) 552-4FUN. Sun.–Thurs., 10–8; Fri., 10–9; Sat., 9–9. Mon.–Fri., before 5 P.M., $4.95. Mon.–Thurs., after 5, $2.95. Fri., Sat., Sun., $5.95 for two hours; toddlers, $2.95 for two hours. Adults must be on the premises. Everyone must wear socks. Free parking. Cafe. Shop. **All ages.** *W.*

The West Coast's largest indoor play facility is a two- and three-level play structure. Kids and their parents can crawl in tube tunnels, run in fun forests, soar through the air like Tarzan on track glides, climb on cargo nets, and slide and jump.

There's a separate section for toddlers and infants. The Big Game room offers 15 challenging games to play on the swings.

❖ Planet Hollywood

2 Stockton Street, between Market & O'Farrell, San Francisco 94108. (415) 421-7827. Daily, 11 A.M.–2 A.M. No Reservations. **Ages 5 & up.** *W.*

Although owners Sylvester Stallone, Bruce Willis, Arnold Schwarzenegger, and local Danny Glover are rarely on hand to greet you, kids will love downing burgers, fajitas, and pizzas (moderately priced) amid the movie memorabilia posters and artifacts from classic and favorite movies. Dirty Harry's Smith & Wesson .44 Magnum, Stallone's glittering cowboy suit from *Rhinestone,* Mary Pickford's costume as *Little Lord Fauntleroy,* a hat from *Dr. Quinn, Medicine Woman,* Warren Beatty's herringbone suit from *Reds,* a gorilla suit from *Planet of the Apes,* Peter

Sellers's shirt from *The Pink Panther,* the "Mel's" neon sign from *American Graffiti,* and the teddy bear left on the top of the Empire State Building in *Sleepless in Seattle,* are the real attractions here. Movie trailers add to the fun.

⇉ The Asawa Fountain

Grand Hyatt Hotel, 345 Stockton Street, between Sutter and Post, San Francisco 94108. Free. **All ages.**

Ruth Asawa, artist and creator of the Mermaid Fountain in Ghirardelli Square, has given the people of San Francisco a one-stop tour of the people and places that make up the City. This fountain, 14 feet in diameter, on the steps of the plaza of the Grand Hyatt on Union Square, was molded in bread dough—the same dough children use for sculpting—and cast in bronze. And the little people, trees, Chinese dragon, Painted Ladies, and school buses demand to be touched. At the bottom of the fountain is the Ferry Building; as you go around it, you'll see Coit Tower, Broadway, Aquatic Park, the Cannery, the zoo, and the Mission district. Everything is laid out in the same general direction as it is in real life. A group of Noe Valley schoolchildren created one of the fountain's 41 plaques, which depicts the children of San Francisco. Your kids will enjoy figuring out which one it is.

⇉ Museum of Money of the American West

Bank of California, 400 California Street, downstairs, San Francisco 94104. (415) 765-0400. Mon.–Fri., 9–5. Free. **Ages 8 & up.**

This tiny but nicely mounted collection of money and gold provides a glimpse of banking and mining in the Old West. Each coin is a piece of history. Privately minted coins from Utah, Colorado, and California show the kind of money used before the U.S. Mint was set up in San Francisco. Ingots, gold bullion, currency, and early bank drafts are here, along with counterfeit coins and counterfeit detectors. One method of counterfeiting, "the platinum menace," used hollowed-out coins filled with platinum, then worth much less than gold. Is that why an Oregon two-ounce copper-alloy coin reads "In Gold We Trust"?

⇉ Wells Fargo History Museum

420 Montgomery Street, San Francisco 94104. (415) 396-2619. Weekdays except bank holidays, 9–5. Group guided tours by appt. Free. Gift shop. **Ages 5 & up.** *W.*

Ever wanted to bounce along in a stagecoach? Or send a telegraph message? Or rock a gold-panning cradle? The youngsters can relive the romance of the West in this beautifully designed bilevel museum. Here you'll find gold, money, treasure boxes, art, tools, photos, a map of Black Bart's 28 stagecoach robberies, iron doors from a Wells Fargo office in the Gold Country, Pony Express memorabilia, and a rocking Concord Stage Coach with an audio tape of one young man's trip from St. Louis to San Francisco.

❋ Chinatown

A visit to San Francisco would not be complete without a visit to Chinatown, along Grant Avenue from Bush to Broadway and along Stockton Street from Sacramento to Vallejo. For the curious, there are fortune-cookie factories, fish stores, and temples, as well as shops and restaurants.

The **Golden Gate Fortune Cookie Factory** (415-781-3956. Weekdays, 10–noon) on Ross Alley, between Washington and Jackson, above Grant, sometimes leaves its doors open so you can see the row of tiny griddles revolving under a hose that squirts dough onto each pan. The pans cook the dough on their way to the cookie-maker, who picks up each browned wafer, pushes it onto a spur for the first fold, inserts the paper fortune, presses the final fold, and puts the cookie in a muffin tin to harden.

Tin Hou Temple (125 Waverly Place, Fourth Floor. 415-391-4841. 10–5 daily) is dedicated to the Queen of Heaven and boasts a ceiling filled with carved wood mythological figures. Just follow the scent of incense up the stairs.

One of our favorite lunchtime meals is *dim sum*, which means "heart's delights." With dim sum, also called Chinese tea or tea lunch, there's always something to entice every palate. Dim sum are simply little bites of good things. You choose small plates of delicacies such as shrimp rolls, curry cakes, beef dumplings, spare ribs, mushroom turnovers, custard pies, or steamed barbecued-pork buns, *bao*. Usually, you pay by the number of plates you have piled on the table. So if there are only two of you, and what you want is, for example, scallop dumplings, and they're presented on two plates, ask for a half order. That way you only get two dumplings on one plate—and have room for more tastes. In Chinatown, we recommend **Lychee Garden** on Powell, between Broadway and Stockton. Our two favorite dim sum restaurants are not in Chinatown proper. **Yank Sing** (427 Battery near Clay. 415-781-1111) has been called the best in the world. And at **Harbor Village** (#4 Embarcadero Center. 415-398-8883) you can get a peek at the bay and the Bay Bridge, then shop in the four buildings that make up Embarcadero Center.

Cultural, historical, and artistic exhibitions are presented in **The Chinese Culture Center,** the forum for the Chinese community (750

Kearny, in the Holiday Inn, third floor. 415-986-1822. Tues.–Sat., 10–4; Sun., 12–4. Gallery, ages 7 & over, free). The center is especially popular during the Chinese New Year Celebration in February. The Culinary Walks offered are fun for whole families and school groups who want to learn more about Chinatown—and they always end with a dim sum lunch.

➤ Chinese Historical Society of America

650 Commercial Street, between Montgomery & Kearny, San Francisco 94111. (415) 391-1188. Tues. & Thurs., 10–2. Donation. Gift shop. **Ages 7 & up.**

Chinese societies throughout California have contributed to this small, hidden museum to show how the Chinese have played an important part in California's development. Ceremonial swords, printing blocks, an altar, porcelain pillows, clothes worn by 19th-century laborers and the high born, opium pipes, photographs, and documents crowd the display space. There are changing exhibits, such as one on the first women to vote in America and another on the first telephone system in San Francisco.

Pacific Heritage Museum

608 Commercial Street, between Montgomery & Kearny, San Francisco 94111. (415) 399-1124. Weekdays, 10–4. Free. **Ages 7 & up.** *W.*

The Bank of Canton has integrated the historic 1875 U.S. Subtreasury Building, once the U.S. Branch Mint, into its architecturally acclaimed world headquarters in San Francisco's Financial District. Exhibits of Pacific Rim culture and history change every 12 to 18 months. During our visit, we were fascinated with "Wings Over the Pacific," which recreated the colorful history of flight throughout the Pacific Rim with hundreds of artifacts, models, engines, and rare photographs.

Cable Car Barn Museum

1201 Mason Street, at Washington Street, San Francisco 94108. (415) 474-1887. Daily, 10–5. Closed holidays. Free/Donation. Museum shop and bookstore. **Ages 4 & up.**

All three cable car lines in San Francisco are run by the huge revolving red and yellow wheels in the brick cable car barn, built in 1887. Visitors can watch the wheels from a gallery, where there are samples of the cable itself and charts explaining how the cable cars work. You can see scale models, earthquake mementos, old cable car seats, photographs, and the cable cars on display, including the first one to operate in San Francisco, in 1873. An exciting underground viewing room lets you see the cables running under the city streets from the car barn at nine-and-a-half miles an hour. A 16-minute video offers more information.

➤ North Beach Museum

1435 Stockton Street, upstairs in Eureka Bank, San Francisco 94133. (415) 391-6210. Mon.–Fri., 9–4. Tours by appt. Free. **Ages 10 & up.**

Photographs and artifacts in changing thematic exhibits celebrate the City's, and especially North Beach's, colorful past, from the Gold Rush to the 1906 earthquake and fire, to the growth of the neighborhood as the center of the City's Italian community, to the Beat Generation.

➤ The Hard Rock Cafe

1699 Van Ness Avenue, at Sacramento, San Francisco 94109. (415) 885-1699. Daily, 11:30–11:30; Fri. & Sat., until 12:30. Reservations for lunch only. Valet parking on Sacramento. Gift shop. **Ages 5 & up.** *W.*

The Hard Rock Cafe is just as much a rock-and-roll shrine as it is a restaurant. It's a mecca for rock fans of all ages. Sounds of the great rockers greet you as you walk into a large, two-level room, the walls of which are covered with posters, gold and platinum records, and the guitars of rock stars. The room has a California openness punctuated by a "dodge 'em" car, a motorcycle, and a standard Hard Rock fixture: half of a Cadillac over the entranceway. The menu's California touches lighten the load of affordable golden oldies such as ribs, fries, hamburgers, shakes, and banana splits. Expect a wait most of the time. Justin wrote, "My favorite restaurant is Hard Rock Cafe. Why I like this particular place so much is because of the food and what there is to look at. While I'm waiting for my food I can just look around and keep myself entertained. I also like the pinball games they have there. . . . They also play loud rock and roll music which you can sit in your comfortable seats and listen. . . . Hard Rock Cafe is a great and fun place to eat."

➤ The Haas-Lilienthal House

2007 Franklin Street, San Francisco 94109. (415) 441-3000. Tours Wed., 12–3:15 & Sun., 11–4:15, and by appt. Pacific Heights Walk, Sun. at 12:30. Donation. **Ages 10 & up.**

"We would like to thank you for our tour at The Haas-Lilienthal House. We learned so much about the family that used to live there, the utensils and furniture they used, and what they did in the rooms we visited. Thanks again!"—middle schoolers Jennifer and Wendy. Forty-five-minute docent-led tours will show you this glorious Queen Anne Victorian, built in 1886, a completely furnished memory of yesterday.

➤ The Octagon House

2645 Gough Street, at Union, San Francisco 94123. (415) 441-7512. Open on the second Sunday and second & fourth Thursdays of each month,

12–3. Groups by appt. Closed on holidays and in January. Free/Donation.
Ages 9 & up.

Built in 1861, this unusual eight-sided home is the headquarters of the National Society of the Colonial Dames of America in California as well as a gracious museum of Colonial and Federal artifacts. A framed pack of Revolutionary War playing cards, a 13-star flag, dishes taken in battle from the USS *Constitution* (Old Ironsides) and a 1789 leather fire bucket from Philadelphia make this a pleasantly educational stop. In one room is a display of documents from 54 of the 56 signers of the Declaration of Independence. Paper models of the house, 50 cents, are popular with young visitors. Next door is Allyne Park, a lovely picnic spot.

❖ Ghirardelli Chocolate Manufactory

Ghirardelli Square, 900 North Point, at Larkin, San Francisco 94109. (415) 771-4903. Daily, 10:30–10; later in summer. Parties: 474-3938.
All ages. *W.*

Since the beginning of the century, Ghirardelli Chocolate has been a popular trade name throughout the West. This red brick, aromatic ice cream and candy shop invokes that name in a nostalgic corner of the old Ghirardelli factory. After filling out an order form and paying the cashier, you claim a table, then take turns watching the chocolate-making machinery in the back of the room until your order number is called. We always dream of diving into the big vats where the chocolate is conched after the beans are roasted, cracked, husked, ground, and mixed with other ingredients. Instead, we dive into a hot fudge sundae, or a delicious extravaganza such as the Emperor Norton, with bananas, or the Chocolate Decadence. Or we could have a soda or cone.

The square itself is three stories full of more than 70 stores and restaurants, many with great views of the bay. Here you can find shoes, popcorn, cookies, crafts, books, perfume, clothes, jewelry, gadgets, and gifts galore. Jugglers and street entertainers perform on weekends and in summer in the flower-bedecked plazas, free. Ruth Asawa's mermaid fountain is wonderful.

❖ Museum of the City of San Francisco

The Cannery, 2801 Leavenworth, Third level, Beach Street & Leavenworth, San Francisco 94133. (415) 928-0289. Wed.–Sun., 10–4. Free/Donation. Gift Shop. **Ages 6 & up.** *W. (Call first, since the museum is scheduled to move to the City Hall area after City Hall renovations are completed.)*

San Francisco treasures capture the imagination in this small, glistening museum space. The Main Room focuses on the earthquake and fire of 1906 and the earthquake of 1989. Photographs and memorabilia such as dishes and letters that survived are featured in free-standing displays. A favorite is the supersize head of the Goddess of Progress, which crowned City Hall before 1906. The hand-carved wooden ceiling is from a 13th-century Spanish palace purchased by William Randolph Hearst. Kids love the dioramas featuring the Gold Rush era. A 1913 player piano delights young and old.

Naturally, since the Cannery, once the biggest peach cannery in the world, is a shopping complex, there are many gift and crafts stores and restaurants to browse through. Toddlers will certainly enjoy the **Basic Brown Bear Factory** on the second level. Older kids will head for the holograms at the **Light Wave Gallery. Q-Zar** (10–10 in summer; 1–5 in winter. 415-775-6700. Fee, $7), a laser game that's fun for everyone over seven years old, offers a video arcade and virtual reality games. Spectacular views from the third-floor walkway extend from the Golden Gate Bridge to the Berkeley hills.

❧ The Maritime Museum (San Francisco Maritime National Historic Park)

900 Beach Street, at the foot of Polk Street, San Francisco 94109. (415) 556-3002. Daily, 10–5; until 6 in summer. Call for calendar of events. sfnmm@aol.com. Free. **Ages 5 & up.** *W.*

The Maritime Museum, housed in an historic art deco *streamline modern* building that resembles a cruise ship, is a mecca for ship lovers of all ages. The maritime history of San Francisco lives on here in models of clippers, British ships, iron ships, schooners, barkentines, cutters, and cod fishers; and in photos, figureheads, tools, scrimshaw, guns, harpoons, diaries, maritime paintings, and ships' logs. The 19-foot sloop *Mermaid*, which one man sailed from Osaka to San Francisco, is on the veranda. Models of the *Queen Mary* along with cargo and warships from World War I to the present chug along in the steamship room.

❧ Hyde Street Pier (San Francisco Maritime National Historic Park)

Hyde Street Pier (Hyde & Jefferson), San Francisco 94109. (Mail: P.O. Box 470310, San Francisco 94147-0310.) (415) 556-3002. Daily, 10–5, later in summer. Tours & Environmental Living Programs by appt. Adults, $3; ages 12–17, $1; under 12 & seniors, free. First Tuesday of each month, free. Family ticket (2 adults, 4 children): $7. sfnma@aol.com. Store. **All ages.** *W (limited).*

The only "floating" National Park, Hyde Street Pier is home to several historic ships. On the *Balclutha*, one of the last surviving square-rigged Cape Horners, you can spin the wheel, visit the "slop chest" and galley, check out the captain's quarters with its swinging bed, ring bells, and read sea chanties and rousing tales of the Barbary Coast below decks, while the movement of the boat on the water stimulates the imagination.

You can also go below decks on the 1895 schooner *C. A. Thayer*, a salmon packet, to see the captain's family cabin. There are antique cars waiting for the next docking on the 1890 ferry *Eureka*. Other boats are docked on occasion such as the 1891 scow *Alma*, the last remaining San Francisco Bay schooner, the six-room *Lewis Ark* houseboat, the 1914 paddlewheel tug *Eppleton Hall*, the 1907 steam tugboat *Hercules*, or the 1915 steam schooner *Wapama*. Some of these are boardable, and the *Alma* and *Hercules* still sail and steam on the bay. On land, there are engine room showings, boat-building classes, movies and videos, and changing exhibits.

❖ USS *Pampanito*

Pier 45, Fisherman's Wharf, San Francisco. (Mail: P.O. Box 470310, San Francisco 94147-0310.) (415) 929-0202. Daily, 9–5; later in summer. Adults, $5; ages 6–12 & seniors, $3. Self-guided audio tours included. **Ages 6 & up.**

Experience what life was like for submariners during World War II by stepping aboard this fully restored floating exhibit. Now a National Landmark, *Pampanito* saw heavy duty during WW II, rescuing 73 prisoners of war from the Pacific Ocean during one particularly heroic effort in 1944. Captain Edward Beach narrates the tour as you explore the torpedo room, crew's quarters, control room, and fully operational galley.

❖ Jeremiah O'Brien Liberty Ship

Pier 32, San Francisco. (Mail: P.O. Box 470310, San Francisco 94147-0310.) (415) 441-3101. Weekdays, 9–3; weekends, 9–4. Adults, $5; seniors, $3; ages 11–18, $2; ages 10 & under, $1. Rentals. Guided tours by appt. **Ages 6 & up.**

The last intact liberty ship carried food and ammunition to England, ferried troops during the Normandy invasion, and transported supplies to the South Pacific. Volunteers, who are always welcome, have restored the ship and enjoy showing visitors around. On the third weekend of each month, they show the kids how a 50-year-old triple-expansion steam engine works. In 1994, volunteers sailed the ship on a five-month voyage to re-enact the WW II invasion of Normandy. In 1996, they sailed to the Pacific Northwest.

❖ Ripley's Believe It or Not! Museum

175 Jefferson, at Fisherman's Wharf, San Francisco 94133. (415) 771-6188. Sun.–Thurs., 10–10; Fri. and Sat., until midnight. Adults, $6.95;

ages 13–17, $5.50; under 12, $4. School tours by appt. **Ages 8 & up.**

This two-story collection of oddities and puzzles is almost unbeliev-able. Where else could you see a cable car made from 270,836 match sticks? A stegosaurus made of chrome car bumpers? Here you can walk through an animal kaleidoscope and a rotating tunnel, experience a disas-ters gallery, and wonder at the man with two pupils in each eye. The museum is always on the look-out for new unbelievable facts or unusual items, so if you send one in, you too can become part of the legend of Robert Ripley's *Believe It or Not!*

⇒ Wax Museum at Fisherman's Wharf

145 Jefferson, at Fisherman's Wharf, San Francisco 94133. (415) 202-0400/885-2023. Daily, 10–10; Fri. and Sat., 9 A.M.–11:30 P.M. Adults, $9.95; seniors & military, $6.95; children, $4.95. Group rates. Parties. One-price tickets available for Wax Museum, Haunted Gold Mine, and Medieval Dungeon. **Ages 8 & up.** *W (limited).*

Meet Prince Charles and Princess Diana, Abraham Lincoln, Mona Lisa, Michael Jackson, King Tut with his Treasures, Elvis Presley, General MacArthur, Joe Montana, the Phantom of the Opera, Peter Pan and Snow White, and heroes and villains, in four floors of scenes recreating the past, the present, and the world of the future. The Chamber of Horrors on the lower level is "not recommended for cowards, sissies, and yellerbellies." That includes us.

The Haunted Gold Mine, in the same complex, is a cute Disneyland-type ride that pretends to take youngsters through the early days of Cali-fornia with occasional scares and murders. **Medieval Dungeon,** next-door, is proud to be a horrifying collection of relics from the Dark Ages—and is only for brave teenagers and oldies.

⇒ Alcatraz Island Cruise and Tour (GGNRA)

Pier 41, San Francisco 94133. (415) 546-2653/556-0560. Frequent departures on the Red & White fleet daily. Advance ticket purchase by phone (415-546-2700) with a charge card is strongly suggested. Once docked, you can walk with the self-guided audio tour available, for an extra charge, when you purchase your ticket. Call for up-to-date schedules and prices. Bookstore & mini-museum. **Ages 6 & up.**

Wear walking shoes and take a sweater on this educational, fascinat-ing-yet-depressing, self-guided walking tour of Alcatraz. One friend calls the two- to two-and-a-half-hour trip a sure-fire way to stop juvenile delin-quency. Try spending time in a nine by five foot cell, all alone, just for a few minutes. Alcatraz is part of the Golden Gate National Recreation Area, a nationally protected park land along the coast.

❧ Bay Cruises

On a sunny day in San Francisco, there's nothing nicer for the family than getting out on San Francisco Bay. You can take a ferry that goes to Sausalito, Angel Island, Tiburon, or Marine World, or simply take a guided-tour cruise of the bay, under the Golden Gate and Bay bridges. The **Red & White Fleet** offers a one-hour cruise with audiotours in English, German, Japanese, Mandarin, Spanish, and French. Daily commuter trips to Sausalito and Tiburon leave from Pier 41 and Pier 43½. The Red & White Fleet also connects tourists to **Heli USA, Helicopter Tours** of San Francisco (800-443-5487 Ext. 2). In California, call (800) 445-8880 or (415) 546-2896.

The **Blue & Gold Fleet** has a one-and-a-quarter-hour Bay Cruise looping under the Golden Gate, past Alcatraz, under the Bay Bridge and back to the sea lions at Pier 39. For schedules and prices, call (415) 705-5555. Group rates. W. Three-hour dinner/dance or holiday cruises from May to December are also available. Blue & Gold Fleet also operates the Alameda/Oakland and Vallejo ferries with frequent daily departures. Special ferry packages are available to destinations such as Angel Island, Marine World Africa USA, and the Napa Valley Wine Train and Wine Tour.

San Francisco Seaplane Tours take off from both a walk-up dock on Pier 39, hourly, 10 to dusk, and from Sausalito. Call (415) 332-4843 for reservations. Adults, $89; under 12, $59. The Canadian-built seven-passenger de Havilland Beaver, a beautiful, rugged bush plane, has bubble center windows and enlarged rear windows for easy, fun sightseeing on forty-five-minute tours.

Pier 39 is also the place to find cute little tour taxi-boats or sailboats such as the *Andiamo,* a 65-foot MacGregor seating up to 19 passengers, (415) 788-4920. One-and-a-half-hour sails are $20 per person. Charters are available.

To ride the wind on a '92 Race Winner, try *Yukon Jack,* a 52-foot sloop. Embark from Pier 40 at 12, 2:30, or 5 P.M., but call for reservations: (415) 241-1803. Remember, Pier 40 is, with all the other even-numbered piers, south of the Bay Bridge.

❧ Underwater World at Pier 39

Pier 39, P.O. Box 640386, San Francisco 94164-0386. (415) 623-5300. Daily, 10–8. Adults, $12.95; seniors, $9.95, ages 3–11, $6.50. Groups, family and low-income discounts available. School tours by appt., free. (415) 705-5500. Gift shop. **All ages.**

After seeing an introductory video to set the scene, travel beneath the sea, riding a conveyor belt along the simulated bay floor in a 400-foot acrylic tunnel that allows over 200 species of local underwater life to swim above and around you in 707,000 gallons of water. Kids can get nose to nose with sharks or schools of herring, lingcod, or lizardfish. A 40-minute audio tour is available that explains the fish and their world along with the work that goes into underwater exploration and making an aquarium.

⇶ Secret of San Francisco

Pier 39, San Francisco 94133. (415) 956-FILM. Daily, every forty-five minutes, 10–10 in summer; 10:30–8 in winter. Adults, $7.50; seniors, $6; under 12, $4.50. **All ages.** *W.*

An original destination motion picture by Academy Award–winning director Keith Merrill captures the historical and cultural wonders, the myth, magic, and beauty of San Francisco. There's lots of aerial photography and vignettes of local personalities. The Chinese New Year's Parade, the Bay to Breakers race, windsurfing on the bay, and a high-speed chase on San Francisco's hills are highlights. 49ers quarterback Steve Young plays a gold miner, and the film ends with the cast of *Beach Blanket Babylon* singing "San Francico."

Pier 39 is a shopping/restaurant complex set right on the water. There's a double-decker merry-go-round for the children, with bumper-cars, a recording studio, and **Cyberstation:** a huge 100-game arcade (Summer, Sun.–Thurs., 10–11. 415-399-9907). Kids can also try the "Turboride" right outside, a kind of bungee-cord swing. Sailing sessions and lessons and buggy and rickshaw rides are available. On weekends, street entertainers stroll the boards.

The **Information Center for the Marine Mammal Center** on the Marin Highlands is worth a stop. But the star of the show is the honking, smelly, boisterous community of **sea lions** who have taken over Pier 39's K-dock. Be sure to pick up the free flyer on "39 Fascinating Facts" about the California Sea Lion, one of the best free shows in the city!

⇶ Fort Mason Center

Once a lonely barracks with deserted piers, Fort Mason, at the foot of Marina Boulevard and Laguna, is now a flourishing center for the arts. Non-profit organizations from the Oceanic Society to Western Public Radio are based here, and performing arts groups give shows in the three theaters. **The Oceanic Society** (Bldg. E, Second floor, 441-1106) offers Whale Watch and Farallon Islands day cruises as well as national and international trips for wildlife enthusiasts. **Sailing Education Adventures** (Bldg. E, Second floor, 775-8779) offers sailing camps, lectures, and field trips featuring marine environment or maritime history topics.

Greens, a fine vegetarian restaurant, has a phenomenal view of the docks, the bay, and the Golden Gate Bridge (771-6222 for lunch and dinner reservations).

The **San Francisco Museum of Modern Art**'s rental wing is in Building A, as is the **San Francisco Craft & Folk Art Museum.** The **City College of San Francisco Fort Mason Art Campus** is in Building B. Call (415) 979-3010 for a list of events each week.

On Free Museum day, the first Wednesday of each month, all five galleries are open late, until 7, and admission is free. The following (all are in San Francisco zip code 94123) are of special interest to the young:

Museo ItaloAmericano. *Building C. (415) 673-2200. Wed.–Sun., 12– 5 & by appt. Adults, $2; students & seniors, $1; under 12, free. Gift shop. W.* Preserves and displays Italian and ItaloAmerican art, history, and culture in changing exhibits. Classes, community activities, and films are presented.

San Francisco African American Historical & Cultural Society. *Building C. (415) 441-0640.* Call for hours and presentation information, since this museum is in a state of change at this writing.

Mexican Museum. *Building D. (415) 441-0404. Wed.–Sun., 12–5. Adults, $3; students, $2; under 10, free. Tours by appt. La Tienda gift shop has a wide selection of handcrafted gifts from Mexico and Latin America.* The Mexican Museum's vision is to generate new perspectives of American culture that shape the way we perceive ourselves as a nation. It collects, preserves, exhibits, interprets and promotes the artistic expression of Mexicano and Latino people through the visual arts and other multi-disciplinary media. Six Sundays a year, the Museum invites families to come together, free, to create crafts projects connected with Mexican cultural and religious holidays.

Children's Art Center of San Francisco. *Building C., First floor. (415) 771-0292. Party facilities available.* Children ages two to 10 draw, paint, sculpt and print in small classes with individual attention, exploring the organized freedom of the studio.

❖ Japan Center

With stores and restaurants, the Japan Center (*Nihonmachi*) can really be another world. The Peace Plaza with its reflecting pools and five-tiered Peace Pagoda is the center of entertaining festivals and celebrations during the year. You can see music and dance programs as well as judo, karate, and kendo matches. Inside the center, you can fish for an oyster with a pearl in it, or have a Japanese fish-shaped *tai yaki*, a warm, filled, waffle-like pastry. Kids like the Mikado store, which sells Sanrio Hello Kitty products.

Introduce children to sushi at **Isobune** (1737 Post Street, San Francisco 94115. (415) 563-1030. W). Here you sit in front of a circular stream. Boats float by you carrying little plates of sushi. You take off what looks good and pay by the plate. Start with *maki*, cucumbers in rice wrapped in crunchy seaweed, or *tamago*, a slice of omelet, or *ebi*, cooked shrimp, for the wary. My 10-year-old nephew, Alan, was hooked by the *unagi*, broiled eel with barbecue sauce. **Mifune,** across the way in the Kintetsu Mall (922-0337) is noted for its many nourishing, inexpensive noodle dishes.

❖ San Francisco Fire Department Museum

655 Presidio Avenue, between Pine & Bush, San Francisco 94115. (415) 861-8000, ext. 365. Thurs.–Sun., 1–4 & by appt. Free. **All ages.** *W.*

Awe-inspiring photos of today's firefighters mingle with uniforms, bells, trophies, and mementos of men and machines, the silver speaking trumpet, leather buckets, a buffalo-leather fire hose, and other relics of yesteryear. Lillie Coit, the darling of the San Francisco Fire Department, has her own case full of mementos. A 1912 fire chief's buggy, an 1890 American LaFrance Steam Fire Engine, and other machinery fill the room.

❖ Mission Dolores

3321 16th Street, at Dolores, San Francisco 94114. (415) 621-8203. Daily, 9–4 in winter; 9–4:30, in summer. Adults and group tours for those 10 or older, Adults, $2; children $1. Audio tour, $5. **Ages 6 & up.**

Built in 1776, the *Mission San Francisco de Asis*, as it is properly named, is the City's oldest structure. The unique Corinthian and Moorish architecture is not at all like other California missions. Inside, two elaborate late 18th century *reredos* flanking the altar have been restored, as have the Indian designs painted on the ceiling. The gardens have been completely rethought and revivified, winding around a cemetery that contains the remains of some of the City's first settlers, from Francisco de Haro, first Alcalde of the City, to James Casey, a fireman hanged for murder by the 1856 Vigilance Committee. To young Alana, her "favorite part of the Mission was when you rang the bells in the Basilica."

❖ The Randall Museum

199 Museum Way, San Francisco 94114. Off Roosevelt, Upper Market Street area, at 14th Street, west of Castro. (415) 554-9600. Tues.–Sat., 10–5. Animal Room, 10:30–1 & 2–5. Free. Classes, workshops, nature walks. **All ages.**

San Francisco's children's museum is situated on a 16-acre hill overlooking the Bay. It features live animals, a petting corral, changing exhibits, a hiking trail, and the Golden Gate Model Railroad (open second and fourth Saturday afternoons). The theater, woodshop, ceramics studio, art studio, lapidary shop and darkroom are used for hands-on programs in the arts and sciences for ages three to adult. Drop-in family classes occur every Saturday at 10 and 1 ($4–$10 per person, sliding scale).

❯❯ Golden Gate Park

From Fulton and Stanyan Streets, west to the ocean. The park office is in McLaren Lodge, San Francisco 94117. (415) 666-7200.

There are more than 1,000 acres of lakes and greenery in San Francisco's Golden Gate Park and at least 100 things to see and do. You can go boating or feed the ducks, cheer model boat races, picnic, ride horses, play tennis or golf or handball, go lawn bowling, watch the grazing bison, bicycle, skate, watch soccer and polo matches, pitch horseshoes, shoot arrows, play cards or chess, fly cast, or make water rings in the fountains. Stow Lake is the place to rent rowboats, motor boats, and pedal boats. Visit the magical, silvery Golden Gate pavilion from China, located on Stow Lake's island.

The Children's Playground, located on the Lincoln Avenue side of the park, features the slide with the fastest ride in the West, plus three other slides, geometrical shapes to climb (handicapped accessible), and swings.

The nearby **Herschel-Spillman 1912 Carousel** (Wed.–Sun., 10–4:15. $1) has been perfectly and wonderfully restored, with 62 menagerie animals, mostly in sets of two—cats, dogs, zebras, tigers, roosters, storks, giraffes, reindeer, frogs, pigs, goats, and beautiful horses—like Noah's Ark, plus a love-tub and a rocker.

Older children might enjoy a walk through **Shakespeare's Garden** to identify the plants he wrote about. You can climb a drum bridge in the **Japanese Tea Garden** (daily, 9–6:30. Adults, $2.50; children and seniors, $1. Tours, 752-1171) and then sit down to tea and cookies in the Tea House (daily, 10–6:30. $2.50. School tours: 415-666-7024).

Drive by the spun-sugar Victorian **Conservatory of Flowers** on Kennedy Drive to see displays of flowers. Ring the Mexican Bell in the **Strybing Arboretum's Garden of Fragrance,** where you can test your sense of smell, touch, and taste (weekdays, 8–4:30; weekends and holidays, 10–5. Tours, theme walks, plant sales & bookstore. 415-661-1316).

Gaze at the **Portals of the Past,** the marble columns that are all that was left of a Nob Hill mansion after the 1906 earthquake and are now the guardians of a duck-filled lake. Don't forget to say thank you to John McLaren—whose statue is tucked in a dell of rhododendrons across from

the Conservatory, though he hated statues in parks—for turning former
sand dunes into an oasis of greenery gracing the City.

⇒ M. H. de Young Memorial Museum

*75 Tea Garden Drive, Golden Gate Park (north side of Music Concourse),
San Francisco 94118-4501. (415) 750-3614. Information Hotline:
863-3330. Wed.–Sun., 10–4:45. Adults, $6; over 65, $4; ages 12–17,
$3; college student annual pass, $10; students, K–12, free. Same-day
admission to the Palace of the Legion of Honor, plus $1. Free first Wed. of the
month, 10–8:45. Lectures, events, docent tours, and school programs (415)
750-3658. Cafe Wed.–Sun., 10–4; until 8 on first Wednesday. Gift stores.*
Ages 5 & up. *W.*

The de Young's romantic Pool of Enchantment, with water lilies and
a sculpted boy playing his pipes to two mountain lions, beckons visitors
to this land of enchantment. The West Coast's best collection of American
painting, sculpture, and decorative arts includes Georgia O'Keeffe's *Petu-
nias*, Frederick Church's *Rainy Day in the Tropics*, and The John D. Rockefeller 3rd Collection of American Art with several works by the Ash Can
school. Art from pre-Columbian Latin America and Africa is also included. Gallery One is a hands-on exhibit, reading, and computer room
dedicated to children. "Doing and Viewing Art," is a special program for
children, 7–12, and "Big Kids/Little Kids" is for children 3½ to 6, with
their families.

⇒ Asian Art Museum, Avery Brundage Collection

*Golden Gate Park (north side of Music Concourse), San Francisco 94118.
(415) 379-8801. Reservations & information: 379-8879. TDD: (415)
752-2635. Wed.–Sun., 10–4:45; until 8:45 P.M. on the first Wed. of the
month. Adults, $6; over 65, $4; ages 12–17, $3. Free the first Wed. of each
month. Tours by appt. A limited number of wheelchairs are available at the
museum entrance, free.* **Ages 6 & up.** *W.*

Chinese galleries on the first floor display objects from prehistoric
times to the 19th century, including a magnificent collection of jade in
a jewel-box setting, the Magnin Jade Room. Second-floor galleries exhibit
art from Japan, Korea, India, Southeast Asia, Tibet, Nepal, and Iran.
Both floors overlook the Japanese Tea Garden at the west end. An interactive video display in the first floor China gallery allows visitors of all ages
to explore the structure and contents of a 10th-century tomb. A story-
telling program for children accompanied by an adult is given each Sunday at 1.

⟫ California Academy of Sciences

Golden Gate Park (south side of Music Concourse), San Francisco 94118. Taped information, (415) 750-7145; switchboard, 750-7000. Daily, 10–5 in winter and 9–6 in summer. Adults, $7; ages 12–17 & seniors, $4; ages 6–11, $1.50. Free the first Wed. of the month. Rates for groups by appt. Special programs and lectures. Gift shop. **Ages 3 & up.** *W.*

Earth, Ocean, and Space, all in one place! Wander through the innovative Wild California Hall and the Hall of Gems and Minerals. The African Safari Hall teems with sights and sounds of Africa. Don't miss the Earth and Space Hall, with the Safe-Quake, a ride that simulates an earthquake. The Far Side of Science Gallery features the work of cartoonist Gary Larson. In the Life Through Time hall, you'll discover facts about the evolution of life on Earth and find out how our planet's remote past affects our world today. Robotic saber-toothed cats, woolly mammoth, giant sloths, and a buck-toothed, long-snouted Platybelodon are some of the Ice Age animals re-created in unique sound-and-movement exhibits. The Discovery Room is a hands-on touch and learn room for tiny explorers, by reservation. (750-7154).

The whale fountain courtyard leads to the Academy's **Steinhart Aquarium**'s swamp, inhabited by crocodiles and alligators. Thousands of fish and reptiles live in 243 colorful tanks, all low enough for children to see into easily. Sea horses, black-footed penguins, deadly stonefish, piranhas, and shellfish of all colors, shapes, and sizes are here. Upstairs, the Fish Roundabout puts you in the middle of a huge tubular tank where fish swim quickly around you. The penguins are fed at 11:30 and 4. For information, call (415) 750-7145.

In the **Morrison Planetarium,** a unique Sky Theater with a 65-foot hemispherical dome presents simulations of the heavens as seen from earth at any time in history. Special-effects projectors take the audience through space into whirling galaxies and black holes. Shows change regularly. For daily shows, call (415) 750-7141. There are shows on weekdays at 11, 12:30, 2, and 3:30; on weekends at 11, 12, 1, 2, 3, and 4. Adults, $2.50; ages 6 to 17 and seniors, $1.25; under 6 by special permission. "Exploring the Skies of the Season," $1 for all, is shown at noon on weekends and holidays.

Laserium is a state-of-the-art "cosmic" laser show in which brilliant colorful images pulsate, float, and dance to today's music against a background of stars. One-hour long LaserRock 3-D shows have been added to the line-up. Shows are on Wednesday through Sunday evenings after the museum closes. Call (415) 750-7138 for titles, times, and prices. Not recommended for those under 6. Group reservations.

❖ The Exploratorium

Palace of Fine Arts, 3601 Lyon Street, between Marina Boulevard and Lombard, San Francisco 94123. (415) 561-0360. Tues.–Sun., 10–5; Wed. until 9:30. Memorial Day to Labor Day: Daily, 10–6, Wed. until 9:30. Closed Thanksgiving and Christmas. Also closed Mondays, except open on holiday Mondays. Adults, $9; seniors, $7; ages 6–17 and those with disabilities, $5; ages 3–5, $2.50. Tactile dome reservations, $12: 561-0362. Groups: 561-0308. www.exploratorium.edu. Parties. Cafe. Gift Shop. **All ages.** *W.*

This touchingthinkingpullingsplashingblinkingspinning amazing museum of science, art, and human perception contains over 650 exhibits. It's the best combination of learning while playing in California. Clap and make a tree of lights blink, blow a two-foot bubble, learn about light, language, patterns, vision, color, and motion, and more. Shrink your mom. Play with purple power. Laser beams, computers, holograms, stereophonic sound testers, and radio and TV sets are here to play with. Lively scientific exhibits demonstrate natural phenomena. "Play Base" is an interactive environment for toddlers and their parents. In the Tactile Dome, you crawl, slide, and climb in and through a black maze of strange textures. An extension into the Presidio will make the Exploratorium bigger and better than ever.

Cristy from El Portal Middle School wrote, "Thanks to you guys for even letting us touch things. Like an alien phone, a shadow screen, and a lot of lights!"

❖ Fort Point National Historic Site

San Francisco 94129. Foot of Marina Drive, on Presidio grounds, under San Francisco end of the Golden Gate Bridge. (415) 556-1693. Wed.–Sun., except holidays, 10–5. Guided tours and demonstrations throughout the day. Audio tours, $2.50 & $1. Gift shop. Free. **Ages 5 & up.** *Partially W.*

Nestled below the underpinnings of the Golden Gate Bridge, Fort Point, the guardian of San Francisco Bay, was built during the Civil War and is the only brick coastal fort in the West. With the icy Pacific slamming into the retaining wall and the wind whistling around the point, this is one of the coldest spots in the City. Two exhibits housed in the fort feature the contributions of women in the military as well as the history and achievements of black soldiers in the Army. Roam throughout the officers' and enlisted men's quarters and walk through the huge casements where once were mounted more than 100 huge cannon. Ask one of the park rangers to demonstrate how to load and fire a cannon. You may end up earning a cannoneer certificate. Videos on the history of Fort Point and on the construction of the Golden Gate Bridge are shown throughout the day.

✺ California Palace of the Legion of Honor

34th Avenue & Clement Street, Lincoln Park. (Mail: Fine Arts Museums of San Francisco, 75 Tea Garden Drive, San Francisco 94118-4501.) (415) 863-3663. Tues.–Sun., 10–4:45, until 8:45 on the first Sat. of the month. Free on second Wed. of the month, 10–8:45 P.M. *Adults, $7; seniors, $5; ages 10–17, $4; college student annual pass, $10; San Francisco students, K–12, Free. Legion Cafe, Tues.–Sun, 10–4, until 8 on first Sat. night. Saturday afternoon drop-in art classes for children, docent tours, lectures, events.* **Ages 5 & up.** *W.*

San Francisco's European art museum includes a major collection of sculpture by Rodin, a Cycladic figure dated 2500 B.C., medieval tapestries and jeweled objects, and paintings by El Greco, Rembrandt, Rubens, Watteau, Seurat, and Picasso. Begin your tour by walking under a 15th-century Spanish carved and polychromed ceiling and finish in an impressionistic world of Monet's *Water Lilies* and works by Van Gogh, Renoir, and Pisarro.

The Ceramics gallery and the Achenbach Foundation for Graphic Arts also offer study centers available to the public. For information on "Doing and Viewing Art" for ages 7–12, and "Big Kids/Little Kids," ages 3½ to 6, call (415) 750-3658.

✺ The Cliff House

1090 Point Lobos Avenue, San Francisco 94121. Geary Avenue and the Great Highway. (415) 386-3330.

"A drive to the 'Cliff' in the early morning . . . and a return to the city through the charming scenery of Golden Gate Park tends to place man about as near to Elysian bliss as he may hope for in this world," wrote B. E. Lloyd in 1876. A drive to and from the Cliff House can still place you in Elysian bliss. At certain times of year, seals bask on the Seal Rocks. There are restaurants with great views.

A **Visitors Center** downstairs (415-556-8642) shows the Cliff House in its various incarnations throughout the years, along with rotating natural history displays. Here you can also find information about Farallon Islands tours, visiting the Whale Center (654-6621), and other adventures. The **Camera Obscura** exhibit on the deck can be intriguing (415-750-0415).

The crammed **Musée Mécanique** (415-386-1170; daily, 11–7; 10–8 in summer, free) houses over 100 coin-operated machines, old and new. Swiss music boxes, a mechanical carnival, a mechanical 1920s farm, old-time movies, and music machines sit alongside electronic games and modern cartoon-themed challengers.

❧ Polly Ann Ice Cream

3142 Noriega Street, between 38th & 39th Avenue, San Francisco 94122. (415) 664-2472. Fri. & Sat., 11–11; Sun–Thurs., 11–10.

In 1955 a wonderful man named Ted Hanson retired and went into the ice-cream-making business, creating over 400 exotic flavors and plastering his tiny stand-at-the-counter store with funny signs and jokes. New owners have retained the signs and flavors and added a few of their own from the Far East, such as Jasmine Tea, Mung Green Bean, Durian, Ube, and other Thai and Philipino fruits. But kids under 3 and dogs "accompanied by a human being" still get free mini cones. Junior cones are available for $1.15, and the price goes up by the scoop. With so many flavors, such as American rose petal, ginger (that bites back!), Batman (grape vanilla with lemon swirl), Lemon Chippee (lemon with chocolate chips), Irish Coffee, Strawberry Rocky Road, and Cinna-Mint, it's really hard to choose. The pure-of-heart may choose the creamy green Vegetable, made with 14 kinds of veggies, including parsley, beets, and corn.

❧ San Francisco Zoo

One Zoo Road, Sloat Boulevard at 45th Avenue, San Francisco 94132. (415) 753-7083/753-7061. Daily, 10–5. Adults, $7; seniors and youth, $3.50; ages 3–11, $1:50; under 3, free. Zoo Keys, for exhibit Storyboxes, $2. Additional charge for Children's Zoo, Carousel, and Zebra Train tour. Parties. Adopt-an-Animal programs. Summer junior volunteer programs. Group tours. Strollers for rent. Gift store. Picnic areas. http://www. SFZoo.com. **All ages.** *W.*

Do you have an urge to pet a hissing cockroach? Ride a zebra train? Walk about an Australian setting? The San Francisco Zoo, located adjacent to the Pacific Ocean, provides a natural, open-air setting for a variety of endangered and exotic animals. A premier education and conservation facility, the Zoo offers children a chance to see and learn about wild animals from many different countries. Animal highlights include black rhinos, cassowary birds, ring-tailed lemurs, kangaroos and koalas, white alligators, domestic animals in the Children's Zoo barnyard, and big cats, such as African lions, Sumatran and Siberian tigers, and a white Bengal tiger, fed daily (except Mondays) at 2 P.M. (They don't eat every day in the jungle, either.)

Visitors can observe endangered snow and Persian leopards in the 20,000-square-foot naturalistic Feline Conservation Center, watch the antics of African warthogs, and see the playful North American river otters at Otter River. Gorilla World, one of the nation's largest exhibits for gorillas, is a tranquil and quiet setting for a group of Western lowland gorillas. Koala Crossing, patterned after an Australian outback station, allows visitors to see koalas both outdoors in a peaceful eucalyptus yard and indoors through a glass panel. Australian WalkAbout is a 2-acre retreat for many marsupial species and emus. The Primate Discovery Center features open atriums housing many endangered primate species. Other highlights include Penguin Island, home to Magellanic penguins, and the Insect Zoo, where visitors can see over 30 different arthropod exhibits—and pet a tarantula. "Bone Carts" bring certain birds and animals to visitors for close-up learning. The 1921 Dentzel Carousel near the entrance is still as beautiful and dream-inspiring as ever.

❖ Public Relations Tours

Basic Brown Bear & Company Teddy Bear Factory. (444 DeHaro Street, at Mariposa on Potrero Hill, San Francisco 94107. 415-626-0781. Mon.–Sat., 10–5. Tours at 1 daily, at 11 on Saturday, and by reservation.) While learning about the history of the teddy bear, from spats to safety eyes, visitors can see 30 kinds of teddy bears cut and stuffed right in front of them—and even stuff their own. Clothing, ribbons, and accessories are available for personalizing your teddy bear.

Levi Strauss Jeans Manufacturing & Museum Tour. (250 Valencia, at 14th Street in the Mission district, San Francisco 94103. 415-565-9159. Tours, Tues. at 10:30; Wed., 10:30 & 1, by appointment.) Hour-and-a-half-long tours begin with a 10-minute video and show the history of Levis and how blue jeans are made, from fabric to fanny. You'll see some of the winners of the 1973 Levi's denim Art Contest on the walls of the mini-museum.

Marin County

Marin County is a land of mountains and seashore just north of the Golden Gate Bridge. Most of the "places to go" with children in Marin are natural wonders. You can drive to the top of Mt. Tamalpais and walk the trails overlooking miles of ocean, land, and city. You can explore the silent redwood groves of Muir Woods, then travel on to Stinson Beach or one of the lesser-known beaches for picnicking by the seaside, collecting driftwood, or wading in the icy sea. You can also spend hours fishing in the Marin lakes or hiking the beautiful Point Reyes National Seashore. And when you feel the need for civilization, you can head for the bayside villages of Tiburon or Sausalito, which will enchant the children as much as they do you.

And you don't have to have a car to get there. **Golden Gate Transit Bus Route 63** starts at the Golden Gate Bridge Plaza and takes the Panoramic Highway out to Stinson Beach, stopping at the Discovery Museum, Tam Junction, Mountain Home, the Boot Jack trailhead, and the Pan Toll ranger station in Mount Tamalpais State Park on the way. (415-332-6600 or 453-2100. Varying schedules weekends & holidays, March–Nov., $3.50.)

Golden Gate Ferry Transit operates daily from San Francisco's historic Ferry Building to Larkspur and Sausalito. Call (415) 923-2000 from San Francisco or (415) 455-2000 from Marin for fares and schedules.

⇻ Marine Mammal Center

Fort Cronkhite, Sausalito 94965. From San Francisco: cross the Golden Gate Bridge, take the first exit after Vista Point, and follow signs to park entrance and beach. On the Marin Headlands in the Golden Gate National Recreation Area, near the batteries and bunkers on Rodeo Beach. (415) 289-SEAL. Daily, 10–4. Tours and classes. Free. Gift store. **All ages.** *W.*

The Marine Mammal Center is where we finally learned the difference between sea lions and seals. Sea lions have outer ear flaps; seals have small holes for ears. Sea lions walk on all four flippers, and seals move on their bellies, like inchworms. The purpose of this center—which always needs volunteers—is to rescue and then release marine mammals stranded on the coastline. Stranded pups are fed herring milkshakes. (Please remember that just because a seal appears on the beach it doesn't necessarily need rescuing. Don't touch it unless you have a permit.) There are critters in cage-tanks to see, and informative illustrated panels to learn from. An exhibit center is in the works. After a visit, one third-grader sent this poem as a thank you:

Dolphins are pink
whales are red
and seals blue and green like the ocean where they live.

The Pacific Energy & Resources Center in the Marin Headlands
(415-332-8200) has a small informational museum on the property.

❧ The Point Bonita Lighthouse
*Marin Headlands Visitor Center. Ft. Cronkhite. (415) 331-1540. Week-
ends, 12:30–3:30. Free. Reserve for sunset or full-moon tours.* **Ages 5 & up.**

Called one of the "Guardians of the Golden Gate," Point Bonita
lighthouse is open to the public. Built in 1877, the lighthouse has been
meticulously renovated and restored, replacing a century of rust with
aluminum and shiny stainless steel. The 1000-watt lightbulb is surrounded by a magnificent Fresnell lens, built in Paris in the 1850s and
shipped to California around Cape Horn. Today, the light is controlled by
computer. The trail across the rocks has also been strengthened and restored. Nonetheless, while walking through a tunnel and over seven small
footbridges, you'll understand why one lighthouse keeper's wife kept her
children tied to ropes, so they wouldn't fall off the yard into the sea.

❧ Sausalito
After stopping for a moment to look back at the Golden Gate Bridge
from Vista Point, spend a few hours in Sausalito, the Riviera by the Bay.
Noted for years as an artists' colony, the village of Sausalito is now a mecca
for tourists and young people. There are clothing and toy stores, ice cream
parlors and coffee houses, art galleries and restaurants for every age, taste,
and budget.

❧ San Francisco Bay–Delta Model
*2100 Bridgeway, Sausalito 94969-1764. (415) 332-3870. Tues.–Fri.,
9–4; weekends and holidays, 10–6. Free.* **Ages 6 & up.** *W.*

Cheryl wrote, "Dear Ranger Suzette, Thank you for taking us on
the tour. I learned about the tides. I just moved here from Utah, and this
place is wonderful. Anyway, that movie was great. I hope I can come
again. Thank you." The U.S. Army Corps of Engineers has constructed a
huge hydraulic scale model of San Francisco Bay and the Sacramento–
San Joaquin Delta. The model shows the action of the tides, the flow and
currents of the water, and the mixing of seawater and fresh water. Guided
tours take an hour, or you can use the self-guided written information or
the tape-recorded audio program, which provides extensive information

about the model and its operation. The model only operates when testing is scheduled, but there's so much to see—pictures, slides, models, and more—you won't be disappointed. Robert wrote, "I liked learning the word 'estuary,' salt and fresh! I especially liked exploring the ship display."

⇒ Bay Area Discovery Museum

557 East Fort Baker, Sausalito 94965. From San Francisco: take Highway 101 north to Alexander Avenue exit and follow signs. (415) 487-4396. Tues.–Sun., 10–5 in summer; Wed.–Sun., 10–5 in winter. Adults, $7; children, $6; seniors, $4. Parties. Discovery Cafe. Gift shop. **Ages 2–13.** *W.*

"The Bay Area Discovery Museum: A boppin' jammin' dancin' happenin' place to be!" So wrote Jez. And Fran called it a "Cool Place! Best museum in the world!" This hands-on museum for children and families is located in a spectacular setting at the foot of the Golden Gate Bridge. Its six historic buildings house the permanent San Francisco Bay and Building the City exhibitions, the Art Spot, a science lab, a media center, the Maze of Illusions, the Tot Spot, and a cafe. The museum features ever-changing activities and workshops focusing on the arts and sciences. The surrounding area provides picnic spots, hiking trails, and tide pools for the entire family to enjoy. A not-to-be-missed attraction is the handmade carousel created especially for the museum by master carousel maker Bill Dentzel.

⇒ Tiburon

Named **Punta de Tiburon,** or Shark Point, by Spanish explorers, Tiburon is a nice place to spend a sunny afternoon. Having lunch, indoors or out, while enjoying the view of the City from one of the restaurants on the bay can be heaven. Nautical shops, a Swedish bakery, and the bookstore are all fun to browse through. Our favorite restaurant is right next to the ferry landing: **Guaymas** (5 Main Street; 415-435-6300) for the kind of grilled fish and fowl you'd have in a seaside Mexican village.

The Landmarks Society (415-435-1853) maintains three historic sites: Hardy walkers can head up the hill to **Old St. Hilary's Church** (Juanita Lane off Esperanza, Apr.–Oct., Sun. and Wed., 1–4, and by appt.; donation) to see a changing photo exhibit and 217 species of plants that grow nowhere else in the world. The **China Cabin Maritime Museum** (Wed. and Sun., 1–4 and by appt.; free), on the cove in nearby Belvedere, is the restored 20- by 40-foot Victorian social saloon, from the SS *China Cabin*, a steam sidewheeler. It looks exactly as it did when it left New York for San Francisco in June 1867, on its first voyage. The **Railroad-**

Ferry Depot (Mon.–Fri., 9–4; free) at 1920 Paradise Drive in Shoreline Park displays photos of Tiburon during its heyday as a railroad town from 1884 to 1964.

❖ Richardson Bay Audubon Center

376 Greenwood Beach Road, Tiburon 94920. (415) 388-2525. Wed.– Sun., 9–5. Lyford House, Jun.–Sept. Sundays only; Oct.–May, Wed.–Sun., 1–4; $2, children $1. Public Nature Programs on Sun. Call for schedule. **Ages 5 & up.**

Richardson Bay Audubon Center and Sanctuary provides a habitat for wildlife and is an environmental education center, a "window on the bay." Youngsters can explore sea life and observe birds on nature trails. Programs, films, and classes help make visitors aware of the wonders around them. Lyford House is a Victorian mansion with period furnishings and Marin County history displays.

❖ Angel Island State Park

P.O. Box 866, Tiburon 94920. For tours, events, and transportation information call (415) 435-3522. For groups, classes, and assistance for disabled contact: Angel Island Association, (415) 435-3522. For ferry schedules from San Francisco, call (415) 546-2815. Ferry from Tiburon daily in summer; on weekends or by arrangement in winter. Call (415) 435-2131. Adults, $6; children, $4; bikes, $1, includes State Park entrance fee. **All ages.**

Most visitors ride the ferries to Ayala Cove, where lawn, beach, and barbecue pits beckon. The Visitors Center has interpretive nature and history displays, a free video, and a gift shop. Tram tours take visitors to the other side of the island. On weekends, April to October, Camp Reynolds, a Civil War site, Fort McDowell, a site from World War I and World War II, and the Barracks Museum at the Immigration Station (Angel Island was the Ellis Island of the Pacific for Asian immigrants) are staffed by volunteer docents who give tours and tell stories. Young Alexis wrote: "When you first set foot on Angel Island you see the green of the trees and the yellow of the houses but what you really see is the gray of the people . . . even though the colors may be of joy—you can feel the sorrow." Angel Island is a wonderful place to spend the day or camp overnight (call for reservations: 415-435-1915).

❖ San Quentin Museum

Highway 580 at the Richmond-San Rafael Bridge. San Quentin Prison. (415) 454-8808. Mon., Wed., Fri., 10–1; Tues. & Thurs., 11–3; Sat., 11:45– 3:15. Adults, $2; children under 12, seniors & military, $1. **Ages 7 & up.**

If your kids still think about the life of a criminal after visiting Alcatraz, a visit to San Quentin should put them on the straight and narrow. Artifacts, memorabilia, photographs, and records trace the history of the state's oldest and best known prison, founded in 1852.

❖ Marin County Historical Society Museum

Boyd Park, 1125 B Street, off Third Avenue, San Rafael 94901. (415) 454-8538. Thurs.–Sat., 1–4. Gift shop. Research & photographic records room. Free. **Ages 6 & up.** *W.*

Designed to "stir the imagination and bring back panoramas of the past," this newly refurbished museum reflects themes in Marin's history. The displays range from transportation, with models of the trains and ferries that once served Marin, to the once extensive dairy industry, with a large collection of old milk bottles. One upstairs room is devoted to the late 19th-century fashions and lifestyles of Marin families. Others focus on the Miwok Indians, Mission San Raphael, and military history. Louise Boyd, a famed Arctic explorer and philanthropist, stars in the Marin Pioneer rooms. Exhibits, such as one on filmmaking in Marin, are changed regularly. A favorite with youngsters is the entrance bell from the ferryboat *Donahue*.

Down the block is the **Mission San Rafael Archangel** (1104 Fifth Avenue. 415-456-3016. Daily, 11–4; gift shop; free). Inside this replica of the original Mission built in 1817, the six flags under which the mission has served still fly: Spain, Mexico, the California Republic, the United States of 1850, the Vatican, and the United States of America.

Budding architects may wish to tour the Frank Lloyd Wright–designed **Marin County Civic Center** (3501 Civic Center Drive off Highway 101. 415-499-7407. Business days, 8:30–5. Free). Said the architect: ". . . We know that the good building is not one that hurts the landscape, but is one that makes the landscape more beautiful than it was before that building was built. In Marin County you have one of the most beautiful landscapes I have seen and I am proud to make the buildings of the County characteristic of the beauty of the County."

❖ Wildcare: Terwilliger Nature Education & Wildlife Rehabilitation

76 Albert Park Lane, off B Street, San Rafael 94915. (415) 456-SAVE. (415) 453-1000. Daily, 9–5. Donation. **All ages.** *W.*

This volunteer-run wildlife rehabilitation hospital cares for and releases back into the wilderness over 4,000 birds and mammals each year. The center operates a *Living With Wildlife Hotline* to answer questions about how to live harmoniously with wildlife. Summer and holiday camps, field trips, and nature walks are offered throughout the year. A small interpretive center houses native birds and mammals unable to survive in the wild because of injuries. A museum with hands-on activities for children is open all year.

❖ China Camp Village

China Camp State Park. Off North San Pedro Road from Highway 101. Museum in a shed on piers over the water. 1-800-444-7275; (405) 456-0766. Daily, 10–5. Parking, $3; camping by reservation. **Ages 7 & up.**

In 1889, nearly 500 Chinese processed about 200,000 pounds of shrimp a year on the beach near this 1,400 acre park. Today, the caretaker considers 10 pounds a day a good catch. The little museum displays photographs of Chinese fishermen along with some of the simple furnishings and fishing gear that were part of life in the village. Boilers and a shrimp sheller still toil in the nearby processing shed. The old diner-style bait and snack shop is open on sunny afternoons at the foot of a pier where old timers still catch bass and perch. Birding and bike trails are excellent in this protected, critical wildlife habitat.

❖ Muir Woods National Monument

Muir Woods Road (Off Highway 1), Mill Valley 94941. (415) 388-2595. Daily, 8 to sunset. Group reservations and special events: 388-2596. Free. **All ages.** *W.*

This lovely forest of giant coast redwoods, some more than 200 feet high, is a breathtaking place to start the day. Among these magnificent trees, you'll encounter many other species of plant life, as well as an occasional black-tailed deer and, in summer, young coho salmon swimming through Redwood Creek. Naturalist John Muir wrote, "This is the best tree lover's monument that could be found in all the forests of all the world." A snack bar, gift shop, and ranger's station are near the park entrance. There are several self-guided trails, including one with signs in braille. During a spring visit, we spent a long time just counting all the ladybugs coming awake on the fence posts. Junior-ranger packs are offered free to young naturalists. Ecosystem seminars: (415) 388-2596.

❖ Audubon Canyon Ranch

4900 Highway 1, Stinson Beach 94970. From Stinson Beach, north 3 miles. (415) 868-9244. Mid-March to mid-July, weekends and holidays, 10–4, and by appt. School programs. Bookstore. Picnic areas. Donations. **Ages 5 & up.** *W.*

This 1,000-acre wildlife sanctuary bordering on the Bolinas Lagoon is a peaceful spot to view birds "at home." From a hilltop, you can watch the nesting activities of the great blue heron and the great egret. The ranch's pond, stream, and canyon are a living demonstration of the region's ecology—the delicate balance between plant and animal life and their environment. The display hall/museum shows local fauna and flora and offers information on the San Andreas fault. Ranch guides will explain all.

⇢ Point Reyes National Seashore

National Park Service, Point Reyes 94952. On Highway 1 near Olema. (415) 663-1092. The park is never closed, but no overnight parking is allowed unless you're camping. Free. **All ages.**

When Francis Drake landed here in 1579, his chaplain wrote of a "Faire & Good Baye, with a good wind to enter the same." Today's visitors will agree. The beauty of the cliffs, the surf (swimmable in some places), the tide pools, lowlands, and forest meadows make you wonder why he went back to England. You can follow nature trails, birdwatch, backpack, picnic, rent horses, and camp. We like Drake's Bay best, and before we set out, we call the ranger's office there (669-1250) to check the weather. The cafe at Drake's Bay is nicely protected and even serves fresh oysters.

Start your visit at the **Bear Valley Visitors Center** (weekends, 8–5; weekdays, 9–5). You can get maps with suggested itineraries and all the information you may need while the kids watch a movie or slide show or explore the beautifully designed "walk-through diorama" of the world of Point Reyes. Our favorite of the interactive exhibits is a large log attached to a handle. When you press down, the log lifts up to show all the creepy-crawlies living underneath. Classes and special programs are listed on the schedule.

From Bear Valley, you can walk to the Morgan Horse Ranch (daily, 9–4:30; 415-663-1763), along the Earthquake Trail, or to **Kule Loklo,** the replica of a coastal Miwok village. A granary, sunshade, sweat house, and *Kotcas*, "the place where real people live," have been reconstructed with authentic materials by volunteers. On weekends there are demonstrations on skills such as hunting, sewing, weaving, and preparing acorn mush (sunrise to sunset; interpretive programs on request; 415-663-1092).

The **Ken Patrick Visitors Center** at Drake's Beach has displays on marine paleontology, 15th- and 16th-century exploration, Native Americans, and the marine environment. A saltwater aquarium has critters collected from the bay (weekends, 10–5; 415-669-1250).

The **Point Reyes Bird Observatory's Palomarin Station,** located at the southern entrance to Point Reyes National Seashore, is open to the public for bird-banding demonstrations, nature walks, and educational field trips. Visitors Center and Nature Trail. (415) 868-1221, Ex. 40.

The **Point Reyes Lighthouse** is open, with tours (Thurs.–Mon., 10–4:30). You have to walk down 300 steps to get there, because the light was meant to shine *below* the fog line on Marin's rocky coast. The first wreck occurred here when the Spanish galleon *Sam Agustin* sank in a storm on November 30, 1595. The beacon finally went into service in 1870 and has been saving ships ever since. Because whalewatching is increasingly popular, and the best place for viewing is the lighthouse, the park supplies free weekend shuttlebus service, January to March, from Drake's Beach to the Point Reyes Lighthouse. Visitors are welcome, Thurs.–Mon., 11–4:30. 415-669-1534.

Tomales Bay State Park (daily, 8–8 in summer; until 6 in winter; 415-669-1140; $5 per car) has beaches for swimming and picnic facilities. The tide pools—rocky pockets that retain seawater when the tide goes out—provide endless hours of fascination, as long as you watch very quietly as the tide pool's occupants move through their daily routines. Seaweeds, anemones, barnacles, jellyfish, sand dollars, tiny fish, and flowery algae can hide if they want to!

❯❯ Johnson's Drakes Bay Oysters
Sir Francis Drake Boulevard, on the way to Drake's Bay in Point Reyes National Seashore. (415) 669-1149. Daily, 8–4:30.

Follow the crushed-oyster-shell driveway to the "farm" to see how oysters are raised, and buy a small succulent sample to taste in the sea air. Signs tell you interesting facts about oyster farming. For example, did you know that it takes 18 months for an oyster to grow?

❯❯ Tomales Bay Oyster Company
P.O. Box 296, Point Reyes Station 94956. 115479 Highway 1, Marshall. (415) 663-1242. Daily, 9–5. Picnic area and barbecue.

Families are welcome and, if the tide is out, rubber boots and old clothes are suggested for the kids who want to catch crabs and "slosh" in the mud while looking at intertidal life. The farm is bordered by state park land that is open for hiking and exploring. Founded in 1909, TBOC is the oldest aquaculture facility in the state. Its many "fields" of stakes are spread out in the bay, each stake holding about 100 oysters. Different holding tanks contain seed, juvenile, and harvest-size oysters. Bay mussels are also grown on the farm. Kids love the bags of "empties." And the staff loves answering questions.

❧ Hog Island Oyster Co.

Highway 1, P.O. Box 829, Marshall 94956. (415) 663-9256. Fri., Sat. & Sun, 9–5 & by appt.

Oysters, clams, and abalone are farm-raised and sold alive and in the shell. Built in the late 1860s on the site of Marshall's original general store and railway station, Hog Island welcomes picnickers and provides shucking knives and BBQ kettles for your use. The staff offers "Day on the Farm" educational programs in schools and love to share oyster lore and shucking tips on site.

❧ Marin Museum of the American Indian

Miwok Park, 2200 Novato Boulevard, P.O. Box 864, Novato 94948. (415) 897-4064. From Highway 101 take San Marin Drive west to Novato Boulevard. Tues.–Fri., 10–4; weekends, 12–4. Docent tour Sun., 1:30. Free.
Ages 5 & up.

"Thank you so much for being our guide! I would love to come back! . . . I loved your visitors exhibit. I have been using my crow call a lot and wearing my arrowhead necklace a lot too. I learned a lot about the artifacts and boat materials, clothing, food, money, and their religious ceremonies. I loved the diorama. I also enjoyed grinding acorns and drilling holes into the soapstone. I was fascinated about what they wore for religious ceremonies. It was so very interesting examining their money, blankets, and games. Hope to see you soon!" This was from Kylie, fifth grade.

The hands-on education room downstairs in the Museum invites visitors to explore Coast Miwok Indian culture through replicas of clothing, tools, animal skins, mortars and pestles, shell bead money, basketry, and hunting implements. Changing exibits focus on other aspects of Indian cultures of the western United States. Classes, lectures, films, and docent-led fieldtrips, summer day camps, and weekend programs are offered, so call for fees and schedules. A newly refurbished California Native Plant Garden including a tule pond with miniature replica tule kochcha (house) flank the museum building.

To walk in the world of the Miwok, drive north on Highway 101 a mile past the Marin airport to San Antonio Road, and cross west off the highway to the **Olompali State Historic Park and Gardens,** the former site of an old Miwok Indian village. The Olompali people are working as a cooperation association to restore the historic adobes that were saved, in 1863, when Maria Black married Dr. Galen Burdell and they encased the Miwok adobes in wooden siding as part of their first home. To help, call (415) 892-3383.

In downtown Novato, the **Novato History Museum** (815 DeLong Avenue. 415-897-4320. Wed., Thurs., Sat., 12–4. Free), in the home of the town's first postmaster, focuses on the history of northern Marin County.

✧ Dollhouses, Trains & More/Dollhouses & Crafts of Marin

14 Commercial Boulevard, #111, Novato 94949 (415) 883-0388. Mon.– Fri., 9–6; weekends, 10–5. **All ages.**

An 800-square-foot dollhouse village, a "lake with waterfalls" for floating boats, a Lego room, and other playrooms bring fans into this combination store and crafts center, which offers special classes.

✳ The East Bay: Alameda and Contra Costa Counties

Mount Diablo crowns the East Bay, which ranges along the east shore of San Francisco Bay. There's even a visitor's center and observation near the top of Mount Diablo (Wed.–Sun., 11–5; free, 510-837-6119). The places of interest in the East Bay are some distance from each other, so plan ahead and call for up-to-the-minute times and prices. Boaters, fishermen, picnickers, hikers, and nature lovers of all ages will find public parks to visit here.

⇒ Treasure Island Museum
Building 1, Treasure Island, off the Bay Bridge, San Francisco 94130. (415) 395-5067. Weekdays, 10–3; weekends, 10–4:30. Fee: 12 & over, $3. Walking tours and groups by appt. **Ages 5 & up.** *W.*

The drive to Treasure Island and its art deco masterpiece built for the 1939 World's Fair provides one of the great views of San Francisco. Inside the building is a large, airy collection of naval memories. The activities of the Navy, Marine Corps, and Coast Guard in Pacific waters, from before the Civil War to tomorrow's space ventures, are well presented. See the Farallon Islands Lighthouse lens, a 1919 diver's suit, ship models, World's Fair mementos, and Pearl Harbor photos. One of the changing displays includes African American naval heroes. Towering over all is Lowell Nesbitt's vast mural of the past, present, and future of American armed services in the Pacific.

⇒ TJ's Gingerbread House
741 Fifth Street, Oakland 94607. Take the Broadway exit from Highway 880. (510) 444-7373. Breakfast, 8–10; lunch, 11–3; dinner (by reservation), 6–8:30, Tues–Sat. Gazebo & Pink House downstairs are available for parties. **All ages.** *Partially W.*

Hansel and Gretel's wicked witch would be envious of this restaurant, which looks good enough to eat. In a tiny shop downstairs, you'll find gingerbread cookies, puppets, dolls, T-shirts, soaps, tea—even gingerbread bubble bath. Upstairs, in a fantasy land of dolls—"a dream come true!"—TJ Robinson serves copious Cajun-Creole breakfasts, lunches, and dinners. Prices range from $13, for vegetarian rice and beans, to $35 for Pheasant "Von Temps." Try Bayou Spiced-Baked Catfish and "Spoon" Jambalaya, or Pick-Your-Heart-Out-Chicken. Each meal comes with fruit salad, Cajun come-back dirty rice, vegetables, sassy corn bread, beverage, and ice cream with a gingerbread cookie. For a nominal price, children can order just their own fruit salad, rice, and dessert.

❧ Museum of Children's Art (MOCHA)

560 Second Street, Jack London Square, Oakland 94607. (510) 465-8770. Mon.–Sat., 10–5; Sun. 12–5. Free. **Ages 2–12.**

Right from the entrance, where the garbage container on the sidewalk has been tiled by kids, you can tell this is a special place. What makes it so special is that everything in the museum has been made by children. Gallery exhibits change monthly, whether it's story quilts made by second graders or clay sculptures done by fifth graders. The museum was created to make art accessible to all children, regardless of race or socio-economic background. Programs are held both onsite and in schools, shelters, and hospitals. On Friday and Sunday afternoons, parents and children can work on art projects together.

❧ Ebony Museum

#30 Jack London Village, Suite 208–9, Oakland 94607. (510) 763-0745. Tues.–Sat., 11–6; Sun., 12–6. Donation. Gift shop. Guided tours by appt. **Ages 5 & up.** *W.*

This grassroots museum specializes in African and African-American arts and artifacts. Benin royal tribal busts, 300-year-old Lobi ancestor figures from Zaire, and chieftain headdresses mingle with graceful wooden statues and rows of weathered masks. The "Degradation" collection of early racist art is an eye-opener, but the owner, Aissatoui Vernita, believes in waking kids (and adults) up. The "soul" jewelry—necklaces of gold chitlins, fatback earrings, peanut pendants—is fun.

A life-size statue of Jack London greets visitors to Jack London Village, now being restored as a center for shopping, dining, play, and the arts. Heinold's First and Last Chance Saloon, where Jack London hung out, is still open. Nearby is the log cabin Jack London supposedly lived in when in the Yukon and a tiny Jack London Museum. To take advantage of the estuary, take a tour at the Oakland East Bay Water Tours (510-835-1306) or California Canoe and Kayak, which also offers classes and rentals (510-893-7833). Jack London Village can be reached by Amtrak and the Alameda/Oakland Ferry (510-522-3300).

❧ Center for African American History & Life

Golden Gate Library, 5606 San Pablo Avenue, Oakland 94612. (510) 597-5023. Wed., Thurs., Sat., 10–5:30; Fri., 12–5:30, and by appt. Free. **Ages 6 & up.**

California's African Americans and their history are the theme of this lovingly put together collection that focuses on local families and recalls especially African American athletes, musicians, scientists, politicians, gold miners, cowboys, farmers, and doctors. Some of the people youngsters will "meet" here are Pio Pico, an early governor of California; black mountaineer James Beckworth; "Mammy" Pleasant; William A. Leidesdorff, who built one of San Francisco's first hotels and launched the first steamer in San Francisco Bay; and Colonel Allensworth, a black Army chaplain who founded one of the state's first black communities.

❧ Oakland Museum of California

1000 Oak Street, Oakland 94607-4892. (510) 238-2200. Wed.–Sat., 10–5; Sun., 12–7. Closed holidays. Adults, $5; students & seniors $3; children 5 & under, free. Sundays 4–7, free. Cafe. Gift shop. **Ages 5 & up.** *W.*

The Oakland Museum of California is actually three first-rate museums in one: California art, California natural sciences, and California history. You can always be sure of finding an afternoon's worth of interesting things for children of all ages.

One level concentrates on art from the days of the Spanish explorers to the present. Panoramic views of San Francisco and Yosemite, cityscapes and landscapes, and contemporary jewelry, ceramics, photos, paintings, and sculpture create a historic continuity in the visual arts.

The natural sciences gallery takes you across the nine zones of California, from the coast to the snow-capped eastern Sierra with its ancient bristlecone pines. Dioramas and displays of mammals, birds, rodents, and snakes in their native habitats provide fascinating replicas of the real thing.

Kids will like the California history level best of all. Begin with the Native Californians, the many Indian tribes, and walk through the superbly furnished "rooms" of the state's history, from the Spanish explorers and *Californios* to the gold miners and cowboys, the pioneers, the Victorian San Franciscans, and on to the California dream, from *Beach Party* to *American Graffiti* and the "Summer of Love."

We always head for the 1890s shiny red fire pumper and the pioneer kitchen with the chair outside the glass—to bring the visitor into the picture. The "information TV centers" provide instant answers to kids' questions with demonstrations and discussions by noted authorities.

Concerts, films, and special exhibits are scheduled regularly. One young visitor wrote in the guest log, "I think that using junk to create art is very ingenious."

❧ Paramount Theatre

2025 Broadway, Oakland 94612. Take Highway 980 to the Downtown exit. (510) 893-2300. Public tours, first and third Sat. of the month, 10 A.M. & by appt. $1. Not advised for those under 10.

The Paramount, which has programs of interest to children, is the best example of art deco architecture on the West Coast. A metal grill-work ceiling teeming with sculpted life, gold walls with sculpted motifs from the Bible and mythology, and elegant embellishments almost compete with what's on stage.

❯❯ The Camron-Stanford House

1418 Lakeside Drive, Oakland 94612. (510) 836-1976. Tours Wed., 11–4; Sun., 1–5; and by appt. Donation. Children 12 and under free. **Ages 8 & up.**

This 1876 Italianate-style Victorian, once the Oakland Museum, shows life in the days of horse cars and gas lighting. Museum displays in the basement show local history as well as the restoration of the mansion. The multimedia Academy Award–winning documentary, "Living in a House," inspired by the life and letters of Franklina Gray Bartlett, shows what it was like to live in a house in Oakland from 1876 to 1936. Upstairs, the elegant rooms have been restored to gracious splendor and include a portrait of Franklina as a 14-month-old bacchante, as well as newspaper stories about her wedding here. Multimedia shows, special exhibits, and engaging docents add to the young visitor's enjoyment.

❯❯ The Pardee Home

672 11th Street, near Castro Street, in Preservation Park, Oakland 94607. (510) 444-1287. One-hour tours by reservation, Thurs., Fri. & Sat., 11, 1, and 2:30. Adults, $4; seniors $3; under 12, free. **Ages 7 & up.**

Youngsters who want to step back in time will also enjoy visiting Governor George C. Pardee's art-laden family home, water tower, carriage house and barn. Built in 1868 at a cost of $12,000, the home is one of the finest remaining examples of the bracketed Italianate villa style in the area and still stands on the original lot. Pardee's daughters, Madeline and Helen, lived in the house until 1980–81. They maintained their mother's extensive collections of candlesticks, minerals, teapots, ceramic pottery, glassware, rocks, scrimshaw, art and textiles from Asia, Africa, North America, and South America just as she'd left them. Scholars will be interested in the extensive archive of photographs and documents related to the Pardee family. Somehow, children are fascinated by all of the collections in this home.

Another historic home in downtown Oakland is the **Cohen-Bray House,** which is a perfect example of "fly in amber" preservation. It is a nearly perfect representation of Anglo-Japanese style in 1884 because it was a wedding gift to Emma Bray and Alfred Cohen on February 28,

1884. Their daughter Emelita lived there—and never redecorated—until she died in 1991. Today the house serves as a study center of late-19th-century decorative arts. For tours call the Victorian Preservation Center at (510) 532-0704.

❧ The Fortune Cookie Factory

261 12th Street, at Harrison, Oakland 94607. (510) 832-5552. Mon.–Sat., 10–3. Tours, $1; groups by appt. Free cookies. **Ages 5 & up.**

Fortune cookie machines are huge and black and make a lot of noise. You can see the flames inside them. Small round pans march relentlessly in and out of the flames. A giant dipper drops cookie batter into each pan, and by the time the rounds emerge, they are browned and just soft enough to bend. A worker grabs the soft round, puts a fortune in the cookie, and folds it over a small metal bar, then sets it on a cooling rack. The fortune cookies also come in flavors. And you can write your own fortune.

❧ Lakeside Park

Off Grand Avenue at Lake Merritt, Oakland 94612-4598. **All ages.**

A narrow strip of grass around Lake Merritt creates a peaceful oasis in the center of a busy city. In the Kiwanis Kiddie Korner, children can slide down double and triple slides and play on swings or climb on rocks in the Astro Circle, which looks like the Jetsons' home or a UFO rocket/spaceship. The **Rotary Nature Center** offers an educational exhibit of native reptiles, mammals, and birds as well as turtle ponds and an observation beehive (510-238-3739; daily, 10–5; free; parking, $2 on weekends). One young visitor wrote, "I enjoy your animals. The toad felt like mashed potatoes. I want to come back soon."

Lake Merritt is the oldest wildlife refuge in the United States for free-flying waterbirds, which include an occasional pelican. Sailboats, houseboats, and paddleboats are available for renting. The *Merritt Queen*, a replica of a Mississippi riverboat, takes half-hour tours of the lake on weekends and in summer for a nominal fee.

❧ Children's Fairyland

Lakeside Park, at Grand & Bellevue Avenues, Lake Merritt, Oakland 94612. (510) 452-2259. Spring and fall, Wed.–Sun., 10–4:30; winter, Fri.–Sun. and school holidays, 10–4:30; daily in summer, 10–5:30. Adults, $2.25; children, $1.75. Gift shop. Parties by reservation. **Ages 2–13**.

Duck through The Old Woman's Shoe to meet Alice, the Cheshire Cat, and the Cowardly Lion. Then slide down a dragon's back or sail on a pea-green boat with the Owl and the Pussycat. Pinocchio, Willie the Whale, slides, mazes, rides, and enchanted bowers come to life. This 10-acre playland is where young children can explore, play, and let their imaginations run free with rides, puppet shows, animals, and storybook settings.

Junior Center of Art and Science

558 Bellevue Avenue, Oakland. (510) 839-5777. Tues.–Fri., 10–6; Sat., 10–3. Weekends, groups, and outreach programs by reservation. Free. **Ages 3–12.**

Changing art and cultural exhibits on subjects such as the birds of Lake Merritt, California Native Americans, and African-American heroes greet the drop-in visitor and those scheduled for weekend or after-school art classes. On Discovery Row, visitors will enjoy childsize displays of five animal habitats at their eye level. Then they can use the Drawing Surface to make their impressions of the leopard geckos, the seven-inch-long African millipede, the Canadian garden snake, fish, turtles, bugs, and the hissing cockroaches. Jake, the miniature lop-eared rabbit, is a family favorite.

Knowland Park–Oakland Zoo

9777 Golf Links Road, Oakland 94609. At 98th Avenue off Highway 580. (510) 632-9523. Park open 9–5 daily, except Christmas and Thanksgiving, weather permitting. Park admission: $3 per car. Zoo: daily, 10–4, later on summer weekends. Adults, $5.50; ages 2–14 and seniors, $3; group discounts. Rides: 75 cents & $1.50. **All ages.** *W.*

This beautifully arranged zoo is one of the nicest in the state. Glide over the African veldt and up into the hills on the 1,250-foot Skyfari Ride, or ride a miniature train for a breathtaking view of the bay. Over 330 animals from around the world make their home in 525 acres of rolling green parkland. The Children's Petting Zoo will make tots' barnyard tales come alive. Picnic, barbecue, and playground facilities are located throughout the park.

Brookdale Discovery Center

2521 High Street, Allendale, Oakland. (510) 535-5657. Tues.–Sat., 2–8 P.M. Free. **Ages 5 & up.** *W.*

This new hands-on science workshop for kids is a homemade mini-Exploratorium created by volunteers. The group's inspiration, Rich Bolecek, looks at it as a toolbox or tinkerer's basement for the neighborhood apartment-dwelling kids, who flock to his treasure house full of wires, plastic tubes, glue guns, batteries, magnets, drills, milk crates, and a hamster named Sunflower.

⇌ Western Aerospace Museum

8260 Boeing Street, Oakland Airport North Field, P.O. Box 14264, Oakland 94614. Near Doolittle Drive and Hegenberger. From Highway 880, west until you reach Earhart, right on Earhart to Hanger 6, Alaska Airlines, then right onto Cook. (510) 638-7100. Wed.–Sun., 10–4. Adults, $4; ages 6–12, $2; 6 and under, free. $2 for Short Solent flying boat tour. Gift shop. **Ages 6 & up.** *W.*

Nineteen antique and retired aircraft, along with a space shuttle and a space shuttle simulation cabin can be seen in this exciting museum. Among the aircraft you'll find a Navy jet A-3 bomber, a Navy A-7 fighter, a Navy A-6 attack aircraft, a NASA "jump jet," a TBM torpedo bomber, a Lockheed 10E like Amelia Earhart's (without the camera modifications), a Yugo trainer, an aerobatic flyer, and a Bucker Jung-meister stunt plane. The pride of the fleet is the Short Solent, a large flying boat used in *Raiders of the Lost Ark.* Twelve exhibit rooms show flying photos and memorabilia on subjects such as Jimmy Doolittle, early Oakland aviation, African-American aviators, and women pilots. Little kids like to look at the planes, older ones like to sit in them and "pretend fly."

The museum offers a discount on the Otis Spunkmeyer hour-long tours in a historic 18-passenger DC-3 ($99; 510-649-5900).

⇌ Dunsmuir House and Garden

2960 Peralta Oaks Court, Oakland 94605. Take the 106th Avenue exit from Highway 580. (510) 562-0328/3232. Mar.–Sept. Grounds open Tues.–Fri., 10–4. Drop-in Mansion tours, Weds. 11 & 12; advance reservations required for Thurs. & Fri., 11 A.M. Adults, $5; seniors and youngsters 6–12, $4; under 6, free. Call for group rates and box lunch reservations. Special Family Sundays throughout the season, such as Easter, Father's Day, 4th of July, Scottish Highland Games, "Music on the Meadow" concert series, and annual December Holiday Faire. Admission varies for special events. Call (510) 615-5555. **Ages 7 & up.**

This 37-room Colonial Revival mansion is set in a 40-acre estate in the East Oakland foothills. A visit will provide an enlightening sense of another way of life through architecture, photos, and garden strolls. Dunsmuir is the site of movies, weddings, and private events.

⟫ Chabot Observatory & Planetarium

4917 Mountain Boulevard, Oakland 94619. MacArthur Freeway (Interstate 80) and Warren Freeway (Highway 13). (510) 530-3480. Fri. & Sat., 7:30 P.M. Adults, $5; children 6–17, $3. Group rates. Reservations advised (call 9–5, Mon.–Fri.). The Chabot Science Center is not open on a regular schedule, so call ahead. **Ages 6 & up.**

The changing two-hour show here includes a movie, science demonstrations, planetarium program, and observation of the heavens through two large telescopes. Locating the Big and Little Dippers during the planetarium show is always a popular part of the program. Recent shows included "The Sky Tonight" and "The Dark of Night."

⟫ Crab Cove Visitor's Center

1252 McKay Avenue, Alameda 94501. (510) 521-6887. Wed.–Sun., 10–4:30. Tours by reservation. Free. **All ages.**

This East Bay Regional Park District center is where the old Coast Guard Station was, on Crown Beach. The museum displays marine life and San Francisco Bay animals such as a saltwater hawk, a turtle snake, and a mountain toad.

⟫ Alameda Historical Museum

2324 Alameda Avenue, Alameda 94501. (510) 521-1233. Wed.–Sun., 1:30–4; Sat., 11–4. Free. Walking tours. **Ages 6 & up.** *W.*

The official repository of objects relating to the history of Alameda, the museum owns collections of vintage clothing, household furnishings, toys, and art. The museum's pride and joy is quite modern, however: "Paint an Alameda House" is a hands-on exhibit of color design for older homes featuring computerized images of 16 of Alameda's homes; it's an electric coloring book that teaches as it amuses.

⟫ UC Berkeley Art Museum and Pacific Film Archive

2626 Bancroft Way (Mail: 2625 Durant Ave., Berkeley 94720-2250). (510) 642-0808. Wed.–Sun., 11–5; Thurs. until 9. Ages 18–64, $6; ages 12–17 and over 65, $4; under 12, free. Free admission Thurs. 11–12 and 5–9. **Ages 7 & up.** *W.*

The UC Berkeley Art Museum is a natural for children, not so much for the art but for the building itself. Its unique multileveled, concrete-slab construction enables a young visitor to see its spacious interiors from any of the many corners and balconies. The outdoor sculpture garden is fun and strikes a chord with young people. The Pacific Film Archive, part of the museum, shows classic, international, and children's films for all ages. Call (510) 642-1124 for schedules.

❧ Lawrence Hall of Science

Centennial Drive, University of California, Berkeley 94720. Up Hearst to the top of the University, to Gayley Road, to Rim Way, to Centennial. Just south of Grizzly Peak Boulevard. (510) 642-5132. Daily, 10–5. Adults, $6; students and seniors, $4; ages 3–6, $2. Galaxy Snack Bar. Parties. **Ages 4 & up.** *W.*

There are young scientists who'd rather spend a day here than anywhere else in the world. The Lawrence Hall of Science has an outstanding variety of exhibits, science workshops, tests of your mathematical and logical ability, tests of knowledge, computers to play with, visual oddities, and a hundred different things to tantalize and amuse. That brightly colored structure on the outdoor plaza isn't just something to climb on, it's a replica of a DNA molecule. Tots love the growling apatosaurus. Many kids are fascinated by "Within the Human Brain," in which visitors step inside a simulated "rate cage" of learning activities. "Math Rules!," a collection of hands-on math challenges, sweeps others away. The Biology Lab is the place to investigate the world of living things (weekends and holidays, 1:30–4:30; daily in summer). Holt Planetarium shows, the Science Discovery Theater, and special events offer ever-changing inducements to learning.

As one visitor wrote "The LHS is the best science place to visit in the world. I learned a lot!! Have a good day!!" Another simply said "This place is cool!"

❧ Phoebe Hearst Museum of Anthropology

Kroeber Hall, Bancroft Way, at College Avenue, University of California, Berkeley 94720. (510) 643-7648. Wed.–Fri., 10–4:30; weekends, 10–4:30; Thurs. until 9. Adults, $2; seniors, $1; children, 50 cents. Museum store. **Ages 6 & up.**

Ten-year-old Mary wrote, "This place is really cool and interesting. I especially liked the rock statue of Phoebe Hearst. It was beautiful. I liked looking at the pottery too. P.S. How did you get all this stuff here?" Gena wrote, "I liked the headphones, the cows, and the baby carrier from Borneo." Many of the museum's rotating exhibits are developed from its vast holdings of ethnographic, archaeological, and archival materials. On occasion, the museum hosts traveling exhibits related to anthropology and ethnic studies. A visit will help children understand other peoples' worlds, past and present.

School groups may request tours of all major exhibitions and children's activity sheets will be provided. A special presentation on Ishi and the invention of Yahi Culture is given for school groups year-round. In addition, a limited number of teaching kits that complement

state-mandated social science curricula are available for loan at no charge.
Reserve early! Lectures, movies, and slide presentations are also available.

➣ The Campanile

Sather Tower, University of California, Berkeley 94720. (510) 642-5215.
Mon.–Sat., 10–3:30; Sun., 10–1:45. 50 cents. **Ages 6 & up.**

From the top of this tower, you can see San Francisco, Alcatraz,
Mt. Tamalpais, the Golden Gate and Bay bridges, and the entire campus.
Above you, 61 bronze bells, the largest weighing 10,000 pounds, ring out
melodies three times a day. You can see them being played.

➣ Hall of Health

2230 Shattuck Avenue, lower level, Berkeley 94704. (510) 549-1564.
Tues.–Sat., 10–4. Groups by appt. Drop-in visits encouraged. Free. **Ages 5
& up.** *W.*

"Your body is yours for life . . . take care of it yourself" is the motto
here. The Hall of Health, sponsored by Children's Hospital Oakland and
Alta Bates Medical Center, is a free hands-on health museum full of interactive exhibits that encourage you to learn with all your senses. Kids can
ride an exercycle that counts calories burned, put together a life-size mag-
netic bone puzzle, look at cells in microscopes, watch films, and much
more. Younger children can listen to their heart beat, visit the organ cut-
out table, and draw their insides on a human-shaped chalkboard. There
are interactive exhibits on safety, drugs, addiction, and the heart and
circulatory system. On the third Saturday of each month, the Hall of
Health sponsors Kids on the Block puppet shows to promote acceptance
and understanding of physical, mental, medical, and cultural differences.
The puppet characters represent diverse cultures and have conditions such
as cerebral palsy, Down syndrome, and blindness.

A 7-year-old wrote, "I liked all of the computers and the junk food
man. The eyeball looks funny. The bladder sounds funny. I could not put
the brain together." One second grader reported, "I never knew so much
about the body. Doesn't it seem kind of impossible for 206 bones to fit in
a body?"

➣ Judah L. Magnes Museum

2911 Russell Street, one block north of Ashby off Pine, Berkeley 94708.
(510) 549-6950. Sun.–Thurs., 10–4. Tours Wed. & Sun. Groups by
reservation. Donation. Children free. Gift shop. **Ages 6 & up.** *W.*

Prints, photographs, maps, prayer books, and ceremonial art from
the museum's collections illuminate the city's place in Jewish, Christian,
and Muslim traditions. The changing exhibits of art and artifacts always

include something that is of special interest to children. Afterwards, they can picnic in the garden.

⇶ Tilden Regional Park

Canon Drive, off Grizzly Peak Boulevard, Berkeley 94708. (510) 525-2233. Nominal prices for rides (weekends, 10–5; weekdays, 11–5). The Little Farm is open daily, 8:30–5. Free. **Ages 2–13.**

Tilden Park has a pony ride, historic merry-go-round, and miniature train. Native California botanical gardens, an Environmental Educational Center, wooded hiking trails, and swimming in Lake Anza are also popular. But the chief attraction for youngsters is the Little Farm in the Nature Area. Here they can meet barnyard animals such as sheep, goats, cows, pigs, chickens, geese, rabbits, and a sociable donkey.

⇶ Pixieland Park

2740 East Olivera Road, at Willow Pass Park, Concord 94519. (510) 689-8841. Daily in summer, and Wed.–Sun. in winter, 10:30–6. Rides 90 cents, 10 for $7. Unlimited weekday pass, 10:30–4, $7.50. Special pack: 60 rides for $35. **Ages 2–10.**

This small amusement park is strictly for very young children. Spinning Tea Cups, a Jungle of Fun, and a Flying Dragon Roller Coaster are new additions to this sweet little park. Old favorites such as the merry-go-round, train, boat ride, car ride, and airplane are still there. There's a little concession stand and a picnic area reserved for birthday parties.

⇶ McConaghy Estate

18701 Hesperian Boulevard, Hayward 94541. Off Highway 880 between Bockman and A Streets. (510) 276-3010. Thurs.–Sun., 1–4. Last tour at 3:30. Groups: (510) 278-0198. Adults, $3; seniors, $2; ages 6–12, 50 cents. Classes, $10. Special Christmas program and rates. Closed holidays, Thanksgiving week, and January. **Ages 7 & up.**

This elegant 1886 farmhouse is so completely furnished it looks as if the family still lives here. One bedroom is filled with toys, games, books, and clothes used by a turn-of-the-century child. The dining room is lavishly decorated for each holiday. A tank house and a buggy-filled carriage house adjoin the house, handily located next to Kennedy Park with its picnic tables, merry-go-round, and train.

⇶ Hayward Area Historical Society Museum

22701 Main Street, at C, Hayward 94541. (510) 581-0223. Mon.–Fri., 11–4; Sat., 12–4. Closed holidays. Adults, $1; children 6–12, 50 cents. **Ages 6 & up.** *W.*

The large brick 1927 post office is now a lovingly presented album of Hayward area history. A 1923 fire engine, an 1820s hand-drawn fire pumper that was shipped around the Horn to San Francisco in 1849, and a 1930s post office present an engaging glimpse of the lifestyle of the past. Exhibits change three times a year to keep visitors returning. A favorite is the holiday collection of toys, trains, dolls, Christmas ornaments, and cards.

❯❯ Sulphur Creek Nature Center

1801 D Street, Hayward 94541. (510) 881-6747. Tues.–Sun, 10–5. Free. Animal-lending library, 10–3, $7. SlphrCreek@aol.com. Picnic tables. **Ages 3 & up.** *W.*

Sulphur Creek Park is a charming spot in which to introduce children to wildlife native to Northern California. Coyotes, opossums, foxes, rabbits, hawks, owls, song and garden birds, a variety of reptiles and amphibians, and invertebrates are displayed in natural habitats. There are changing exhibits and a wildlife garden. Nature study classes, wildlife rehabilitation, and volunteer opportunities are available. A fan wrote, "I liked the opossum, when you brought it out! I like the crow. While you were with the other group the crow said 'hellow.' I learned that there are more animals and bigger habitats. Thank you for talking to us."

❯❯ Hayward Shoreline Interpretive Center

4901 Breakwater Avenue, Hayward 94545. (510) 881-6751. Daily, 10–5. Free. Hayshore@aol.com. Gift store. Volunteer opportunities. Summer day camps. **Ages 6 & up.**

Located on the Hayward shore of San Francisco Bay, this center displays exhibits of local estuary animals and is the hub of a 1,800-acre marshland park. You can explore marine life in a hands-on Wet Lab, search for animal life under the microscope, see a variety of exhibits on the shoreline area, check out a free family discovery pack or binoculars, and hike on eight miles of trails. Public naturalist programs on weekends. Aaron wrote, "Thank you for taking us around Hayward Shoreline and showing us insects under the water. I liked picking up scum in the nets. I liked the Mud Dobber! I think it's amazing how God has made creatures great and small. There is also something else that I noticed. A dragonfly came up to me and stared at me in the face and then flew away."

❯❯ Ardenwood Farm

Ardenwood Regional Park, 34600 Ardenwood Boulevard, at Highway 84, Fremont 94555. (510) 796-0663/796-0199. Apr.–mid-Nov., Christmas *events and holidays, Thurs.–Sun., 10–4. Adults, $6; ages 4–17, $3.50; seniors and disabled, $4. Special events, extra. House tours by appt. on a first-come first-served basis. Wagon rides. Rain may close the park.* **All ages.** *W.*

Ardenwood Farm leaped onto our "top 11" list on the first visit. The 205-acre farm is a look into the Bay Area's farming past. Its motto:

> May learning, science, useful art,
> Adorn thy life, improve thy heart.
> May kind affection, love so dear,
> Hereafter bless, and guide you here.

At Ardenwood, kids of any age can visit a remarkably well restored Victorian farmhouse, built in 1857 by George Patterson, a '49er who found gold in the land. Costumed docents tend the Victorian flower garden, demonstrate Victorian crafts such as as lacemaking, and show off farming skills. Farm produce and flowers can be purchased. The Deer Park train is fun. There are lots of animals in the farm yard. There are also picnic and party areas, and concerts are given in the gazebo. Amy said, "I learned that history can be real fun by the way you girls made it." Juliane expounded, "I learned that women were very fancy. They wore corsets laced very tightly, which rearranged their internal organs. They wore swimsuits which you couldn't swim in. They wore a hatpin and always carried an umbrella. They had small beds. I learned this from your presentation. When some of my classmates got to put something on, I found it really hilarious."

↠ Mission San Jose

43300 Mission Boulevard, Fremont 94539. (510) 657-1797. Daily, 10– 5. Closed holidays. Adults, $2; children 12 and over, $1. Group tours by reservation. **Ages 7 & up.** *W.*

"Dear Mission San Jose, I appreciated you letting us come to your mission. It was fun and exciting to see how the missioners lived and I liked the slide show about the mission and the church. I had a good time. My favorite thing was the fountain and the olive trees. Thank you very much. Sincerely, Lakisha."

Founded in 1797, Mission San Jose holds an exciting place in California history. A highlight of the museum tour is an exhibit on the Ohlone, the native people of the Bay Area. Father Duran, who arrived in 1806, taught some of the 2,000 Ohlone neophytes to play the original mission bells and musical instruments now on display. Original mission vestments, the original baptismal font, a pioneer cradle, and the sanctus bells are housed in the adobe living quarters of the mission padres. The mission church has been carefully reconstructed from hand-hewn beams and more than 180,000 adobe bricks.

San Francisco Bay National Wildlife Refuge

Highway 84, Fremont 94539. At the east end of the Dumbarton Bridge, near the toll plaza, off Thornton Avenue. (510) 792-3178. Visitors Center, Tues.–Sun., 10–5. Free. **Ages 5 & up.**

Weekend interpretive programs, nature study walks, slide and film presentations, and a self-guided trail through the marsh and diked ponds help introduce youngsters to the world around them. Discover packs are available free for checkout and further exploratory fun.

Stephanie rhapsodized, "Thank you for the presentation you gave us. I like making tule rope. Angie and I made four ropes. When I looked through the binoculars I saw a squirrel and a white rabbit. I also saw ducks on the pond. When we played predator or prey I guessed them quickly. When I was on the bus I saw a snowy egret. I went on the board-walk with Michelle's grandfather. We saw pickle weed and we smelled sage. It smelled good. I liked the Indian games with stick, dice, marble game, and the relay game too. The stuffed animals looked like they were alive. I liked the way the pheasant felt. I liked the noisy musical instru-ment. It sounded like an airplane propeller. . . . It was interesting to see and learn how the Indians cooked, fished, caught things, and played games. Right then I knew it was difficult to live in the Indian times. I hope I can come again sometime."

Wind Farms of Altamont Pass

On windy days you can often hear them before you see them—the more than 7,500 giant wind turbines, perched on towers, on either side of Interstate 580. The world's largest "wind farm" produces electricity from the wind. A seven-mile drive just north of and paralleling I-580, begun either from Greenville or Mountain House roads, east of Livermore, tours the heart of the wind farms.

Livermore History Center

2155 Third Street, Livermore 94550. (510) 449-9927. Wed.–Sun., 11–3. Free. **Ages 8 & up.**

This exhibit on the history of the Livermore Valley from prehistoric times to the present is housed in the old Carnegie Library. Pictures, maps, artifacts, and mementos from local families, businesses, and groups are on display. A 19th-century drugstore exhibit has been installed. The mu-seum members are currently working on the restoration of the historical

Duarte Garage/Lincoln Highway Museum in Livermore at North L Street and Portola. Early-day fire trucks, wagons, and other apparatus can be viewed by appointment.

Ravenswood, the Victorian-era home and gardens of San Francisco's "Blind Boss" Christopher Buckley, is occasionally open to the public (on Arroyo Road; call 510-373-5770 for an appointment). Visitors will see cloisonne chandeliers, an ornate billiard table, clothing, pictures, and mementos of the Buckley family.

➢ Amador-Livermore Valley Museum

603 Main Street, Pleasanton 94566. (510) 462-2766. Wed.–Fri., 11–4; Sat. & Sun., 1–4. Donation. **Ages 8 & up.** *W.*

Housed in the 1914 Town Hall, this museum features platform exhibits of yesteryear including a blacksmith shop. Changing cultural exhibits explore the Tri-Valley area's history from fossil remains to the present. The Museum Art Gallery exhibits change regularly and feature local artists in all media.

➢ Clayton Historical Museum

6101 Main Street, P.O. Box 94, Clayton 94517. (510) 672-0240. Groups & reservations: (510) 672-4786. Wed. & Sun., 2–4. Free. Gift shop. **Ages 8 & up.**

Located at the base of Mount Diablo, this city of 9,000 owes its existence to a fear of developers—it's a small, quaint old town. The Museum, the home of the town founder, miner Joel Clayton, is one of several older buildings that occupy the downtown district and whisper about yesteryear. Period furnishings, photos, coal mining artifacts, and British family memorabilia bring this 1860s home to life. Clayton was so wealthy that he loaned money to William Randolph Hearst's father, George, but he died in 1872 while tending cattle.

➢ The Behring Automotive Museum

3700 Blackhawk Plaza Circle, Danville 94506. (510) 736-2280. Wed.–Sun., 10–5. Adults, $7; students & seniors, $4. Lectures & programs. Tours by appt. Gift Shop. **Ages 7 & up.** *W.*

The Behring Classic Car Museum shows rare classic automobiles as works of art. It showcases Kenneth Behring's $100 million collection of custom-built and one-of-a-kind automobiles created during the years between the two world wars. There are rotating exhibits of the 120 autos as well as video interactive presentations with the designers of the Tucker, Duesenberg, 1955 Ford Thunderbird, and other classics. The 1897 Leon

Bollee three-wheeler, the oldest existing GM automobile, and the nickel-silver-bodied Daimler built for the Maharaja of Rewa are favorites.

The UC Berkeley Paleontology Gallery, on the lower level near the gift shop, is free and showcases artifacts dating back to 3,500 B.C. The museum is especially proud of a nine-million-year-old mastodon found just two miles away in the Blackhawk Quarry Site. "Lucy," the oldest known human skeleton, is part of the exhibit of fossils.

✦ Richmond Museum

400 Nevin Avenue at 4th Street, P.O. Box 1265, Richmond 94802. (510) 235-7387. Wed.–Sun., 1–4, except holiday weekends, and by appt. Free.
Ages 8 & up. *W.*

Life in the Richmond area up to the mid-1940s is portrayed in the history gallery with the aid of room re-creations, photographs, panel displays, and text. Old-time vehicles such as a peddler's wagon and a Model A Ford are a thrill to young and old alike. In addition to the permanent history gallery, changing exhibits draw on a wide variety of topics of local interest.

✦ Diablo Valley College Museum & Planetarium

321 Golf Club Road, Pleasant Hill 94523. Off Willow Pass Road from Highway 680. (510) 685-1230 ext. 330. Hours change each semester. Groups by appt. **Ages 8 & up.**

In this museum youngsters can see a seismograph working, a Foucault pendulum swinging, and changing oceanography and anthropological exhibits on Native Americans. Local animals, especially the nocturnal moles, weasels, and owls, are fun to see, as are the star shows.

✦ The Lindsay Museum

1931 First Avenue in Larkey Park, Walnut Creek 94596. Highway 680 to Geary/Treat exit, left on Geary. From Geary, turn left onto Buena Vista, right onto First Avenue. (510) 935-1978. Wed.–Sun., 11–5, in summer; 1–5 during the school year. Adults, $4.50; ages 3–17, $2.50; seniors, $3.50; under 3, free. Wildlife Rehabilitation training for ages 12 and up.
All ages. *W.*

More than 50 species of live California wild animals including a bobcat, coyote, bald eagle, and roadrunner are displayed in an exhibit hall that focuses on learning to live with nature. Special programming all day includes videos, eagle feeding at 1:30 P.M., bat feedings at 2 P.M., and storytelling at 2:15 and 3 P.M. Innovative children's programs, nature classes for adults, and a unique Pet Library that allows Family Members to "check out" a rabbit, guinea pig, rat, or hamster. Wildlife rehabilitation hospital cares for injured and orphaned native wild animals brought in by the public. There are ample volunteer opportunities for docents and animal care-givers, lots of hands-on activities, festivals, and other special events year-round.

Every once in a while, the Walnut Creek model railroad society runs their Diablo Valley Line in Larkey Park. The miniature handmade models in the "mining town" make this fun for everyone (510-937-1888—but the office is not open every day).

❧ Virtual World

1375 North Main Street, Walnut Creek 94596. (510) 988-0700. Mon.– Thurs., 11–11; Fri. & Sat., 10–1 A.M.; Sun., 10 A.M.–11 P.M. Prices are $7, $8, or $9 depending on the day and time of day. http://www.virtualworld .com. **Ages 7 & up.**

Older kids will find challenges and fun in this cockpit-based virtual reality entertainment "digital theme park," where human pilots do the unexpected at every turn. In "Red Planet," you choose a hovercraft ride to fly into the canals of Mars. In "BattleTech," you pilot giant work robots, *Battlemachs*, as they move around the battlefield.

❧ Old Borges Ranch

1035 Castle Rock Road, near Northgate High School and Shell Ridge Open Space, Walnut Creek 94596. (510) 934-6990. Daily, 8–dusk. Visitor center, Sat., 1–4; first Sun. of the month, 12–4. Free. Group tours by reservation. **All ages.**

Visitors to this 1899 working cattle ranch can see goats, lamb, pigs, chickens, geese and cattle, check out the antique farm machinery, peek in the farm buildings, and draw water at the windmill. Or they can fish or hike the many trails.

History buffs will also want to visit **Shadelands Ranch Historical Museum**, in town, a restored time capsule/home with a gazebo in back (2660 Ygnacio Valley Road, Walnut Creek 94598. 510-935-7871. Wed., 11:30–4; Sun., 1–4. Adults, $2; picnics and parties; W).

❧ Eugene O'Neill National Historic Site

P.O. Box 280, Danville 94526. Tours by reservation only, Wed.–Sun. at 10 A.M. and 12:30 P.M. (510) 838-0249. Free. **Ages 13 & up.**

Tao House, built in 1937, is where Eugene O'Neill wrote *Long Day's Journey into Night* and *A Moon for the Misbegotten*. It's now a museum run by the National Park Service and will interest high school and college students. The dark blue ceiling, white concrete walls, and deep red floors give the place an Asian air with art deco accents. O'Neill's study, with two desks, ship models, sharpened pencils, and a wastebasket full of crumpled paper, captures the author's life. The beauty of the Las Trampas Hills echo the solace O'Neill found here.

➤ Niles Canyon Railway

Boarding area: the corner of Main Street and Kilkare Road, Sunol. Along Highway 84, just west of Interstate 680. (Mail: P.O. Box 2247, Fremont 94536-0247.) (510) 862-9063. First & third Sundays of the month, 10–4. Adults, $5; children, $2. **Ages 5 & up.**

Volunteers with the Pacific Locomotive Association operate 18 vintage steam and diesel locomotives, and passenger and motor cars through six miles of sun-dappled curves of Niles Canyon. A 1924 steam locomotive and a "skunk" car, with its trademark yellow sides, silver room and skunk logo, are favorites. Niles is best known for the over 400 Charlie Chaplin, Ben Turpin, and Zazu Pitts silent movies filmed here at the Essanay Film Manufacturing company. Chaplin's cohort, Bronco Billy, would be right at home here today.

➤ Waterworld

1950 Waterworld Parkway (two blocks east of Interstate 680 off Willow Pass Road), Concord. (510) 609-WAVE. Adults, $19.99; children under 48 inches tall, $13.99; under age 3, free. Parking $4. **All ages.**

The old swimming hole was never like this! There are free-fall slides, rubber-tube wars, river-runs, double-tubing in total darkness, and splash landings sure to cool you off fast. Always call ahead for discount deals, schedule updates, picnic possibilities, and health considerations. Wear waterproof sports sandals or watersocks.

➤ The Alvarado Adobe & Blume House Museum

1 Alvarado Square, San Pablo 94806. At the intersection of San Pablo Avenue and Church Lane. (510) 215-3092. Open third Sunday of each month and by appt. Donation. **Ages 7 & up.** *W.*

The Alvarado Adobe has been precisely reconstructed on its original site. The owner, Juan Bautista Alvarado, husband of Martina Castro, was the Mexican governor of Alta California from 1836 to 1842 and lived here from 1848 to 1882. The house was built in the early 1840s by the Castro family. Furnished in a mix of Rancho and Early California styles, it offers visitors showcases of artifacts including *cascarones*—painted eggshells that were filled with confetti or cologne and cracked open on party-goers. And from local Indian mounds there are Indian shell games and samples of *amole*, the soap plant, which was roasted and eaten; boiled for glue; pounded into a paste that stupefied fish when thrown into a stream; used for twine, shampoo, and soap; and dried to stuff mattresses.

The Blume Museum is a 1905 farmhouse now refurnished to look as it did then, with oak furniture, early plumbing fixtures, and an iron stove in the kitchen.

⇻ Crockett Historical Museum

900 Loring Avenue, Crockett 94525. At the foot of Rolph Avenue, in the old S.P. Depot alongside the railroad tracks. (510) 787-2167. Wed. & Sat., 10–3. Free. **Ages 7 & up.** *W.*

Exhibits of C & H Sugar Refining Co., a world record sturgeon, an 8-foot model of the National Cathedral, pictures of Crockett and the Carquinez Strait, ship models, and artifacts of 20th-century life in Crockett are part of this exhibit. Visitors can see the "N" track model railroad display with the small trains in action.

⇻ Benicia Capitol State Historic Park

First and G Streets, Benicia 94510. (707) 745-3385. Daily, 10–5. Closed Tues. in winter and closed holidays. Adults, $2; ages 6–12, $1. **Ages 8 & up.**

Benicia was named for General Mariano Vallejo's wife, Benicia. Today the town is a mecca for artists and antique collectors.

Benicia was, briefly, the first capital of California, and the Capitol building still looks much as it did in 1853. The exhibit rooms capture a bit of California history—right down to the whale-oil lamps, quill pens, shiny brass cuspidors, and varied headgear on all the desks. The Senate is on the first floor, the Assembly on the second. Interactive displays also bring the past to life.

The **Fischer-Hanlon House** (weekends, 12–3:30) next door is also part of the state historic park complex. This fine old Federal-style house has been lovingly restored by volunteers. Included are the creamery and the carriage house with buggy and cart (with horses and manure). This is a proper, upper-class merchant's home of the 1880s, and the Hanlon sisters enjoyed it until they gave it to the state in 1969.

Don't forget to go across town to the **Camel Barn Museum** (2024 Camel Road. 707-745-5435. Tues.–Sun., 1–4; Donation. W.), in the Arsenal on Camel Road off Park. These large sandstone warehouses now serve as nicely designed art galleries and a historical town museum, but they actually housed 35 Army camels from 1856 to 1864. A donation is requested, and tours are by appointment only. Other buildings in Benicia Industrial Park include a clocktower and the 1860 Commandant's Home, where poet Stephen Vincent Benet lived while his father was commanding officer of the post.

The **Benicia Fire Museum** (160 Military West. 707-745-1688, by appt.) is one of five such museums west of the Mississippi. On display are antique fire extinguishers, a collection of water grenades up to 150 years old, two antique fire engines, and many more items appealing to fire-fighting buffs.

⇉ John Muir National Historic Site

4202 Alhambra Avenue, Martinez 94553. Off Highway 4. (510) 228-8860. The house is open for self-guided tours Wed.–Sun., 10–4:30. Guided tours and Environmental Living Programs by reservation. Adults, $2; $4 a carload; children, free. **Ages 6 & up.**

"I hold dearly cherished memories about it [the house] and fine garden grounds full of trees and bushes and flowers that my wife and father-in-law and I planted—fine things from every land. . . ."

The book John Muir wrote these words in is still in his "scribble den." After a beautiful film narrated with John Muir's words and scenes of the natural wonders that inspired it, visitors tour Muir's large 19th-century ranchhouse, one of the most authentically presented houses you can visit. The closets are still filled with clothing. Muir's suitcase is on the bed, ready for travel; his glasses and pencils are on the desk in his "scribble den." Pictures of his friends President Theodore Roosevelt and naturalist John Burroughs are on the walls, and you can look through some of the scrapbooks in the parlor. You can go up to the attic and ring the ranch bell in the bell tower.

The **Martinez Adobe**, built in 1849 by the son of the Mexican don for whom the town was named, is in the garden, where you can wander at will. Muir's daughter and her family lived there. Muir also advised, "Climb the mountains and get their good tidings. Nature's peace will flow into you as sunshine flows into trees. The winds blow their open freshness into you, and the storms their energy, while cares will drop off like autumn leaves." This is a great place to start.

⇉ Black Diamond Mines Regional Preserve

5175 Somersville Road, Antioch 94509. Take Highway 4 to Somersville Road and head south on it toward the hills. (510) 757-2620. Free. **Ages 8 & up.**

Black Diamond Mines Regional Preserve was the site of 19th-century coal mining and 20th-century sand mining. There are six public-access mine openings that are available for exploration by older children, with adults, during park hours. Prospect Tunnel, 200 feet deep, was named by miners prospecting unsuccessfully for coal. Two of the other tunnels are powder magazines that were created by miners to store explosives.

The surrounding 4,000-acre preserve was once home to three thriving towns. Now, only Rose Hill cemetery, ghosts, and trails remain. Historic photographs and videotapes on the area's history are available for viewing daily, 8 A.M. to 4:30 P.M. There are weekday and weekend naturalist programs and hikes and talks on the natural and cultural history of the area. Most are free.

⇝ Pittsburg Historical Society

40 Civic Avenue, off Richmond, Pittsburg 94565. (510) 439-7501. Tours Sun., 1–4:30 and by appt. Donation. **Ages 8 & up.**

"Were it not for the preservation of memorabilia, the history of this area would fade and pass without record." This is the motto of the Pittsburg Historical Society.

Gifts from local families have helped make this a fine collection. Visitors will enjoy the barbershop and the little school room, the kitchen with the collection of old irons, and the World War II army camp with mannequins in uniform. Displays honor the commercial fishermen of the area, as well as the Indian, Mexican, and ranching eras.

The Peninsula and San Jose Area

The Peninsula and the San Jose area offer many days of happy "attraction" hunting. Here one can explore the past, at the historic town that is the San Jose Historical Museum, and the future, at Silicon Valley's finest Tech Museum. Or you can dig beneath the sea at Coyote Point or search the skies at Lick Observatory. For sheer pleasure, there's a blustery amusement park, Great America.

Since the area grows ever more crowded and less suburban, city street maps are especially helpful.

❖ Sanchez Adobe

1000 Linda Mar Boulevard, off Highway 1, Pacifica 94044. (415) 359-1462. Tues. & Thurs., 10–4; Sat. & Sun., 1–5 and by appt. Free.
Ages 7 & up.

In 1842, the alcalde, or mayor, of San Francisco, Señor Sanchez, built his home in the farmland that once produced food for San Francisco's Mission Dolores. The adobe still stands, sparsely decorated—as it would have been 100 years ago—with Sanchez's rancho mementos, and the Victorian furniture and clothes of several Sanchez generations. Today's youngsters can participate in hands-on programs that take place in the historic garden. Activities include adobe brick making, junior archeology workshops, Native American games, and Native American skills workshops put on by the San Mateo County Historical Association.

❖ Half Moon Bay Jail

505 Johnston Street, Half Moon Bay. (415) 726-7084. Self-guided tours: Fri.–Sun., 1–4. Guided tours, by appt. Adults, $3; free for schoolchildren.
Ages 7 & up.

The Spanishtown Historical Society is restoring the little 1850s jail cell as a photo-packed museum. Behind it, the barn built by Thomas Johnston in the late 1860s displays old farm equipment, and docents give hands-on tours of early coastside farming. Both buildings should be open under the name of The Mary Vallejo History Center soon.

The nearby **James Johnston House** (The White House, Higgins Purissima Road, just south of downtown) is now becoming an interpretive museum with a community garden. Historical walking tours of this sweet, gallery-filled beach town are also available. There are beaches, redwood parks and perfumed nurseries to walk through as well as Pescadero Marsh for free weekend bird walks (415-879-2170).

✥ Phipps Country

2700 Pescadero Road, P.O. Box 349, Pescadero 94060. (415) 879-0787. Daily, 10–6 in winter; until 7 in summer. Closed Christmas week. Free. Tours, by appt. **All ages.**

This working farm, with a roadside stand, nursery, barnyard, gardens, and picnic areas, makes a very pleasant outing. Pick your own berries in season. While parents buy fresh produce, herbs, an intriguing selection of dried beans, and plants in the nursery, kids can explore out back. There are several aviaries filled with colorful, exotic birds. In the barnyard is Eeyore the donkey, a huge potbellied pig named Arnold, a sweet small potbelly named Margaret, and momma goats with babies. There is a large poultry enclosure with chickens and other exotic birds and a pond for the ducks and geese to play in. Kids of all ages will enjoy looking at the antique farm equipment. Take a picnic and enjoy the country.

Little Loryn wrote, "Dear Phipps Ranch Friends, I liked picking strawberries at your ranch. I also liked it when the donkey (Eeyore) yelled at us. I also liked that big black pig. I got to touch the goat's horn, too, and I liked that. Thank you very much!"

✥ Coyote Point Museum for Environmental Education

1651 Coyote Point Drive, San Mateo 94401. Coyote Point Park, off Poplar Avenue from Highway 101. (415) 342-7755. Information: (415) 342-9969. Tues.–Sat., 10–5; Sun., 12–5. Closed Christmas, New Year's Day, and Thanksgiving. Adults, $3; seniors, $2; ages 6–17, $1. First Wed. of the month, free. Gate fee for park, picnic areas, playgrounds, and beach, $4 per car. **Ages 5 & up.** *W.*

The Environmental Hall takes visitors on an imaginary trip from San Francisco Bay over the Santa Cruz Mountains and down to the Pacific shore. Six ecological zones of the Bay Area are interpreted. The display emphasizes the need to preserve and protect nature's resources and creatures. Models, exhibits, hands-on games, and computers serve as educational tools. The adjacent Wildlife Habitats house over 40 live mammals, amphibians, birds, and reptiles native to the Bay Area. The gardens are planted to attract hummingbirds and butterflies. One area shows how Native Americans used plants, trees, and shrubs. First-grader Jestina wrote, "Thank you for letting us touch the animals. The one I like is the 'possum and the mice or rat or whatever, but I thank you."

✥ Japanese Tea Garden

Central Park, San Mateo 94403. (415) 377-4640. Mon.–Fri., 10–4; Sat. & Sun., 11–4. Free. **Ages 6 & up.** *W.*

This proper, gracious Japanese garden is a soothing spot in the midst of city bustle. Quaint bridges and rock pathways take the visitor past a waterfall, a pond thick with waterlilies and *koi* (carp), and in the springtime, pink cherry blossoms. The teahouse is open, irregularly, in summer.

⇉ San Mateo County Historical Museum
1700 West Hillsdale Boulevard, San Mateo 94402. Off Highway 101 at Highway 92. (415) 574-6441. Mon.–Thurs., 9:30–4:30; Sun., 12:30–4:30. Free. **Ages 7 & up.** *W.*

A walk through this museum is a walk through history. You begin with the Pleistocene period—14 million years ago—and view bones and fossils from that age found in San Mateo. Then on to the Costanoan Indians of 3,000 years ago, and the description of their magic dances, boats, tools, and food. The Mission Rancho period is well represented. Exhibits of lumber mills, an old general store and bar, settlers' wagons, and unicycles recall the past. Galleries change exhibits to focus on subjects such as 19th-century fire fighting, the many mansions of San Mateo, and transportation. There are also lectures and audiovisual programs.

⇉ Lathrop House
627 Hamilton Street, Redwood City 94063. (415) 365-5564. Tues.–Thurs., 11–3. Donation. **Ages 7 & up.**

In 1863, Benjamin G. Lathrop, the county's first clerk, built this handsome Gothic Revival mansion, "Lora Mundi," on a lot bought from the Arguello family.

The house has been relocated twice and has been restored—right down to the top hats on the hall rack—by the Redwood City Heritage Association. The ground floor kitchen is equipped with a woodburning stove and butter churn. Naturally, kids like the children's bedroom best.

⇉ Marine Science Institute
500 Discovery Parkway, Redwood City 94063. (415) 364-2760. Mon.–Sat., 8–5. Call for prices of the Shoreside and Discovery Voyage programs. **Ages 10 & up.**

"I enjoyed geo/chem—using the VanDorn bottle to get water samples and sticking your fingers in 'Benthic Oooze'! I liked putting out the otter net and catching the fish and giving birth to some fish. I thought that looking at Phytoplankton, Zooplankton, and Circumplankton was fun." This is one San Jose student's response to the four-hour Discovery Voyage on the 85-foot research vessel *Inland Seas*. Groups of 40 to 45, over 10 years old, learn about marsh and marine life and the sea around us.

⇻ Filoli House and Gardens

Canada Road, Woodside 94062. Filoli Nature Hikes: Individual and group tours and nature hikes by reservation; (415) 364-2880/366-4640. Fee. Children must be accompanied by an adult. **Ages 12 & up.**

Explore the many trails in the remote areas of Filoli. You can learn about the Indians who lived here many years ago and touch the San Andreas fault line. Learn about the animals, plants, ecosystems, and history of a fascinating place in the Bay Area. The two-hour hikes are two to three miles long. Filoli's House and Garden Tour is not open to children under the age of 12, including babies in backpacks and strollers. Gustavo wrote, "I had a real good time. . . . My favorite part was when we went to the wildlife center. I also liked the Indian dig. Even if we didn't really see a turkey vulture or a redtailed hawk, the turret spider was pretty amazing!"

⇻ The Woodside Store

Kings Mountain and Tripp roads, Woodside 94062. (415) 851-7615. Tues. & Thurs., 10–4; Sat.& Sun., 12–4 . Tours by appt. Free. **Ages 7 & up.**

The San Mateo Historical Society has preserved, stocked, and opened the 1850s lumber/general store that started in 1854 as a stage stop. A slide show explains more of the site's history.

⇻ NASA Ames Research Center

Moffett Field 94035. Off Highway 101. (415) 604-6274. Visitors Center open Mon.–Fri., 8–4:30; free. Outdoor two-hour tours, two miles long, by appt., for those in 4th grade & over: (415) 604-6497. Closed federal holidays. Gift shop. **Ages 9 & up.** *W.*

After an orientation lecture and film, visitors can see the world's largest wind tunnel, centrifuge operations, research aircraft, or flight simulation facilities, depending on the center's schedule. In one section, tiny robots roam in a simulated lunar landscape. The center focuses on space exploration and artificial intelligence, developing new ways to link humans and the highly advanced computers needed for the future space missions now on NASA's drawing boards. Films, telelectures, and school presentations are also available.

⇻ West Bay Model Railroad Association

1090 Merrill Street, Menlo Park 94025. (415) 322-0685. Free. **Ages 5 & up.**

Three different-sized trains run on the club's 2,000 feet of track, whistling past miniature towns and painted scenery and over tiny bridges and turntables. Adding to the effectiveness of the show is a tape of special sound effects interspersed with the story of how the club came about. The club also has a railroad-stationery display, a library, and a workshop. The members' special Christmas show on the second weekend in December is a favorite with local youngsters.

⇶ Stanford University

Stanford University Campus, Stanford 94305. Highway 101 to Stanford exit. (415) 723-2300. Stanford Guide & Visitors Service, 723-2560/723-2053. Daily, 10–4. Visitor's Information Center: Daily, 9–5. Hoover Tower Observation Platform, 723-2053: Mon.–Sun., 10–4. Adults, $2; children and seniors, $1. **Ages 7 & up.**

In addition to the breathtaking view from the 250-foot-high observation platform at the top of the Hoover Tower, the **Hoover Exhibit Rooms** display some of the treasures collected by Herbert Hoover and his wife, Lou Henry Hoover, and document some of their remarkable accomplishments. Among the items on display are a priceless gold Peruvian mask, one of Hoover's fishing rods, a model of the Hoover Dam, Lou Henry's Stanford diploma, and the original copy of one of the earliest Soviet-American agreements (1921).

The Visitor's Center will also provide information on the following attractions of interest to teens and older: **Leland Stanford, Jr., Museum** (723-3469: scheduled to open in 1998), **Stanford Linear Accelerator Center** (926-3300 ext. 2204; tours by appt., free), **Jasper Ridge Biological Preserve** (327-2277; tours by appt., free), **campus walking tours** (723-2560; Mon.–Sun., 11 & 3:15, free).

⇶ Baylands Nature Interpretive Center

2775 Embarcadero Road, at the eastern end, Palo Alto 94303. (415) 329-2506. Tues.–Fri., 2–5; weekends, 1–5. Free. Groups by appt. **Ages 6 & up.**

This bayside nature center is on pilings out in a salt marsh, handy for the nature walks and ecology workshops it excels in. The exhibits show local birds, plants, and a saltwater aquarium. On weekends, there are nature movies and slide shows, as well as nature and bird walks; bike tours; wildflower shows; fish, pond, and geology programs; and workshops.

⇶ Palo Alto Junior Museum and Zoo

Rinconada Park, 1451 Middlefield Road, Palo Alto 94301. (415) 329-2111. Tues.–Sat., 10–5; Sun., 1–4. Free. **Ages 4 & up.** *W.*

This beautifully constructed museum has one major changing exhibition yearly to keep kids coming back for more. Outside, in the poured concrete shelters, there are snakes and reptiles, ravens, owls, bobcats, and raccoons. Ducks nest under the bridge that curves over the pretty pond. The exhibitions program focuses on physical, biological, and cultural themes.

≫ Barbie Doll Hall of Fame

Doll Studio, 433 Waverly Street, Palo Alto 94301. (415) 326-5841. Tues.–Fri., 1:30–4:30; Sat., 10–12 & 1:30–4:30. Admission, $4. **Ages 5 & up.**

Did you know that Barbie was named after the daughter of its creator, Ruth Handler, cofounder of Mattel? Since Barbie mimics society, her Hall of Fame offers a view of the changing culture and style over the past four decades (she was "born" in 1959). The world's largest collection of Barbie dolls—18,000 Barbies and Kens and friends—includes the first black Barbie, a hippie Barbie, Barbie as the first woman astronaut, Barbie as a yuppie, and other incarnations reflecting the changing fashions in clothes, accessories, and hairstyles over the last quarter century. Two Barbies are sold every second, 1.5 million every week. If placed head to toe, they would circle the Earth more than 11 times.

≫ Museum of American Heritage

3401 El Camino, Palo Alto 94306. (415) 321-1004. Fri.–Sun., 11–4. Free. Gift Shop. **Ages 8 & up.** *W.*

Frank Livermore decided to share his love of gadgets, so he created this "celebration of mankind's technical ingenuity of the past as an inspiration for the future." Displays of machinery, appliances, and mechanical items in use during the 100 years before the advent of solid state electronics are combined with special exhibits, featuring items on topics such as automatic musical instruments, a salute to 25 years of Mattel's Hot Wheels, and 100 years of toy trains. There's a turn-of-the-century office, a '30s kitchen, and a '20s grocery store that once "lived" in Chicago. One young visitor saw a typewriter here for the first time. Another was astonished by the crystal radio set.

≫ Los Altos History House

51 N. San Antonio Road, Los Altos (415) 948-9427. Wed., 1–5; Sat., 12–4 & by appt. Free. **Ages 8 & up.**

This 1905 farm house, located in one of the few surviving orchards in Santa Clara Valley, depicts life on the small family-run orchards that dominated Los Altos before World War II. Both the house and surrounding grounds provide a quiet respite from today's bustle.

⇒ Magic Edge Center

1625 North Shoreline Boulevard, on the road to the Amphitheater, Mountain View 94043. (415) 254-REAL (7325). Mon., noon–11 P.M.; Tues.– Thurs., 11–11; Fri., 11 A.M. to midnight; Sun., noon to 10 P.M. Reservations recommended. $2 one-time membership fee. 12-minute session, $14.75; 20-minute session, $19.75. Children under 16 may play before 5 P.M. for $7. Group rates. **Ages 9 & up.**

This Virtual Reality playground allows you to experience the most advanced full-motion flight simulator available. Take a flight aboard the X-21 Hornet and experience the G-forces of a fighter. After your mission, leave your pod and cool your jets at the Magic Edge Cafe.

⇒ Perham Electronics Museum Foundation

Call for information, since this is scheduled to join the Keely Park group in San Jose: (408) 734-4453.

Based on a private collection started in 1893 by 6-year-old Douglas Perham, this is the most extensive display of early electrical and electronic devices in the West. Young scientists will be intrigued by exhibits of the first radio broadcast station, the first Silicon Valley electronics firm, the first TV picture tube (invented by Philo Farnsworth in San Francisco), a 10-foot robot, and hands-on demonstrations of electricity and magnetism.

⇒ Sunnyvale Historical Museum

235 East California Avenue at Sunnyvale Avenue, P.O. Box 61301, Sunnyvale 94088. (408) 749-0220. Tues. & Thurs., 12–4:30; Sun., 1–4; & by appt. Free. **Ages 8 & up.**

This one-room regional museum, set in Martin Murphy Jr. Park, captures the past with artifacts and pictures of area pioneers, including the Murphy family, who acquired their land grant from the Castro family. Originally built as a dirigible hangar, the museum also has a display on Moffett field. And the model of a dirigible is a favorite with the kids.

⇒ California History Center

De Anza College, 21250 Stevens Creek Boulevard, Cupertino 95014. (408) 864-8712. Mon.–Thurs., 8–12 & 1–4:30; closed July & Aug. Free. Parking fee on campus. Call for special Sat. hours. Group tours by appt. **Ages 8 & up.**

Changing exhibits—from "First Californians" to "The Chinese in the Monterey Bay Area" to "Hard Rock Gold Mining"—explore California's rich and varied history. This living history museum is housed in the restored le Petit Trianon, the original house on De Anza land. Visitors may tour this elegant Louis XVI mansion and surrounding garden area with a pavilion reminiscent of Versailles.

⇶ Minolta Planetarium

De Anza College, 21250 Stevens Creek Boulevard at Stelling Road, Cupertino 95014. (408) 864-8814. Call for times and prices, since they change with each class session. Birthday parties. **All ages.** *W.*

The Minolta Planetarium uses the latest audiovisual and video projection systems to present remarkable family shows as well as laser shows and 3-D shows for older kids. The main projector spreads the night sky across a 50-foot dome, while sound surrounds the audience, issuing from a Bose full-spectrum system that includes two 16-foot-long sound cannons. These cannons add "feel" to the music and special sound effects. One hundred fifty other projectors produce dazzling effects, recreating a flight to the moon with the astronauts or a voyage back in time to see the birth of a star. Family programs and astronomy evenings, which include preschool-age children, are a specialty.

⇶ Hakone Japanese Gardens

21000 Big Basin Way, P.O. Box 2324, Saratoga 95070. (408) 741-4994. Mon.–Fri., 10–5; weekends, 11–5. Closed Christmas. Parking: $5 weekends, $3 weekdays; free on Tues. Donation. Gift Shop. Children under 10 must take an adult. Tours for children, 25 cents per child. **Ages 6 & up.**

Walk along curving foliage-lined paths, pass through a wisteria-roofed arbor, and step on three stones to cross a stream next to three waterfalls. Climb a moon bridge to see the goldfish. Discover a moon-viewing house and gazebos hidden in the trees. Spy stone and wooden lanterns and statues of cranes and cats hidden in the flowers. This wonderful garden was designed by a former court gardener to the Emperor of Japan as a hill and water garden, the strolling pond style typical of Zen gardens in the 17th century. The teahouse is open by appointment. Picnic tables are available.

⇶ Villa Montalvo

Saratoga–Los Gatos Road, Saratoga 95070. (408) 741-3421. The hours for the arboreteum, galleries, and park vary from day to day, depending on the performance schedule and season, so please call before planning an outing. Free. **All ages.**

Nature trails traverse a redwood grove, hills and meadows, and flower-covered arbors in this arboretum. The villa's grounds are also a bird sanctuary for over 60 species of birds. The villa takes its name from a 16th-century Spanish author. Montalvo wrote a novel describing a tribe of Amazons living in a fabulous island paradise named "California." The Amazons rode on gryphons, and the many stone gryphons on the grounds will entrance youngsters. Music, dance, and other performing arts events, many geared for children, such as storytelling, puppetry, and children's ballet performances, are scheduled throughout the year. The villa also hosts Environmental Volunteers classes in the spring and a performing arts camp each summer.

❧ Billy Jones Wildcat Railroad & Carousel

Oak Meadow Park, Los Gatos. For tours and special runs, write to P.O. Box 234, Los Gatos 95031. (408) 395-RIDE. Spring and fall: Sat. & Sun., 10:30–4:30; daily in summer. Under 2 with an adult, free; others, $1.
Ages 4 & up.

"Old No. 2," a full-steam narrow-gauge, 18-inch prairie-type loco-motive, toots along a mile-long track pulling four open cars. The water tank, a necessity when operating a steam railroad, was designed and built by volunteers, as were the turntable, station, and engine house. Painted in Southern Pacific's "Black Widow" color scheme of black, orange, red and silver, the "2502" has an interesting history as the newest member of the Billy Jones motive power fleet.

Volunteers restored the William E. "Bill" Mason Carousel and created the building to house it. The carousel is an English 1910 Savage roundabout shipped around the Horn to San Francisco for the 1915 Panama-Pacific exhibition. Twenty-nine hand-carved wooden horses and two chariots ride clockwise, along with five C. W. Parker, two Dare, and two Armitage-Herschel horses installed to replace missing horses. The replicated Wurlitzer organ adds to the fun.

❧ Forbes Mill Regional Museum

75 Church Street, Los Gatos. (408) 395-7375. Wed.–Sun., 12–4. **Ages 8 & up.**

The storage room for a grain mill built in 1854 and 1880 has been transformed into a small museum of Los Gatos history. Amid local school artifacts, desks and books, the display of "Mountain Charlie," who battled grizzly bears, is a favorite.

The nearby **Los Gatos Museum** (Main Street & Tait Avenue, Los Gatos. 408-354-2646. Wed.–Sun., 12–4) was once a firehouse. There are changing art shows (including at least one show of children's art each year) on the main floor. The basement holds a grand collection of fossils, rocks, and natural history panoramas.

❖ Hidden Villa

26870 Moody Road, Los Altos Hills 94022. (415) 948-4690. Daily except Mon., 9–dusk. Organic farm tours, summer programs, environmental education programs, and individualized tours, by appt. Call for schedule and prices. $5 parking fee. **All ages.**

Hidden Villa's 1,600-acre wilderness preserve is relatively unchanged since the days when Ohlone Indians gathered food from its hillsides and took fish from its creeks. A self-guiding tour of the farm area is available, as are four suggested wilderness treks. Visitors can picnic, rent horses, and visit a working vegetable garden, dairy and sheep barn, orchard, and pig and poultry areas. Deanna Fale, who told us about Hidden Villa, wrote, "The preschool tour we took at Hidden Villa was wonderful. The children smelled bay leaves, basil, etc. They held a newly hatched egg. Petted a ewe about to give birth. The guides are knowledgeable and gear their talks to the various age groups. The one-hour tour for 4-year-olds was just about right."

❖ Campbell Historical Museum & Ainsley House

300 Grant Street, off First Street and Civic Center Drive, between the Campbell City Hall and Library (51 No. Central Ave.), Campbell 95008. (408) 866-2119. Thurs.–Sun., 12–4, April–Dec. **Ages 8 & up.**

Docent-led tours of this 1920s historic house museum located in the Tudor Revival mansion of former canning industry pioneer J.C. Ainsley feature life in the Santa Clara Valley in the 1920s and 1930s. (Tours every 30 minutes; adults, $6; seniors, $3; children 12–18, $2, members and children under 12, free.) The Morgan Gallery in the Ainsley House features exhibits and videos on Campbell's history and the Campbell Museum Foundation Store (free).

❖ Mission Santa Clara de Asis

Santa Clara University, 500 El Camino Real, Santa Clara 95053-3217. (408) 554-4203. Daily, 8–5. Free. **Ages 7 & up.** *W.*

Founded in 1777 and now part of the university campus, the present mission is a replica of the third building raised on this site by the mission fathers. An adobe wall from the original cloister still stands in the peaceful garden. The original cross of the mission stands in front of the church, and the bell given by the king of Spain in 1778 still tolls.

The **De Saisset Museum** (Tues.–Fri., 10–5; weekends, 1–5. 408-544-4528) is on campus and makes an interesting brief stop. There are changing art and cultural exhibits. In the basement is a display of artifacts from the Mission era and the early founding of Santa Clara University.

✈ Intel Museum

2200 Mission College Boulevard, Santa Clara; (408) 765-0503. Mon.–Fri., 8–5. Guided tours by appt. Free. **Ages 8 & up.** *W.*

What's a microprocessor? A semiconductor? A megabyte? Discover the answers at the home of the world's largest computer chip manufacturer. The hands-on exhibits teach how electronic chips are created from silicon, the primary component of sand. Get a look at how computers do what they do, see how chips are constructed, and learn how video and computer come together in changing exhibits that give a better understanding of the industry that gave Silicon Valley its name.

✈ Great America

Great America Parkway, off Highway 101, P.O. Box 1776, Santa Clara 95052. (408) 988-1776. Spring and fall weekends and daily in summer, 10–9; later on Saturdays and holiday weekends. Ages 7–54, $27.95; ages 3–6, $13.95; over 55, $18.95. Group rates available. Season passes available at Paramount's Great America and through BASS/TM outlets. **Ages 5 & up.** *W.*

Plummet 224 feet—22 stories—at 62 miles per hour in the Stunt Tower Drop Zone. Get messy in Nickelodeon Splat City, three acres of wet, slimy, mega-messy fun. The thrill-ride capital of Northern California offers 100 experiments in the fast and scary, including Vortex, the West's only stand-up roller coaster; Top Gun, an inside-out roller coaster; Demon, an especially jolting roller coaster; and Grizzly, an old-fashioned wooden roller coaster. At Fort Fun, kids can meet Star Trek aliens and costumed cartoon charters such as Yogi Bear and Fred Flintstone and watch a puppet theater or ride Little Dodge 'Ems, Lady Bugs, and Huck's Hang Gliders.

Concerts, a giant screen movie, a bird show, and live stage shows allow for pleasant respites during a day or night of adventure.

✈ The Recyclery

1601 Dixon Landing Road, Milpitas 95035. (408) 945-2807. Mon.–Fri., 2:30–4:30 for self-guided tours. Education Center & Buy Back Center, Saturday, 8:30–4:30. Groups, third-graders and up, by appt. Free. **Ages 8 & up.**

One of the largest recycling centers in Northern California is spreading the word by showing how it's done. Visitors stand in a glass booth and watch big trucks unloading glass, cans, and newspaper that is sorted by machines on the floor below. Then the material is hauled by conveyor belts to processing machines, where it is packaged for handling by companies that reuse the materials. Visitors are encouraged to bring recyclables for the Buy Back Center. One third-grader wrote, "Thank you for giving us a tour. We liked the video and the 'mrf.' The wall of garbage was neat. I hope we can come and resikel [sic]."

❯❯ Children's Discovery Museum

180 Woz Way, San Jose 95110. (408) 298-5437. Tues.–Sat., 10–5; Sun., 12–5. Open holiday Mondays. Adults, $6; seniors, $5; ages 2–18, $4; members, free. Theater specials, story telling, and programs. Groups by appt. (408) 298-5437, ext. 259. Gift shop. **Ages 2–12.** *W.*

The purple angled Discovery Museum is fun inside and out. Spectacular hands-on exhibits and games capture the imagination of pre- and grade-schoolers instantly. Here they can don helmets and climb behind the wheel of a real fire truck or an old Ford. Or slide down a culvert and clamber through sewer pipes "under the city." They can listen to and talk to traffic controllers working at the San Jose Airport. The Kids' Bank demystifies money, and in Waterworks, children pump pedals and spin big screws to transport water from one level to another. Youngsters can enter an Ohlone hut, make tortillas and adobe bricks, and do farm chores, while learning about the layers of history in their world. The Doodad Dump beckons inventors to glue together infinite varieties of thingamajigs. The museum specializes in creative physical and fantasy play. Our favorite is "Bubbalonga"—especially the bubble-stretcher.

❯❯ The Tech Museum of Innovation

145 West San Carlos Street, San Jose 95110. (408) 279-7150. Summer: Mon.–Sat., 10–6; Sun., 12–6; winter: Tues.–Sat., 10–5, Sun., 12–6. Adults, $6; ages 6–18 and seniors, $4; members, free. Hi-tech gift shop. Lectures, programs, classes. Groups & evening rentals. School trips: (408) 279-7176; public programs: (408) 279-7158. http:///www.thetech.org. **Ages 6 & up.** *W.*

Hands-on interactive exhibits all about high technology with a down-to-earth approach make this a museum for everyone. Plans are to move The Tech a few blocks away into another new building created by the architect Legorreta, across from the San Jose Museum of Art. Meanwhile, the challenges are here: The 23-foot-high tower of 500 telephone books illustrating the amount of information contained in a molecule of DNA will astound. Astronauts-in-the-making can take the controls of a Mars Rover model and guide it around the obstacles of a simulated Martian landscape. Or they can witness the complex interactions that take place on a silicon chip.

Exhibits are devoted to the six industries of Silicon Valley: semiconductors, space, biotechnology, robotics, advanced materials, and bicycles.

Laboratories and a multimedia library draw on the latest technology to allow visitors to explore on their own. Internet stations at each exhibit allow the visitor to get current new information on the web. The Tech's web site allows kids to tackle new technologies at home. One writer said, "I loved it! Multimedia, chemistry, robotics, what more could a kid ask for?" And another wrote, "When people hear the word museum, they think of some boring place, but The Tech Museum was the exact opposite."

❖ American Museum of Quilts & Textiles

60 South Market Street, San Jose. (408) 971-0323. Tues.–Sun., 10–4; Thurs. until 8 P.M. Adults, $4; seniors & students, $3; under 13, free. **Ages 12 & up.**

This is the first museum in the United States dedicated to the exhibition, preservation, and study of quilts. Changing shows include historical, traditional, and contemporary quilts and other fiber arts from around the world. Children's programs may be scheduled.

❖ The San Jose Museum of Art

110 South Market Street, San Jose 95110. (408) 294-2787. Tues.–Sun., 10–5; Thurs., until 8. Adults, $6; seniors, students, and ages 6–17, $3. http://www.sjliving.com/sjma. **Ages 7 & up.**

The San Jose Museum of Art offers changing exhibits of 20th-century art, including painting, sculpture, works on paper, photography, video, and mixed media. A landmark collaboration with the Whitney Museum of American Art in New York City will provide exhibitions of 20th-century masterworks from the Whitney's permanent collection through the year 2000. On our last visit, Nam June Paik's TV world was much more interesting to kids than it was to stick-in-the-mud adults. Call for concert and children's activities programs.

❖ Peralta Adobe & Fallon House Historic Site

175 West St. John Street at San Pedro, San Jose 95110. (408) 993-8182. Guided tours, Wed.–Sun., 11–4. Adults, $6; seniors, $5; ages 6–17, $3. **Ages 8 & up.**

Built in 1797, the Peralta Adobe is San Jose's oldest structure. It is furnished with period pieces and artifacts that help to interpret the early pueblo lifestyle. The *recamara*, or bedroom, is furnished as it might have been in 1800; the *sala*, or living room, looks as it might have in 1860. The Fallon House next door, built in 1855, was the opulent home of one of San Jose's most charismatic mayors, Thomas Fallon. The house's 15 rooms are fully furnished in the Victorian style of the 1860s. Together, the site offers a unique look into San Jose's historic past.

≫ Rosicrucian Egyptian Museum and Planetarium

Rosicrucian Park, 1342 Naglee Avenue, at Park, San Jose 95191. (408) 947-3636. Egyptian Museum: daily, 9–5. Adults, $6.75; seniors and students, $4; ages 7–15, $3.50; under 2, free. Planetarium: daily 9–4:15. Planetarium shows: adults, $4; seniors and students, $3.50; ages 7–15, $3; under 5, not admitted. Call (408) 947-3636 for show times and subjects. Closed Thanksgiving, Christmas, and New Year's Day. Group discounts by reservations. Private planetarium shows and party rentals by arrangement. Gift shop. **Ages 6 & up.**

The wonderful, faraway world of ancient Egypt awaits to mystify and enchant you in an amazingly large and varied collection. Egyptian mummies, sculpture, paintings, jewelry, cosmetics, scarabs, scrolls, and amulets are here in abundance. The ornate coffins, mummified cats and falcons, and descriptions of the embalming process are totally absorbing— especially to youngsters, who want to know how old everything is. Sumerian clay tablets, a model of the Tower of Babel, and a walk-through replica of an Egyptian noble's tomb vie for your attention.

The Rosicrucian Planetarium, a theater of the sky, presents changing programs exploring the myths, mysteries, and facts of the sky of yesterday, today, and tomorrow.

≫ Winchester Mystery House

525 South Winchester Boulevard, between Stevens Creek Boulevard & Interstate 280, San Jose 95128. (408) 247-2101. One-hour tours daily except Christmas: 9:30–4:30 in winter; 9–5:30 in summer. Adults, $12.95; seniors, $9.95; ages 6–12, $6.95. Reduced group tour and catering rates by reservation: (408) 247-2000. Birthday packages available. Cafe. Gift shop. **Ages 7 & up.**

Sarah Winchester, widow of the Winchester Rifle heir, was told that as long as she kept building something, she'd never die. So for 38 years, carpenters worked 24 hours a day to build this 160-room mansion filled with mysteries. Doorways open to blank walls, secret passageways twist around, and the number 13 appears everywhere—13-stepped stairways, 13 bathrooms, ceilings with 13 panels, rooms with 13 windows—all in the finest woods and crystals money could buy. Thirteen stately palms line the main driveway.

A self-guided tour of the Victorian Gardens, the Winchester Historical Firearms Museum, and the Antique Products Museum is included in the tour price.

❯ San Jose Historical Museum

1600 Senter Road, San Jose 95112. Kelley Park at Senter Road. (408) 287-2290. Mon.–Fri., 10–4:30; weekends, 12–4:30. Adults, $4; children, $2; seniors, $3. Group rates, by appt. Party & picnic facilities. Gift shop. **Ages 6 & up.** *W.*

Reconstructed and restored landmarks bring to life the look and feel of late-19th-century San Jose in this 16-acre complex. Walk around the plaza and visit O'Brien's candy store, in 1878 the first place to serve ice cream sodas west of Detroit, the print shop, the 1880s Pacific Hotel, Dashaway stables, the 115-foot electric light tower, the Ng Shing Gung Temple, the Empire firehouse, a 1927 gas station, the Trolley Barn, Coyote post office, Steven's Ranch fruit barn, H. H. Warburton's doctor's office, the 1909 Bank of Italy building, and the many Victorian homes that have been saved and moved to museum premises, including poet Edwin Markham's Greek Revival home. Our favorite is the little Umbarger House, a delicious orange and ochre 1870s "Painted Lady" gingerbread confection that has been completely furnished, right down to the clothes in the closets and the dishes in the sink. New to the Museum is the *Imperio*, a replica of a 1915 chapel where Holy Ghost festivals were held by the Portuguese community. Letters, photographs, diaries, artwork, cookbooks, historical artifacts, and Holy Ghost costumes celebrate the Portuguese culture.

❯ Machu Picchu Museum of the Americas

El Paseo Court, 42, South First Street, Suite D, San Jose 95113. (408) 280-1860. Mon.–Fri., 10:30–5:30; Sat., 11–5 and by appt. School & outreach programs. Free. **Ages 7 & up.**

The Tree of Life guards over the Pre- and Post-Columbian art, artifacts, and textiles from Central, North, and South America in this museum. There are Huichol Indian beaded masks and bowls, finely carved gourds from Peru, hand-embroidered dresses from Central America, *rebosos*, or shawls, and pre-Columbian dolls from the Chancay culture in Peru. A newsletter, tours to Peru, and art and musical events are offered as well.

❯ Japanese Friendship Tea Garden

1300 Senter Road, Kelley Park, San Jose 95112. (408) 277-5254. Daily, 10–sunset. Free. Parking fee, $3. **Ages 5 & up.**

This tranquil garden is patterned after the Korakuen garden in San Jose's sister city of Okayama. The three lakes are designed to symbolize the word *kokoro*, which means "heart-mind-and-soul." Picturesque bridges and waterfalls, shaped rocks and trees, and land and water flowers are wonderful to wander around. Naturally, the children will head over to watch the families of *koi*, fat gold, white, or black carp, who come when dinner is offered.

✦ Happy Hollow Park and Zoo

1300 Senter Road, Kelley Park, San Jose 95112. (408) 277-3000. Open daily; call for hours and fees. Advance group reservations available. Parking fee, $3. **Ages 2–12.** *W.*

Enjoy Danny the Dragon as he prowls through a bamboo forest, or listen as a chorus of sea animals invites you to enter Neptune's kingdom. Climb a stairway in the Crooked House and slide down a spiral slide. Visit the many play areas dotting the park, and view a puppet show at the puppet castle theater. The zoo offers youngsters a chance to see exotic animals from all over the world. They can cuddle a baby goat or pet a baby llama.

✦ Raging Waters

Tully Road, Lake Cunningham Regional Park, P.O. Box 21368, San Jose 95151-3168. (408) 270-8000. Daily, June 14–August 27. Spring & fall days & hours vary. Admissions prices also vary. **Ages 4 & up.**

The San Francisco Bay Area's largest water park features more than 30 slides, a 500,000-gallon fresh water wave pool, and an interactive water fort. Lather-up with sunblock and fly on a seven-story speed slide or on a Shotgun waterfall. Younger children love to climb on the structure at Pirate Island that is designed for super waterfights.

✦ Youth Science Institute—Vasona Discovery Center

296 Garden Hill Drive, Los Gatos 95030. Vasona County Park, off Blossom Hill Road. (408) 356-4945. Mon.–Fri., 9–4:30; weekends, 12–4:30. Free. Parking fee, $3. Picnic facilities. **Ages 7 & up.**

The Vasona Discovery Center is a junior museum focusing on aquatic life and water ecology. Live animals on display include fish, reptiles, and amphibians; other exhibits show fossils and dinosaurs. School and community children's science classes are taught at the center. The Viola Anderson Native Plant Trail winds past the center and overlooks Vasona Lake.

✦ Youth Science Institute—Sanborn Nature Center

16055 Sanborn Road, Saratoga 95070. Sanborn-Skyline County Park, off Highway 9. (408) 867-6940. Wed.–Fri., 9–4:30; weekends,

12–4:30. Parking fee, $3. Picnic tables & hiking trails. **Ages 7 & up.**

The Sanborn Nature Center is a junior museum located in a redwood forest, so there are natural history displays on the redwood forest. Live animals on display include reptiles and amphibians. A geology room, an Ohlone Indian exhibit, and organic gardens are also presented in a "hands-on" fashion. School and community children's science classes are taught at the center. Fourth grader Christine wrote, "I liked the hike and the games the Indians played. I like making the cattail rope and grinding the acorns. I had fun on the field trip."

➤ Youth Science Institute—Alum Rock Discovery Center

16260 Alum Rock Avenue, San Jose 95127. Alum Rock Park, off Highway 680. (408) 258-4322. Tues.–Sat., 12–4:30; Sun., between Easter & Labor Day, 12–4:30. Adults, 50 cents; children, 25 cents. Parking fee, $3.
Ages 7 & up.

The Alum Rock Discovery Center is a junior museum with an extensive collection of live animals, reptiles, amphibians, and birds (including hawks and owls) displayed in renovated exhibits. Bird species are displayed. There is a resource library, and several activities are always in the works. Alum Rock Park has trails, streams, and picnic facilities. Fourth grader Josephine enthused, "I like the hike, because I got to stand in an earthquake fault. The creek was fun. I got wet and I learned about all kinds of animals and creatures."

➤ New Almaden Quicksilver Mining Museum

21570 Almaden Road, P.O. Box 124, New Almaden 95042. (408) 268-1729. Sat., 12–4 & by appt. Guided hikes of the 4,000 surrounding acres dotted with historic buildings: (408) 268-3882. Donation. **Ages 7 & up.**

Step into the world of a 19th-century boomtown in this little museum tracing the history of the area's quicksilver, or mercury, mines, once the most productive in the world. Photographs of miners from China, Europe, and Mexico share space with exhibits on how quicksilver was extracted from the ground to be used in thermometers. Also see the mining artifacts gathered by Constance Perham, who as a young girl accompanied her father on trips to the mines. See how Cinnabar, mercury's red ore, was carved into jewelry, and enjoy the tall tales spun by volunteers.

➤ Gilroy Historical Museum

195 Fifth Street, at Church, Gilroy 95020. (408) 848-0470. Mon.–Fri., 10–5; third Sat. of the month, 11–3. Tours by appt.; closed holidays. Donation. **Ages 8 & up.**

Telephones, tools, and toys are just part of this collection of over 22,000 donated memories from Gilroy's pioneer families. A cigar-store Indian, a school desk, and Ohlone clothing and artifacts are kids' favorites. Rotating exhibits emphasize the tobacco industry that was important in the building of the town, which once was home to the world's largest cigar factory, and to Henry Miller, the local cattle king. Today, it's garlic that's king.

⇥ Lick Observatory

Highway 130, 25 miles southeast of San Jose, Mt. Hamilton 95140. (408) 274-5061. Gallery, daily, 10–5; tours, 1:30–4:30. Closed holidays. Gift store. Free. **Ages 8 & up.**

A long, narrow, winding road takes you to the top of Mt. Hamilton and the awesome domes of Lick Observatory. It was here that four of the satellites of Jupiter were discovered—the first since the time of Galileo. Now star clusters and galaxies are studied with the most modern equipment. The visitor's gallery looks up at one of the largest telescopes (120 inches) in the world, a Shane reflecting telescope. The tour of photos and astronomical instruments is intriguing and educational. The gallery is half a mile from the Visitor Center. Call for public program information. And remember, there are no food or gas facilities nearby.

⇥ Public Relations Tours

Acres of Orchids. (Rod McLellan Orchidary, 1450 El Camino Real, South San Francisco 94080. 415-871-5655. Daily, 9–6; guided tours, 10:30 & 1:30. Free.) Naturalists over 10 can learn the history and technology of raising orchids here. There are orchids in more colors, types, and sizes than you can imagine, for looking, smelling, and buying.

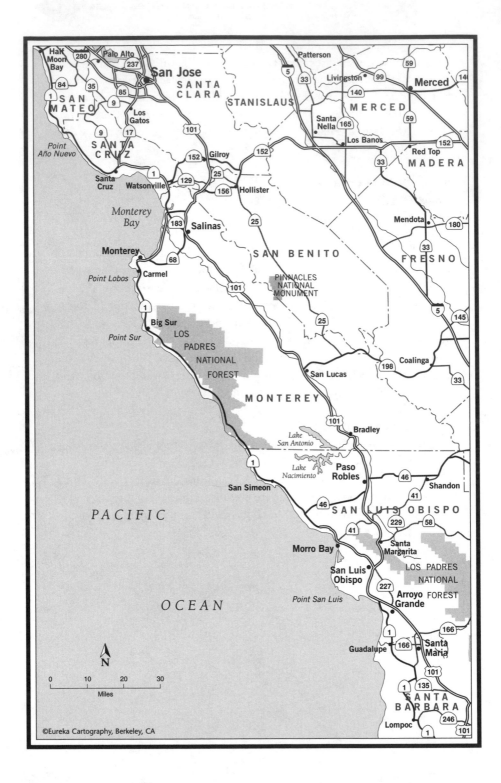

©Eureka Cartography, Berkeley, CA

Heading South by the Sea

DRIVING DOWN THE COAST from San Francisco, curving next to cliffs that head down to the sea, can be breathtaking. If you're driving from San Francisco to Monterey, we suggest you spend the night there before heading back. Getting to and from Santa Cruz is easier. And if you want to make a short stop or two on the way, we have these suggestions:

❖ Capitola City Museum

410 Capitola Avenue, Capitola 95010. (408) 464-0322. Fri., Sat. & Sun., 12–4 & by appt. Donation. **Ages 8 & up.**

Founded in 1966, the Capitola Historical Museum encompasses the history of the town from its founding as Camp Capitola through its transition to today's busy city-by-the-sea. Changing themed exhibits regularly include those mounted in cooperation with the Capitola Arts Commission.

❖ Davenport Jail Museum

2 Davenport Avenue, Davenport 95017. (408) 425-7278. Weekends, 10–2 & by appt. Free. **Ages 8 & up.**

This 1914 county jail, later used for other purposes, was abandoned in 1936. Now it houses a small, intriguing exhibition of local, "North Coast" cultural and natural history, with displays on the people who were here before us.

❋ The Santa Cruz Area

The Santa Cruz area is small, nestled on a bay southwest of San Jose and north of Monterey. Big Basin Redwoods, Natural Bridges (both have visitors centers with exhibits), and Loch Lomond parks are some of the natural sites of interest. Along with Castroville, home of the artichoke, they are perfect day trips from San Francisco. At Wilder Beach State Park, volunteers in period costume operate farm machinery and guide visitors through the Wilder home, furnished as it was at the turn of the century (weekends, 408-426-0505).

Here you can find birdwatching, butterfly watching, whale watching, herb and heritage walks and walks that focus on sea and sky. In Santa Cruz, beaches are the main attraction. If you're coming from San Francisco, be sure to take along car games to while away the two-hour ride. Highway 1, along the coast, is more beautiful and easier to drive than the faster choice, Highways 101 and 17.

⇶ Roaring Camp & Big Trees Narrow-Gauge Railroad and Santa Cruz, Big Trees & Pacific Railway Company

P.O. Box G-1, Felton 95018. Take Highway 17 to the Mt. Hermon Road exit in Scotts Valley, then drive west 3.5 miles to the end of the road at Felton, and left onto Graham Hill Road. (408) 335-4400. Roaring Camp round-trip fares: ages 3–12, $8; over 12, $11. Santa Cruz, Big Trees round-trip: $11 & $14. Group rates available. Call for schedules. **Ages 5 & up.**

Old-time train buffs now have two fabulous train rides to choose from, both originating at Roaring Camp. Great steam locomotives hiss and puff through the redwoods on the steepest narrow-gauge railroad grade in North America and around the tightest turns to the top of Big Mountain. The 1¼-hour trip transports riders back 100 years.

On the two-hour "Picnic Line" between Roaring Camp and the Santa Cruz beaches, passengers ride in historic 1902 wooden and 1926 steel passenger cars and open vista cars pulled by steam and early diesel locomotives, round trip or one way. Back in Roaring Camp, you can explore an 1880s logging town, wander along nature trails, rest beside an 1840s covered bridge, chow down at the Chuck Wagon Bar-B-Cue, and on summer weekends, enjoy country and western music.

⇶ Santa Cruz Surfing Museum

Lighthouse Point, West Cliff Drive, Santa Cruz (Mail: 1305 East Cliff Drive, 95062). (408) 429-3429. Wed.–Mon., 12–4. Donation. Gift shop. **Ages 8 & up.** *W.*

The Santa Cruz Surfing Museum, the first surfing muse
planet, is located in the Mark Abbott Memorial Lighthouse
Point, overlooking "Steamer Lane," the best surfboard inlet in the
On display are photographs, surfboards, and other surfing memorabilia
tracing more than 50 years of surfing in the Santa Cruz area. Kids over 10
love watching the continuous videos and delight in the board that's been
nibbled on by a shark.

⇶ Long Marine Laboratory & Aquarium

*100 Shaffer Road, at the end of Delaware Avenue, near Natural Bridges
State Park, Santa Cruz 95060. (408) 426-4308. Tues., 1–4. Adults, $2;
under 16, free. Group tours by appt.* **Ages 7 & up.**

A marine research facility of the University of California at Santa
Cruz, this is a working laboratory featuring fascinating marine aquariums,
touch tanks, the skeleton of an 85-foot blue whale, and a glimpse of current research. A young visitor named Daniel gives it this review: "I got to
touch the sea star, the sea anemone, and the hermit crab. The crabs were
fighting with each other. One crab bit a smaller crab by the antenna. So I
put one of the smaller crabs in a separate tank. After we finished playing
with the fish we went to the ocean and we saw a sea otter eating oysters
and abalone fish. Also, we went into the training area where they train the
sea lions and the dolphins. . . . I had a lot of fun."

⇶ The Mystery Spot

*465 Mystery Spot Road, Santa Cruz. (Mail: 74 River Street, Suite 209,
95060). (408) 423-8897. Guided tours daily, 9–5 in winter; until 8:30
in summer. Adults, $4; under 11, $2. Group rates available.* **Ages 5 & up.**

All the laws of gravity are challenged in this scary natural curiosity.
Balls roll uphill, the trees can't stand up straight, and you always seem
to be standing either backwards or sideways. One test here is to lay a
carpenter's level across two cement blocks, checking to see that their tops
are on the same level. Then stand on one and see your friend on the other
suddenly shrink or grow tall. You can also walk up the walls of a cabin
that looks cockeyed, but isn't. Alice-in-Wonderland's caterpillar would
feel right at home.

⇶ Santa Cruz Beach and Boardwalk

*400 Beach Street, at Riverside Avenue, Santa Cruz 95060. (408) 423-
5590. Weekends & holidays, 11–5 or 6; closed in December. From the last
week in May until Labor Day, the Boardwalk is open daily from 11–5, 7,
or 10 P.M., depending on the weather. Package tickets for 60 individual rides,*

$24.95; for all day, $17.95. Individual ride tickets and group rates, by reservation. General admission, free. Free off-site picnic tables. Free wheelchairs to borrow. Bike locks, $5 a day. Birthday parties with Captain Ned and Seaweed the parrot by appt. **All ages.** *W.*

The 1924 Giant Dipper, one of the world's top 10 roller coasters, and the classic 1911 Looff merry-go-round, with 72 hand-carved wooden horses, are both magnets for kids at California's only remaining amusement park on the beach. The last of the old-time West Coast boardwalks, Santa Cruz has everything you hope to find on one: a Ferris wheel, bumper cars, skee ball, a penny-video arcade, pinball and interactive games, miniature golf, cotton candy, and sweet and scary rides—including the steel Hurricane roller coaster and the Wave Jammer.

The **Neptune's Kingdom** entertainment complex (free admission, year-round; 408-426-7433) is a two-story treasure island of fun, with theme miniature golf, family pool tables, air hockey, and "foos ball," as well as a state-of-the-art video complex and a "historium" display of historical photos. The **Casino Fun Center** (free admission, year-round; 408-426-7433) beckons with a Sector 7 Laser Tag arena, a fantasyscope maze of black light, Virtualink virtual reality play center, and the Daytona USA Special, a fast interactive race. A Surf Bowl Bowling Center with 26 lanes is across the street.

There are 19 restaurants and fast-food vendors on the well-maintained boardwalk, and the best thing of all, a wonderful white beach, with parasailing and kayaking facilities. On the pier nearby, you can fish and see sea lions swimming around the pilings.

➤ Save Our Shores Interpretive Center

2222 East Cliff Drive, #5A, Santa Cruz 95062. (408) 462-5560. Mon.– Fri., 9–5; Sat., 11–3. Free. **Ages 5 & up.**

This marine sanctuary center provides visitors with an overview of the Monterey Bay National Marine Sanctuary.

To see the Sanctuary up close, take a **Gateway Adventure Tour** (Near Crows Nest restaurant at Lower Yacht Harbor. 408-479-4981. Adults, $8.50; ages 3–12, $5; under 3, free) of the harbor on a glass-enclosed boat. You'll see otters, sea lions, pelicans, cormorants, and perhaps porpoises and whales on one of the 40-minute tours. Sunset tours highlight the glimmer of the boardwalk lights on the water.

➤ Santa Cruz City Museum of Natural History

1305 East Cliff Drive, at Pilkington, Santa Cruz 95062. (408) 429-3773. Tues.–Sun., 10–5. Donation. Reserved parking on Pilkington in summer. Groups by appt. **Ages 6 & up.**

A "gray whale" welcomes you to natural history exhibits of ani
birds, and local plant groups. Learn how local Ohlone Indians live a
grind acorns in a stone mortar. See a mastodon skull from a prehistoric
denizen of the region and honeybees in action in an observation hive.
Touch live tide-pool animals. You can picnic in the park that surrounds
the museum or build a sand castle on the beach across the street.

Youngsters will be right at home in the **Children's Art Foundation**
(765 Cedar Street, Suite 201, 95060. 408-426-5557. Mon.–Fri., 9–5:30
& by appt; free), which collects, preserves, and exhibits children's art from
around the world, publishes *Stone Soup*, a magazine of writing and art by
children, and gives art lessons.

➢ McPherson Center for Art and History

*705 Front Street, Santa Cruz 95062. (408) 454-0697. Tues.–Sun., 11–4;
Thurs. until 8 P.M. Adults, $3; county residents, $2; members, students, &
children under 12, free. Tours available.* **Ages 6 & up.**

The McPherson Center for Art and History is a cultural complex
housing the Art Museum of Santa Cruz County, the History Museum of
Santa Cruz County, the Museum Shop, and the historic Octagon Gallery.

The History Museum of Santa Cruz County is designed for hands-on
exploration by children and their friends and gives history buffs a chance
to embark on an adventure through Santa Cruz County's intriguing past.
Through changing exhibitions, the Art Museum of Santa Cruz County
presents and interprets the art of our times.

➢ Santa Cruz Mission State Historic Park

*School Street, Santa Cruz 95062. (408) 425-5849. Thurs.–Sun., 10–4.
Fee, $2; seniors and those under 12, $1; family, $5. Free Living History
Programs. Gift Shop.* **Ages 6 & up.**

This adobe building is the last remaining structure of Mission
Santa Cruz, active from 1791 to 1834. The state's only authentically restored mission housing for Native Americans, it is a living testament to
the interplay between California's rich Spanish and Native American
heritages. On weekends, docents teach youngsters how to make candles,
tortillas, adobe bricks, paper flowers, and tule reed dolls.

➢ William H. Volck Memorial Museum

*261 East Beach Street, Watsonville 95076. (408) 722-0305. Tues.–
Thurs., 11–3 & by appt. Free.* **Ages 8 & up.**

Local history is lovingly preserved in this community museum featuring items and artifacts from the Pajaro Valley. We like the fine collection
of historic costumes and textiles, from gingham sunbonnets and aprons to

opera hats and ball gowns. The museum plans to move into an 1868 Victorian with garden at 332 E. Beach Street, so call first.

The **Pajaro Valley Arts Council Gallery** (408-722-3062. Wed.–Sat., 12:30–4:30. Free) houses contemporary and historial exhibitions nearby at 37 Sudden Street.

➤ Elkhorn Slough National Estuarine Research Reserve

1700 Elkhorn Road, Watsonville 95076. (408) 728-2822. Wed.–Sun., 9–5. Over 16, $2.50; free for those with valid fishing/hunting license. Weekend guided walks at 10 and 1. Visitors center, free. Gift shop. **Ages 6 & up.** *W.*

Videos are shown and special events are staged in the visitors center, run by the California Department of Fish and Game, which has displays of the natural history surrounding the area. The visitors center also offers hands-on exhibits, an aquarium, and a relief model of the Monterey Canyon. Blooming plants are identified. There are five miles of guided nature trails through oak woodlands, grasslands, and fresh and saltwater marshes.

In spring, the wildflowers are rampant and great blue herons and great egrets nest in the Rookery by the trail. In summer, small leopard sharks and smooth hound sharks come in on the high tide to give birth and feed on crabs and clams. Migrating shorebirds attract visitors in the fall. And in winter, ducks and shorebirds are plentiful.

To see the Elkhorn Slough up close, try an **Elkhorn Slough Safari.** (Reservations: 408-424-3939. 12 passengers per boat. Adults, $22.50; 14 & under, $17.50. Group & senior discounts. Gift certificates. Write: Gideon Charters, 10 Center Street, Salinas 93905.) Ride on a 26-foot pontoon boat, take photos, and listen to stories about the slough, and its ecology and history, on a two-hour adventure. Participants meet at Moss Landing.

➤ Public Relations Tours

Salz Tannery Tour (1040 River Street, Santa Cruz 95060. 408-423-1480. Free. Tours by appt. for groups of 8–25). The oldest tannery west of Chicago, Salz produces fine leather goods and accessories.

The Monterey Area

Since its discovery in 1542 by Spanish explorer Juan Cabrillo, the Monterey Peninsula has been a mecca for vagabonds and visionaries, pioneers in agriculture and art. It was here that California, after being under the flags of Spain and Mexico, was made part of the United States.

The Monterey area offers many sites worth investigating: the state's best-preserved tribute to its early history; a magnificent coastline in Big Sur; Salinas, with its reminders of novelist John Steinbeck; a sweeping windswept valley now turning into fertile farmland; Pinnacles National Monument; and the San Antonio de Padua Mission. From San Francisco, allow three hours driving time on Highway 101, taking the Monterey turnoff, or three and a half hours by the prettier coast route.

❧ San Juan Bautista State Historic Park

Highway 156 exit off Highway 101, P.O. Box 787, San Juan Bautista 95045-0787. (408) 623-4881. Daily, 10–4:30. Adults, $2; children, $1. Separate donation for the mission. Check at ranger station for scheduled interpretive activities. Call for information on Living History Days, when volunteers don period costumes and reenact events from California's past. **Ages 6 & up.**

A mission, a museum, an adobe house, an 1870s hotel and stables, a wash house, blacksmith shop, and cabin all encircle the lovely plaza of San Juan Bautista, representing four periods in California history—California Indian, Spanish, Mexican, and early Californian.

Start your visit at the **Mission of San Juan Bautista** (408-623-4528 for information), founded in 1797 and carefully preserved. The mission is still operated by the Catholic Church, and though it is not part of the State Historic Parks, it still anchors the square of history here. The old adobe rooms house many treasures, including a 1737 barrel organ, gaming sticks of the San Juan, or Mutsun, Indians, and artifacts from the original building. The original bells still call parishioners to mass. In the mission gardens, today's youngsters can learn some of the same things the Indians were taught, and they can bake in the outdoor ovens.

On the main street is the **Castro Adobe,** which also houses General Castro's secretary's office. This should serve as a model for other museums: Every room is completely labeled, with pictures to aid in the identification of the objects. The house is furnished as it was in the 1870s by the Breen family, who survived the Donner Party disaster and eventually found a fortune in the gold fields. You'll see the candlesticks that came west with the Breens and the diary, wardrobe, gloves, fan, and card case of Isabella Breen. The kitchen is complete, right down to the boot pull.

The **Plaza Hotel,** next door, is noted for its barroom with billiard and poker tables standing ready. Built in 1813 as a barracks for the Spanish soldiers, it is now furnished as it might have been in the 1860s. A slide show brings "the early years" to life.

Diagonally across the plaza is the **Zanetta House,** a completely furnished Victorian home, with dishes on the table and singing bird in the parlor, built on the foundation of the adobe that once housed the Indian maidens of the settlement. The **Livery Stable** is jammed with wonderful wagons, including a surrey with a fringe on top, a Wieland's beer wagon, a "tally ho wagon," phaetons, and buck boards.

The streets nearby have interesting shops and restaurants, making San Juan Bautista a perfect place to spend a relaxing morning or afternoon.

✤ Monterey

In *Two Years Before the Mast,* Richard Henry Dana called Monterey "decidedly the pleasantest and most civilized-looking place in California."

In this pleasant, bustling town, The Path of History, natural attractions, and busy shops lure visitors. Fisherman's Wharf is a melange of restaurants, fish stores, and shops. Although seal watching is the favored pastime, you can go fishing (408-375-5951/372-7444), whale watching (408-375-4658) or take a diving bell 30 feet down to look at the ocean's floor. The Nautilus Semi-submersible Underwater Viewing Vessel operates daily (408-647-1400 for reservations). There are also picnic tables near the bocce ball courts. In Monterey, you can go hang-gliding, ballooning, tide-pooling, and on nature walks.

Today's Cannery Row is a far cry from the Cannery Row in John Steinbeck's books. Now it is a growing complex of restaurants, shops, and galleries offering entertainment for all. Its greatest attraction is the extraordinary Monterey Bay Aquarium.

The City of Monterey has made it easy for visitors to get around and to see its beginnings. The Waterfront Area Visitor Express, the WAVE, allows you to park in one spot and then bus everywhere, from the Del Monte Shopping Center, through downtown Monterey, to Fisherman's Wharf and along the water to the Aquarium, Lover's Point, Point Pinos, Asilomar, and back, all for just $1 a day, 50 cents for children, seniors, and disabled, Memorial Day to Labor Day.

And by following the yellow line painted on several streets, you follow **"The Path of History."** Landmark plaques tell briefly who built historic houses, and why the buildings are landmarks.

❖ Maritime Museum of Monterey

Stanton Center, 5 Custom House Plaza, Monterey 93940. (408) 375-2553. Daily, 10–5, ex. Thanksgiving & Christmas, later in summer. Adults, $5; ages 13–18, $3; ages 6–12, $2. Groups by appt. Workshops and children's activities. Research library open Tues.–Fri., 10–5. Gift shop. **Ages 5 & up.** *W.*

A spiffy modern building captures the maritime tradition of Monterey and celebrates a seafaring heritage linking Spanish explorers, mission settlement, trade, fishing, and the U.S. Navy. The First Order Fresnel Lens, standing nearly two stories tall and weighing almost 10,000 pounds, served as a warning to mariners off Point Sur. Today it lights up the museum's ship model exhibit, a sea captain's quarters, navigational instruments, and chronicles of a once thriving whaling industry and Monterey's era as the sardine capital of the world. Fans will recognize the memorabilia from the Allen Knight collection, including the sardine boat and the sailor's ditty box. A personal favorite: the sampler by 9-year-old Laura Green, created aboard the SS *Indove*, January 16, 1868, sailing to Abbyssinia and the Suez. Old sailing accoutrements—octants, ships' bells, sailors' thimbles, Arctic goggles, scrimshaw, and ships' logs—are fascinating.

Special sea chanty sessions, story-telling events, and other programs will bring kids back for more.

❖ Monterey State Historic Park:
Stanton Center, Maritime Museum, State Park Orientation Center & History Theater

Custom House Plaza, between Fishermans's Wharf and Doubletree Hotel, Monterey. (Mail for all buildings in MSHP: 20 Custom House Plaza, 93940.) (408) 649-7118. The Center is open daily, 10–5. Tickets & information for MSHP Individual House Tours at Casa Soberanes, Larkin House, Cooper Molera Complex and Stevenson House: Adults, $2; ages 12–18, $1.50; ages 6–12, $1. Guided walking tours daily at 10:15, 12:30, and 2:30; $2. Special 2-day passes for all house tours and walking tour: $5. Groups by appt. **Ages 5 & up.**

Monterey State Historic Park is California's most authentically presented remembrance. There are more original and restored buildings in one town than there are anywhere else in America—including Colonial Willamsburg. One can drive along the yellow "Path of History" to see them all. Or you can start at the Stanton Center, see the free film, which is presented every 20 minutes, and then walk to each home or building you wish to explore.

⇉ Custom House

1 Custom House Plaza, Monterey. (Mail: 20 Custom House Plaza, 93940.)
(408) 649-7118. Daily, 10–4. Free.

The United States flag was first officially raised in California over this
building, in 1846. It is here that each ship captain presented his cargo for
the customs inspector. Today, you walk into a long room that holds the
cargo Richard Henry Dana wrote about in his novel *Two Years Before the
Mast*. There are casks of liquor, cases of dishes, bags of nails, coffee, flour,
and wagon wheels. A screeching yellow and green parrot rules a roost of
ribbons, ropes, cloth, shawls, soap, paper, tools, and trunks. In one area,
piles of "California bank notes"–cowhides–wait to be used for trading.
The Custom House guard's quarters upstairs feature a carved bed and
chest, a table, and a desk with an open ledger.

⇉ Pacific House

10 Custom House Plaza, Monterey 93940. (408) 649-7118.

The Pacific House, which has been a tavern, a court, a newspaper, a
church, and a ballroom, will be reopening after renovations are completed,
approximately October 1997. Call for information.

⇉ The Boston Store/Casa del Oro

Corner of Scott & Olivier Streets, Monterey. (408) 649-3364. Thurs.–Sat.,
10–5; Sun., 12–4. Free.

Built by Thomas O. Larkin about 1845, this structure housed a
general merchandise store operated by Joseph Boston & Company in the
1850s. The building was later called Casa del Oro because it served as a
gold depository. The safe is still there. Today, the building is again a
general merchandise store operated by Historic Gardens of Monterey with
profits going to preserve the building. The herb garden outside is wheelchair accessible and the store has a booklet of Mr. Boston's herb recipes.

⇉ Monterey's First Theatre/Jack Swan's Tavern

Corner of Scott & Pacific Streets, Monterey. Building information: (408)
375-5100. Theater information: (408) 375-4916. Fri. & Sat., 1–8;
Thurs.–Sat., 11–3. Free.

Jack Swan's lodging house gave its first performance of a stage play
in 1847 to entertain bored soldiers. Since then theatrical productions have
been produced regularly, and now 19th-century melodramas are per-
formed on weekends. During the day you can walk through and look at
the theatrical memorabilia, including a playbill for Lola Montez. The

Troupers of the Gold Coast celebrated its 50th anniversary in 1987. You'll have fun identifying the stars who got their start here.

➤ Casa Soberanes

336 Pacific Street, at Del Monte, Monterey. (408) 649-7118. Tours, Fri., Sat., Sun., Mon. & Wed., 10 & 11. See fees in Monterey State Historic Park listing above.

"The House with the Blue Gate" is an authentic, typical home of Mexican California. Built by Rafael Estrada in the 1830s, it was lived in by the Soberanes family from 1860 to 1922. With its thick walls, interconnected rooms, cantilevered balcony, and lovely garden, Casa Soberanes reflects life in Monterey, from its Mexican period beginnings to more recent times. The furnishings are a blend of early New England and China trade pieces with Mexican folk art. A collection of local art graces the house as well. The garden, which dates to the 1850s, is the oldest in the area.

➤ The Larkin House

510 Calle Principal, at Jefferson Street, Monterey. (408) 649-7118. Guided tours, Fri., Sat., Sun., Mon. & Wed., 1, 2, & 3. See fees in Monterey State Historic Park listing above.

Built by Thomas Oliver Larkin, the first and only U.S. consul to Mexico stationed in Monterey, the house is an architectural and historical gem. It was the first home in Monterey in the New England style, with two stories. Some of the furnishings are original. The early 19th-century rooms hold antiques from many parts of the world, acquired by the builder's granddaughter, Alice Larkin Toulmin, who lived here from 1922 to 1957. Through the rose-covered garden is a small house, now a museum, used in 1847–1849 by Civil War general William Tecumseh Sherman, then an Army lieutenant.

➤ Cooper-Molera Adobe Complex & Store

Polk & Munras Streets, Monterey. (408) 649-7118. Tours, Tues., Thurs., Fri., Sat., & Sun., 10 & 11 A.M. See fees in Monterey State Historic Park listing above. Cooper Store and Visitor Center open daily. Free.

This restored complex contains Captain John Cooper's townhouse (Cooper was Thomas Larkin's half-brother; his wife was Mariano Vallejo's sister, Encarnacion). The site contains several adobe buildings, a carriage house display room, and period gardens complete with scratching chickens. It was occupied by three generations of Coopers from 1827 to 1968.

The gift and book shop features handicrafts that hark back to the town's beginnings, including heirloom seeds from the property's garden.

❯ The Stevenson House

525 Houston Street, Monterey. (408) 649-7118. Tours, Tues, Thurs., Fri., Sat. & Sun., 1, 2, & 3. See fees in Monterey State Historic Park listing above. Nov. 13 is an open house for Robert Louis Stevenson's "unbirthday" because he gave his original birthday away to a little girl born on Christmas Day. Special events and school programs.

In 1879 Robert Louis Stevenson spent a few months in a second-floor room of this boarding house. He had traveled from Scotland to visit Fanny Osbourne, who later became his wife. He wrote *The Old Pacific Capital* here. The house is restored to look as it did then, with several rooms dedicated to Stevenson memorabilia. Be sure to see the doll collection upstairs. There is a rumor of a ghost.

After a visit, third-grader Jennifer wrote, "Thank you for a fun day at the 'French Hotel.' I like Robert Stevenson. I like looking inside his room. I learned that Stevenson gave his birthday to a little girl named Annie. Thank you for the cake."

❯ Casa Gutierrez

590 Calle Principal, Monterey 93940. (408) 649-7118. MSHP. Daily, 10–4.

This adobe was built in 1841 by a young Mexican for his bride. He earned his living as a farmer and rancher, and raised 15 children here.

❯ Colton Hall Museum of the City of Monterey

Pacific Street, between Jefferson and Madison, Monterey 93940. (408) 649-7118. MSHP. Daily, 10–5. Free.

Colton Hall, the first town hall and the first public school of Monterey, was the site of the first Constitutional Convention of the State of California, in 1849. Here the California Constitution was written in Spanish and English and the Great Seal of the state was designed. The large meeting room is furnished as it was then, with displays depicting the scene in 1849 during the convention, as if the delegates had just stepped out for a break. The hall was built by Navy Chaplain Walter Colton, who served as the first American alcalde (mayor) in California from 1846 to 1849.

Behind Colton Hall is the **Old Monterey Jail,** open daily until 5. The walls are granite, two feet thick, the doors are iron, and the cells tell the stories of the jail and its inmates. Believe it or not, this was the city jail until 1959. The Old Monterey Jail was a second home for Danny, in John Steinbeck's *Tortilla Flat*.

❧ Cannery Row

Cannery Row Information Center: (408) 373-1902. Cannery walking tours.

In his novel, *Cannery Row*, John Steinbeck called the Row "a poem, a stink, a grating noise, a quality of light, a tone, a habit, a nostalgia and a dream." Today's visitor will find most of that here, along with restaurants and shops, many with water views.

Three workers' shacks have been restored for public viewing on the Irving Street walkway, between the Recreation Trail and Wave Street. Each looks as it would have when inhabited by a Spanish cannery worker in the 1920s, two Japanese fishermen in the 1930s, or a Filipino reduction plant worker in the 1940s. Just walk by and peek in the windows.

The little theater inside A Taste of Monterey—the wine and produce visitors' center at 700 Cannery Row—offers 3-D showings of **Old Cannery Row in 3-D,** a film that relives the last days of the historic canneries, including their mystique and architectural design. 3-D glasses are provided (408-646-5446).

You could also rent a 1929 Mercedes, a 1929 Ford Model A, or a 1930 Phaeton to go sightseeing. **Rent-A-Roadster** is at 229 Cannery Row (408-647-1929).

Shoppers will happily explore the art, antique, and souvenir shops on the row, along with 45 factory outlets and restaurants at the **American Tin Cannery** (125 Ocean View Boulevard, Pacific Grove, around the corner from the Aquarium. 408-372-1442. Mon., Wed. & Sat., 10–6; Thurs. & Fri., 10–9; Sun., 11–5) and the **Edgewater Packing Company** (11–11 weekdays, later on summer weekends), across from the Aquarium, which boasts shops, restaurants, and a super 34-horse, two-unicorn and two-zebra 1905 carousel that is said to be the fastest in the West. **Oscar Hossenfellder's Ice Cream Fountain** next to it offers breakfast, lunch, and parties.

❧ Bubba Gump Shrimp Co.

720 Cannery Row, Monterey 93940. (408) 373-1884. Mon.–Thurs., 11– 10 P.M.; Fri., until 11; Sat., 8:30–11; Sun., 8:30–10, in summer. Closing hours earlier in winter. **All ages.**

Right behind the park bench with a suitcase, white sneaks you can stick your feet into, and a Box of Chocolates, the Bubba Gump Shrimp Co. celebrates *Forrest Gump* with Gump memorabilia and scrawled "Gumpisms" on every varnished wood tabletop. The movie plays continuously on video monitors and waiters challenge customers with *Gump* trivia questions. Shrimp is served 10 ways, from Mama Blue's Southern Charmed Fried to Jenny's Sweet Ginger and Garlic Shrimp Scampi, along with This Man's Army Bone-in Rib Eye Steak and Bubba's Far Out Dip, among other things. The water view is great.

The store next door sells *Gump* cookbooks, CD-ROMS, videos, mugs, T-shirts, and chocolates.

⇛ Spirit of Monterey Steinbeck Wax Museum

700 Cannery Row, Monterey 93940-1085. (408) 375-3770. Daily, 11–8, longer hours in summer. Adults, $5.95; ages 6–16, $4.95; over 65, $3.95. Tours with special rates by appt. **Ages 6 & up.** *W.*

Dozens of scenes tell the spellbinding story of Monterey and the people who lived it, from the Indians who lived here before the Spanish galleons cast anchor to Steinbeck's rowdy crew. Visitors will meet Conception, who fell in love with a Russian officer and waited in vain for his return; Robert Louis Stevenson; the Spanish dons who ruled Monterey; and Thomas Larkin, who was California's first "ambassador" to the United States. Kit Carson rides up and tells his story, Joaquin Murietta spouts poetry, and Steinbeck reminisces about his friends in the Lone Star Cafe.

⇛ Monterey Bay Aquarium

886 Cannery Row, Monterey 93940-1085. (408) 648-4888. Advance purchase: (800) 756-3737 and all BASS outlets. Daily, except Christmas, 10–6. Adults, $13.75; students and seniors, $11.75; ages 3–12 & disabled, $6. Posted feeding schedules. Workshops and discovery labs for members and school groups. Group rates and tours available. Gift shops. http://www.mbayaq.org/. **All ages.** *W.*

"He's feeding fish to fish," one youngster exclaimed, while standing entranced before the three-story kelp forest. All the wonders of a hidden world come to light at the internationally acclaimed Monterey Bay Aquarium, one of California's "top 11" attractions. In a startling undersea tour of Monterey Bay, visitors will meet more than 350,000 living creatures in more than 100 galleries and exhibits.

California sea otters frolic nose to nose with you in their own naturalistic pool, visible on two different levels. You can investigate with telescopes and microscopes, play with bat rays and starfish, or walk through a shorebird aviary. Special exhibits change every 20 months.

Twice a week, "Live from the Monterey Canyon" lets visitors peek over the shoulders of scientists in a research submarine and look at unusual creatures living 3,000 feet and more below the surface of Monterey Bay.

The spectacular Outer Bay wing is the first in the world to present the life of the open ocean on a grand scale. After you go up an escalator, you discover you're beneath a silvery school of anchovies flashing over you.

Wander through the permanent gallery of "Drifters," graceful, magical jellyfish of all sizes. Banks of microscopes and live exhibits introduce visitors to plankton, the foundation of the oceanic food chain. Some of the animals are included in an aquarium exhibit for the first time ever. Then there's the million-gallon indoor ocean showcasing the sunlit blue waters where Monterey Bay meets the open sea. Sharks, ocean sunfish (3,000 pounds and 10 feet tall!), green sea turtles, barracuda, and schools of tuna swoop by, as visitors watch from a three-story, 54-foot-long window. Imagine that you're 50 miles offshore, 300 feet beneath the surface. It's dark, quiet, awesome.

Then head on out to "Flippers, Flukes & Fun," which is filled with super hands-on exhibits to show younger children all about whales and other marine mammals. They can even don flippers to pretend they're mermaids and wander inside a whale's stomach, make a whale sing, a sea lion bark, and a dolphin whistle.

Films, slide shows, special programs, flip charts, and hands-on interpretive exhibits challenge and intrigue. The aquarium is outstanding, a beautifully designed treat for the whole family. The Portola Cafe features a cafeteria, a full-service restaurant, and an oyster bar, all with ocean views. There's also a snack bar.

Be on the lookout for Deep Sea Galleries, which open around 2001, featuring fishes and animals from the perpetual darkness of the Monterey Canyon, two miles below the ocean's surface.

❧ La Mirada, Monterey Peninsula Museum of Art

720 Via Mirada Street, off Fremont, Monterey. (Mail: 559 Pacific Street, 93940.) (408) 372-5477. Thurs.–Sat., 10–4; Sun., 1–4. Tours by reservation. Adults, $5; students & ages 12–18, $3; under 12, free. First Sunday of the month, free. **Ages 8 & over.**

La Mirada adobe, built in the early 19th century, was the home of Mexican General Jose Castro. Visitors will explore early California history, experience a taste of life on the Peninsula in the 1920s, and enjoy exhibitions of California regional art and art of the Pacific Rim.

❧ Dennis the Menace Playground

Pearl Street, El Estero City Park, off Del Monte Avenue, Camino del Estero and Fremont, Monterey 93941. (408) 646-3866. Daily, 10–dusk. Free. **Ages 2–12.**

Youngsters will want to head to this colorful playspace designed by cartoonist Hank Ketchum. Here, little potential "menaces" can let off steam in a steam switch engine, hang from the Umbrella Tree, sweep down the Giant Swing Ride, and put their heads in the lion's mouth for a drink of water. There's a special play area for the physically challenged.

➤ Pacific Grove Museum of Natural History

Forest and Central Avenues, Pacific Grove 93950. (408) 648-3116. Daily except Mon., 10–5. Closed Thanksgiving, Christmas Eve & Day, and New Year's Day. Groups by appt. Movies & special programs. Free. **Ages 6 & up.** *W.*

Each October, thousands of Monarch butterflies arrive in Pacific Grove to winter in a grove of pine trees until March. The **Monarch Restoration Habitat** (on Ridge Road, off Lighthouse Avenue) is their home. Visitors who arrive in other months can see a marvelous exhibit of the Monarch in this beautifully designed museum. There is also a large collection of tropical and other California butterflies as well as sea otters, fish, mammals, rodents, insects, and birds. The skeleton of a sea otter playing with a clamshell is touching. The life of the Costanoan Indians is revealed in an archaeological "dig."

Dioramas and the amazing relief map of Monterey Bay are also worth a look—if the youngsters can tear themselves away from climbing on Sandy the Gray Whale in front of the museum.

➤ El Cocodrilo Rotisserie & Seafood Grill

701 Lighthouse Avenue, Pacific Grove 93950. (408) 655-3311. Closed Tuesdays.

To sample the spirit and flavor of cuisine from the Caribbean, Central and South America, dine at this award-winning Latin Fusion restaurant. The owners feel that the way to save the Rainforest is to show that its nuts and berries can produce income. So they use spices and nuts from the Rainforest in their chowders, salads, pastas, and entrees. Try the alligator nuggets, the Nicaraguan tamale, the West Indian baby back ribs, spit-roasted Mayan chicken, or the sauteed prawns Rio Coco. Salsa fresca, Costa Rican rice, and fried platanos will appeal to herbivores. The folk art, sculpted birds and animals in brilliant colors, adds to the fun.

➤ Point Pinos Lighthouse

Off Asilomar Boulevard & Lighthouse Avenue, Pacific Grove 93950. Information at Pacific Grove Museum: (408) 648-3116. Thurs., weekends, & holidays, 1–4. Free. **Ages 8 & up.**

Point Pinos—Point of Pines—was named by explorer Sebastian Viscaino in 1602. The lighthouse overlooks the meadows and sand dunes of a golf course on one side, and the whitecapped ocean on the other. Inside the Cape Cod-style building, which is the oldest working lighthouse on the West Coast (1855), newly refurbished and redecorated rooms bring back the homey look of the lighthouse when Emily Fish was the light keeper at the turn of the century. Volunteer docents in period dress tell lighthouse history. Upstairs in the tiny watch room, you can read Fish's logbooks of storms, the 1906 earthquake, and the 1906 Chinatown fire in Pacific Grove.

The short distance to town along scenic Oceanview Boulevard offers many beautiful sights. Along the way you'll pass Lovers Point, with marine gardens, and tree-shaded picnic grounds.

Point Sur State Historic Park (408-625-4419) offers guided tours of a 19th-century lighthouse and support structures on the Big Sur Coast.

❖ Carmel

A visit to the Monterey Peninsula is not complete without an hour or two of browsing in the picturesque village of Carmel. The Pine Inn Block, bounded by Ocean Avenue, Lincoln, Monte Verde, and Sixth Avenue, is bustling with Victorian shops, galleries, gardens, and restaurants. Kids will enjoy the dollhouse miniatures and "Wee forest folk mice" at The Impulse Shoppes, on Ocean, opposite the Pine Inn. The Mediterranean Market at Ocean and Mission (408-624-2022) supplies picnic goodies for your walk on Carmel Beach, at the end of Ocean Avenue.

❖ Carmel Mission, Mission San Carlos Borromeo

Rio Road, off Highway 1, Carmel 93923. (408) 624-1271. Daily except holidays, 9:30–4:30; later in summer. Donation. **Ages 7 & up.**

The lovely mission church and cemetery, museums, and the adobe home of the pioneer Munras family combine to make this mission a "must stop." Father Junipero Serra rests in the church, and in the cemetery lies Old Gabriel, who lived 119 years and was baptized by Father Serra. The small Harry Downey museum in the garden houses pictures of the original mission and its restoration. There are Indian grinding pots, arrowheads, baskets, beads, toys, and other archeological treasures. The long main museum offers fine art from the original mission and a replica of the stark cell Father Serra died in. You'll also find California's first library here—Father Serra's books, bibles, travel commentaries, and technical works. Altar pieces, saddles, the furnished kitchen and dining room, a "clacker" used instead of bells, and a fabulous nativity crèche are also of interest, as are mementos of Pope Paul's visit in 1987.

The Munras Museum is now a memorial to the Munras family. Visitors can see the keys from the original adobe, family pictures, music and provision boxes, a doctor's bag, jewelry, dresses, and a totally furnished living room.

❖ Robinson Jeffers's Tor House

26304 Ocean View Avenue, Carmel 93923. (408) 624-1813. One-hour tours on Fri. & Sat. by reservation: 624-1840. Adults, $5; college students, $3.50; high school students, $1.50. **Ages 12 & up.**

Mature, budding poets over 12 years old will enjoy a visit to the home of California poet Robinson Jeffers on a high bluff overlooking the Pacific. Part English country cottage, part stone monument to the mystery of the human imagination, Tor House celebrates the nature around it. Jeffers himself built the low main cottage of "stone love stone," with memorabilia from his world travels imbedded in the stone walls. The 40-foot Hawk Tower looks like a castle turret. He also built a wonderful "dungeon playroom" for his sons.

❖ Point Lobos State Reserve

Highway 1, south of Carmel, P.O. Box 62, Carmel 93923. (408) 624-4909. Daily, 9–5 in winter; later in summer. Cars: $6, or $5 for senior citizens. **All ages.**

Early Spanish explorers named this rocky, surf-swept point of land *Punta de Los Lobos Marinos*, or Point of the Sea Wolves. You can still hear the loud barking of the sea lions and see them on offshore rocks. Point Lobos is an outdoor museum: Each tree, plant, and shrub is protected by law, as are the cormorants, pelicans, otters, squirrels, and black-tailed mule deer that live here. One of the last natural stands of Monterey cypress is also found at the reserve. There are three picnic areas and 10 miles of hiking trails. Dogs are not permitted in the reserve.

❖ The Steinbeck House

132 Central Avenue, Salinas. Reservations: (408) 424-2735. Luncheon seatings at 11:45 or 1:15, Mon.–Fri. Light lunch and dessert on Saturdays, open seating, 11:30–2:30. Gift shop. **Ages 10 & up.**

John Steinbeck's childhood Victorian home is now a luncheon restaurant offering fresh produce of the valley amid Steinbeck memorabilia. This is where the author of *The Red Pony* and *Tortilla Flat* grew up. The "Best Cellar" features Steinbeck's books. Profits go to Salinas Valley charities, and the house's restoration has been funded by the luncheon proceeds.

The Steinbeck Library (110 W. San Luis, 408-758-7311) displays an extensive collection of John Steinbeck's memorabilia, including reviews and personal correspondence and a life-size bronze statue.

⇒ The First Mayor's House

238 East Romie Lane, Salinas 93901. (408) 757-8085. First Sun. of the month, 1–4. Free. **Ages 8 & up.**

Built in 1868 by Isaac Harvey, the first mayor of Salinas, of redwood lumber hauled from Moss Landing, the house has been moved to its present location. The Monterey County Historical Society has restored and refurnished the home and is continuing to work on its restoration.

⇒ The Boronda Adobe

333 Boronda Road at West Laurel Drive, Salinas 93901. (408) 757-8085. Weekdays, 9–3; weekends, 1–4; and by appt. Free. Archival vault available to researchers. **Ages 8 & up.**

The Monterey County Historical Society has also restored Jose Eusebio Boronda's unaltered adobe, built in 1844, once part of the 6,700-acre Rancho San Jose. The oldest building in Salinas is now a little museum proudly showing many of its original furnishings.

Also on the site is the **Lagunita One Room School House,** built in 1897. This is the school Steinbeck wrote about in *The Red Pony.* A Queen Anne Victorian built by Salinan William Weeks is being turned into a house museum and a research center. A cultural museum and agricultural museum are underway.

⇒ Issei Pioneer Museum

14 California Street, Salinas 93901. (408) 424-4105. By appt. Free. **Ages 6 & up.**

The first and only *Issei* pioneer museum in the United States, housed in the annex of a Buddhist temple, contains over 600 items related to the Issei—the first generation of Japanese to immigrate to the United States, in the 1890s and early 1900s. The museum was opened in 1976, the bicentennial year of our country. Many of the articles were handmade by the Issei during World War II in various relocation camps. The oldest item is a book about Tokyo, printed in 1850. The museum also houses many items of historical significance collected by Y. Takemura.

⇒ Mission Nuestra Señora de la Soledad

36641 Fort Romie Road, Soledad 93960. Highway 101 southwest of Soledad. Arroyo Seco off-ramp, then right on Fort Romie Road. (408) 678-2586. Daily except Tues., 10–4. Donation. **Ages 8 & up.**

Founded in 1791 as the 13th in the chain of 21 California missions, this mission, dedicated to Holy Mary, Our Lady of the Solitude, was in desolate open plains and in ruins by 1859. Volunteers have restored it as a lovely oasis surrounded by gardens. Visitors may visit the museum and chapel and then spend time in the gift shop, graveyard, and picnic area.

San Antonio de Padua Mission

P.O. Box 803, Jolon 93928. On Fort Hunter Liggett, off Highway 101 from King City or Bradley. (408) 385-4478. Mon.–Sat., 9:30–4:30; Sun., 11–4:30, mass at 10 A.M. Donation. Gift shop, 10–12 & 1–4:30. Information for fourth graders may be obtained by a request accompanied by a self-addressed, stamped envelope. **Ages 7 & up.**

San Antonio de Padua is one of the finest of the missions. It was the third mission founded by Fra Junipero Serra, in 1771. A military base around it has preserved its natural setting. To visit is to feel that you're discovering the days of the padres and Salinan Indians of 200 years ago. Inside the mission museum, on a self-guided tour, you'll see artifacts from mission days, tools for candle-making and carpentry, the old wine press, and other old-time implements needed to run a working mission. The grist mill, the aqueduct system, waterwheel, and wine vat stand as the Indians saw them when San Antonio was at its height. The wildflower season in late April and early May is gorgeous. The annual Fiesta Bar-B-Q is held on the second Sunday of June, close to the Feast of St. Anthony. Steinbeck described the mission in a state of abandonment in *To a God Unknown*. Today, it is a working parish and contemplative center and retreat, served by the Franciscan Friars of California.

Public Relations Tours

Roses of Yesterday and Today (803 Browns Valley Road, Watsonville 95076. 408-724-3537). The big rose garden that specializes in old, hard-to-find roses is, in season, a sight to behold. Groups and school visits are encouraged and there are tables and benches for picnics.

Stone Container Corporation (1078 Merrill Street, Salinas 93901. 408-424-1831. Nov.–Apr., by appt. for children over 10. Free). Today's kids sometimes like the boxes toys come in more than the toys. Here's where they can see the manufacture of corrugated boxes and paper laminations.

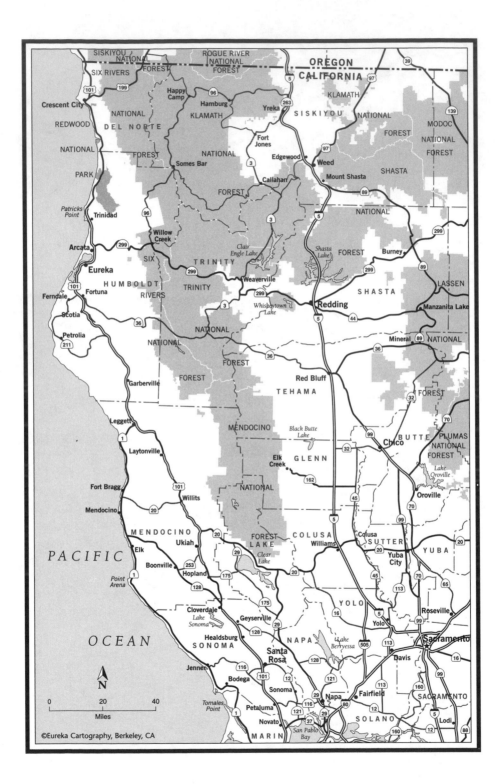

Heading North

✸ Napa, Sonoma, and Lake Counties

The Napa-Sonoma area is best known for the vineyards that grow on rolling hills and in the Valley of the Moon. But the country itself is welcoming and is seen to advantage from the hot-air balloons, gliders, planes, and parachutes now available for the brave of heart. Napa's first American settler, George Yount, was given a land grant by General Mariano Vallejo in 1836. He planted the first grapes so he could have wine for his table.

Wineries can be fun for youngsters to visit, not only because the wine-making process is fascinating but because the wine industry is part of California's history and culture. In most wineries, your tour will follow the direction the grape takes, from vineyard delivery to the crushing and the aging vat, and on to the bottles in the tasting rooms. Many wineries also offer local food products such as jam or olive oil. Tasting rooms, which may charge, may also offer grape juice or nonalcoholic wine. Many wineries have picnic areas, also free of charge. Kid-friendly wineries include **Robert Mondavi** (Highway 29, P.O. Box 106, Oakville 94562. 800-MONDAVI, 9–5:30. Free. W.), which offers free concerts on the lawn; **Sterling Vineyards** (1111 Dunaweal Lane, off Highway 29, Calistoga 94515. 707-942-3300. Daily except holidays, 10:30–4:30. Adults, $6; under 21, $3) with its aerial Skytram ride; **Buena Vista Winery** (18000 Old Winery Road, off East Napa Road, 1 mile from Sonoma, Sonoma 95476. 707-938-1266/800-926-1266. Daily, 10:30–4:30), with its atmospheric limestone caves and great history; and **Matanazas Creek Winery** (6097 Bennett Valley Road, Santa Rosa 95404. 707-528-6454. Daily self-guided grounds tours), amid California's largest lavender plot.

For up-to-date information on tours, balloon rides, resorts, sightseeing, hotels, etc., in eight languages, call the **Napa Valley Hotline,** 1-900-267-NAPA.

❧ Napa Firefighters Museum
1201 Main Street, Napa 94559. (707) 259-0609. Wed.–Sun., 11–4. Groups & tours by appt. Free. **Ages 4 & up.**

Here's a chance to ride a firetruck and have your picture taken. School groups also get free fire chief's badges. The museum is a treasure trove of firefighting equipment, from an 1850 hand-drawn hand-pumper to a 1904 horse-drawn steamer, a 1913 horseless carriage Model T to a 1931 ladder truck. Uniforms, scrapbooks, photographs, hose carts, firefighting toys, and other machinery fill the room. People from the community share their collections for rotating shows of, for example, cameras or tools. There are pictures of firehouses from all over the world, including Ponce, Puerto Rico's black & red striped Victorian, and St. Petersburg. The museum will find a permanent location in 1999, so call first.

❖ Napa Valley Wine Train

1275 McKinstry Street, near Soscol and First Streets, Napa 94559. (707) 253-2111 or (800) 427-4124. By reservation, with deposit only. A Deli Car ride, without a meal, is $25. Brunch, $57; lunch, $63; dinner, $70. Group rates. Gift shop. **Ages 12 & up.**

Older youngsters may find this 36-mile, three-hour adventure a real treat. Brunch, lunch, or dinner is served in a meticulously restored 1917 Pullman dining car replete with etched glass, polished brass, and rich mahogany. You will be pampered as you roll through the vineyards and mustard fields of the Napa Valley.

❖ Yountville-Vintage 1870

Highway 29, 6525 Washington Street, P.O. Box 2500, Yountville 94599. (707) 944-2451. Daily, 10–5:30. **Ages 10 & up.** *W.*

This lovely historic winery complex is part of the original land grant made to Salvador Vallejo in 1838 and was bought in 1870 for $250 in U.S. gold coin. The brick exterior of the building hasn't changed much, but the interior is now a charming complex of 40 stores, including a bakery, toy cellar, and candy store. Restaurants, garden cafes, and picnic areas surround the property.

❖ Napa Valley Museum

473 Main Street, in Vintage Hall, St. Helena 94572. (707) 963-7411. Mon.–Fri., 9–4; Sat. & Sun., 11–3. Adults, $2; children, free. **Ages 8 & up.**

This small museum celebrates the land, the people, and the industries of the Napa Valley with changing exhibitions of art, history, and natural history.

❖ The Silverado Museum

1490 Library Lane, one block east of Main Street (Highway 29), St. Helena 94572. (707) 963-3757. Daily except Mon. and holidays, 12–4. Groups by appt. Book shop. Free. **Ages 5 & up.** *W.*

Robert Louis Stevenson has been associated with the Napa Valley ever since he honeymooned in an abandoned bunkhouse of the Silverado Mine on Mount St. Helena. Today, anyone who grew up on *A Child's Garden of*

Verses or *Treasure Island* will appreciate this tribute to the man who wrote them. Portraits of Stevenson abound, including one showing him as a 4-year-old with long flowing curls. Original manuscripts, illustrations, the author's toy lead soldiers, tea set, doll, chess set, desk with carved faces, and memorabilia from his plantation in Samoa, plus Henry James's gloves, are neatly displayed in this modern, cheerful museum. It makes you want to read a Stevenson book right away.

❖ Bale Grist Mill State Historic Park

3369 St. Helena Highway North (Highway 29), 3 miles north of St. Helena (Mail: c/o Napa Valley State Park, 3801 St. Helena Highway North, Calistoga 94515). (707) 963-2236. Demonstrations every hour from 11:30 on weekends. **Ages 5 & up.**

Walk to the mill from Bothe Park, along the History Trail. This restored water-powered grist mill was built in 1846 and has been milling flour ever since. The 36-foot waterwheel is equipped with French buhrs, quartzite stones used to grind the finest flour. Baking demonstrations (tastings too!) round out the experience. Exhibits provide an orientation to the area as well as descriptions of its natural history. You can buy flour to take home.

❖ Hurd Beeswax Candles at Freemark Abbey

3020 St. Helena Highway North (Highway 29), St. Helena 94574. North of St. Helena. (707) 963-7211. Winery tours daily at 2. Shops open 10–5:30 daily. **Ages 4 & up.**

The old Freemark Abbey Winery also houses the Hurd Beeswax Candle Factory, along with a restaurant and a gift shop. Weekday visitors may see candles being made by hand, 8:30 to 5, seasonally. And all youngsters will be intrigued by the wooden shutter on the far wall of the inside showroom. It opens to reveal a glass-backed beehive full of bees filling their honeycomb. One young fan wrote, "Thank you for letting our class come to see you make candles and letting us see you color them in wax and letting us see the bees make wax."

❖ Sharpsteen Museum & Sam Brannan Cottage

1311 Washington Street, Calistoga 94514. Take Highway 29 to Calistoga; right on Lincoln to Washington. (707) 942-5911. Daily except Thanksgiving & Christmas, Nov.–March, 12–4; April–Oct., 10–4; and by appt. Free. Gift shop. Lectures. **Ages 7 & up.** *W.*

This museum, given to the city of Calistoga by Ben Sharpsteen, a Disney Studios artist, is dedicated to the preservation and presentation of the history of Calistoga. Calistoga's pioneer history comes alive in the scale model dioramas and shadow boxes. The diorama-mural "Saratoga of the West" covers one wall. Other dioramas depict Robert Louis Stevenson, the railroad depot, the Chinese settlement, and more. Sam Brannan, the founder of Calistoga and the first California millionaire, is present in spirit. One of his cottages has been moved to the site, restored, and furnished authentically, a delight for children and adults.

≫ Old Faithful Geyser of California

1299 Tubbs Lane, 2 miles north of Calistoga, Calistoga 94515. (707) 942-6463. Daily, 9–6 in summer, until 5 in winter. Adults, $5; seniors, $4; ages 6–12, $2. Gift shop and snack bar. Picnic tables available. **All ages.**

One of the more surprising results of the 1989 earthquake is that it made Old Faithful "old erratic." Once one of the few faithful geysers in the world, erupting every 40 minutes almost like clockwork, Old Faithful now shoots forth its plume of boiling water and steam, sometimes 60 feet high, every hour or so, with lapses of up to 20 or 30 minutes. But the effect is the same. As one little girl exclaimed, when she viewed the geyser after dark: "Look, Mommy, the geyser is washing the stars."

≫ Petrified Forest

4100 Petrified Forest Road, Calistoga 94515. (707) 942-6667. Daily, 10–5; until 6 in summer. Adults, $3; seniors, $2; ages 4–11, $1. Gift shop. **All ages.** *Partial W.*

Volcanic eruptions of Mount St. Helena six million years ago formed this forest of petrified redwoods, "discovered" in 1870 and written about by Robert Louis Stevenson in "Silverado Squatters." A lovely forest trail passes a 300-foot-long "Monarch" tunnel tree and "the Queen," which was already 3,000 years old when it was buried. On the way out, you'll walk through a specimen shop of fossils and petrified worms, snails, clams, nuts, and wood.

≫ Air Play

The rolling hills and soft wind currents of the area have made the skies here especially accessible. For those who are adventurous, and can afford it, try the following—and check the local Yellow Pages for others. Since companies open and fade with the wind, call for schedules and prices.

Calistoga Gliders. *1546 Lincoln Avenue, Calistoga 94515. (707) 942-5000. Glider rides, instruction, and rental.*

Balloons Above the Valley. *5091 St. Helena Highway, P.O. Box 3838, Napa 94559. (800) 464-6824; (800) GO-HOT-AIR; (707) 253-2222. One hour flights by reservation. Balloon pins for every flyer. Free* *child-care provided, since those under six may be more alarmed than enchanted. Brunch included.*

Napa Valley Balloons, Inc. *P.O. Box 2860, Yountville 94599. (800) 253-2224; (707) 253-2224.*

Sonoma Thunder, Inc. Wine Country Balloon Safaris. *2508 Burnside Road, Sebastopol 95472-9423. (707) 538-7359; (800) 759-5638. Group rates.*

⇒ Whale watching: *New Sea Angler* and *Jaws*

P.O. Box 1148, Bodega Bay 94923. (707) 875-3495. **Ages 8 & up.**

Those seeking more down-to-the-sea pleasures may choose to whale watch on the ocean. *New Sea Angler* and *Jaws* head out twice a day on weekends and holidays, December 28 through April, from Bodega Bay. Both vessels also provide year-round, daily salmon and rock cod fishing trips. Special cruises are also offered, on request.

⇒ Bodega Marine Laboratory

Between Bodega Head and Salmon Creek. (707) 875-2211. 1-hour tours, Fridays, 2–4. Free. **Ages 8 & up.**

The University of California at Davis conducts research here on marine and coastal habitats. In 1775, Francisco Bodega y Cuadra, a Spanish mariner, became the first European to anchor in the harbor. Today, Bodega Bay is the second largest salmon fishing port in California. Just walking along the beaches and dunes around the bay can make you feel like you're the first person to set foot here.

⇒ Petaluma Historical Library-Museum

20 Fourth Street, Petaluma 94952. (707) 778-4398. Mon., Thurs., Fri., Sat., 10–4; Sun., 1–4. Free. **Ages 7 & up.** *W.*

Downtown in "The Egg Basket of the World," the Petaluma Historical Library-Museum shows rotating and permanent displays, such as one on the local poultry industry and another on local river history. The bust of Chief Solano, photos of General Vallejo, and the Knickerbocker No. 5 fire engine are popular. A third-grader from the Meadow School wrote, "I like the stained glass window, the kitchen and where they did the laundry because it was really fun."

⇒ Petaluma Collective Military Antiques & Museum

260 Petaluma Boulevard North, Petaluma 94952. (707) 765-2920. Daily, 10–5:30. Free. **Ages 5 & up.**

Wend your way through the assemblage of antique and second-hand stands downstairs to a mind-boggling collection of military mementos dating back to the Civil War. The retail area offers uniforms, medals, headgear, nonfunctioning weapons, books, ephemera, and personal mementos. Next to the main shop is a 1,200-square-foot military museum with several small dioramas and other items of interest to fighting fans such as wartime posters, "trench art," and a 1945 Ford jeep.

❯❯ Petaluma Queen

The Petaluma Riverboat Company. Golden Eagle Shopping Center, across the downtown pedestrian bridge, then downstairs to the docks. Petaluma 94952. (707) 762-2100; (800) 750-7501. **All ages.**

Have brunch, lunch, or dinner on a three-decker, 350-passenger Victorian "Showboat"-style paddlewheeler.

❯❯ Marin French Cheese Company

7500 Red Hill Road, Petaluma-Point Reyes Road, ¼ mile south of Novato Boulevard, Petaluma 94952. (707) 762-6001. Daily, 8:30–5. Tours on the hour, 10–4. Student programs. Free. **Ages 5 & up.** *W.*

Situated next to a pond in the rolling, cow-speckled hills between Novato and the coast, this is a perfect destination for an afternoon outing or picnic. A 15-minute tour begins with the 4,000-gallon tank of milk and takes you through the different stages of cheese making—heating the milk, adding the three "cheese" ingredients (culture, enzymes, and starter), and aging. You pass shiny steel tubes and tanks and different aging rooms, each with its own smell. They don't make cheese every day, so call to be sure they're doing it when you visit. Picnic tables are available, where you can sit and eat a picnic lunch bought on the spot. Kids like the cheese, but they love the duck pond.

❯❯ Sonoma County Farm Trails

Drive from a cactus nursery and smoked poultry specialist in Petaluma to apple ranches and Christmas tree farms in Sebastopol. The Farm Trails map lists farms that are open to the public and has a handy alphabetical product listing. For a copy of the map, send a self-addressed envelope with 55 cents postage to: P.O. Box 6032, Santa Rosa 95406. There's also a "Friend of Sonoma County Farm Trails" newsletter with a Friends Card for discounts and freebies. Remember that all listed are working farms, and although they may post hours, it's best to call first, to be sure your visit is convenient.

Local favorites are:

Bird Exchange & Honkey Donkey Farm (5355 Hall Road, Santa Rosa 95401. 707-575-0433. Daily 12–5). Sicilian miniature donkeys and exotic birds, reptiles and koi.

Bucher Dairy Farms (5285 Westside Road, Healdsburg 95448. 707-423-2916. May–Oct. Call first). Dairy tours with milking parlor viewing room.

Santa Rosa Bird Farm (1077 Butler Avenue, Santa Rosa 95407. 707-564-1077. Open July–Jan. Call first). Raises exotic pheasants and quail, emus, ostriches, rheas, swans, and parrots.

California Carnivores (7820 Trenton-Healdsburg Road, Forestville. 707-838-1630. Daily; 10–4 in winter, call first). Over 350 kinds of insect-eating plants including the Cobra Lily and Venus fly trap. The sign says, "Please don't tease the plants." B.Y.O.Bugs.

Pet-a-Llama Ranch (5505 Lond Pine Road, Sebastopol 94572. 707-823-9394. Weekends, 10–4 & by appt.). Pet and feed llamas, large and small, see spinning and weaving demonstrations, and buy llama products. Birthday parties (bring your own cake) in the picnic area.

⇒ Petaluma Adobe

3325 Adobe Road, East of Highway 101, Petaluma 94954. (707) 726-4871. Daily, 10–5. Tickets usable at all state parks that day. Adults, $2; children, $1. Picnic areas. Tours, groups, and Living History Programs.
Ages 4 & up.

General Mariano G. Vallejo's ranch house, Rancho Petaluma, was built in 1836 as the centerpiece of a Mexican land grant of 66,000 acres. Here we learned that in Spanish, *adobe* means to mix, and that the thick, naturally insulating bricks were made from clay mixed with water and straw and then dried in the sun. A self-guided tour takes you into the workshop, weaving room, servants' quarters, and the Vallejos' upstairs living quarters—graciously furnished with authentic pieces. Outside, there are huge iron cauldrons, clay ovens, and the racks on which cowhides, the currency of the period, were stretched out to dry. Farm animals add authentic background sounds. At one time, General Vallejo had one thousand workers on the ranch, and it's not hard, standing on the second-floor porch of Rancho Petaluma, to imagine the bustle of yesteryear.

⇒ Sonoma State Historical Park

20 East Spain Street, Sonoma 95476. (707) 938-1519. Daily, 10–5. Tickets usable at all state parks that day. Adults, $2; children, $1. **Ages 5 & up.** *W.*

The flags of seven countries have flown over Sonoma: Spain, England, Imperial Russia, Mexico, The Bear Flag, and the United States. The stories behind them can be found in the plaza at the center of the town.

Lachryma Montis, off Third Street West, which was named after its clear spring, "Tears of the Mountain," was General Vallejo's city house.

Furnished as it might have been when he lived there with his family, the house feels as if Vallejo just stepped out for a moment. One daughter's painting is on a wall, along with family photos. Behind the house is the kitchen building and the Chinese cook's quarters. The Chalet in front was once the storehouse and is now a Vallejo museum containing his books, pictures, saddles, coach, and cattle brand, various remembrances of his family, and biographies of 10 of his 16 children.

On the plaza in town you'll walk by the site of Vallejo's first home in Sonoma. Since a fire in 1867, only the Indian servants' quarters remain. In the reconstructed **Soldiers Barracks** (built in 1836), there are exhibits representative of Sonoma history, an audio-visual show, and other activities on weekends. Also on the plaza, **The Toscano Hotel** (built in 1858) is a carefully restored mining hotel with cards and whiskey glasses still on the tables waiting for the card players to return. (Docents give tours on weekends.)

At the far corner of the plaza is **The Mission San Francisco Solano,** the northernmost and last of the 21 Franciscan missions in California and the only one established under Mexican, rather than Spanish, rule, in 1823. The padres' quarters is the oldest structure in Sonoma. Visitors can walk through the building, looking at interesting exhibits, a restored chapel, watercolors of the missions, furnished rooms of the padres, spurs and leggings of the *vacqueros*, and other interesting artifacts of mission life, including the primitively painted chapel. A *ramada* has been constructed in the garden for blacksmithing, weaving, breadbaking, and other period crafts demonstrations.

During your wanderings you may want to stop in at the **Sonoma Cheese Factory** (on the plaza at 2 Spain Street, 95476. 707-996-1931. Daily, 9–6) to see a video and watch young men rolling cheese bags to make Sonoma Jack cheese. While there, pick up food for a picnic, which you can enjoy in the park across the street.

❖ Traintown

20264 Broadway, Sonoma 95476. On the main road into town from San Francisco. (707) 938-3912. Daily in summer and on winter weekends, 10:30–5:30. Adults, $3.50; children, $2.50. **Ages 2–9.** *W.*

A 20-minute trip on the Sonoma Steam Railroad, a quarter-size reproduction of a mountain division steam railroad of the 1890s, takes you over trestles, past trees, lakes, tunnels, and bridges, and into Traintown. While the train takes on water in Lakeview, you can look through the quarter-size miniature mining town and listen to its recorded history. The ducks are normal size, but you still feel like Gulliver in the land of Lilliputians. You can also ride on a carousel.

❧ Jack London State Historic Park

2400 London Ranch Road, Glen Ellen 95442. (707) 938-5216.
Museum open daily, 10–5; grounds, 8–sunset. For the museum and the
enlarged park, $5 per car; seniors, $4; dogs, $1. On weekends, there's a golf
cart run for seniors and disabled to get to Wolf House and Beauty Ranch.
The cottage where Jack and Charmian lived is open weekends, 12–4. Nature
hikes on weekends. The first floor of the museum and the cottage are accessible.
All ages.

"I liked those hills up there above the ranch house. They were beautiful, as you see, and I wanted beauty. So I extended the boundary up to the
top of that ridge and all along it . . . I bought beauty, and I was content
with beauty for a while. . . . Do you realize that I devote 2 hours a day to
writing and ten to farming?" So wrote Jack London, in 1915.

Charmian London built the House of Happy Walls, the finest tribute
to a writer in California, as a memorial to her husband. Furnished with
the furniture and art gathered for Wolf House, which burned before the
Londons could move into it, this museum covers the life of the adventurous young novelist. Once a sailor, prospector, and roustabout, London
struggled to gain acceptance as a writer—and you can see a collection of
his rejection slips. Photos of the *Snark*, in which the Londons sailed the
South Pacific, and treasures collected on their voyages line the walls. The
rangers sell London's books "signed" with the stamp London used to save
time. A fascinating film taken a few days before his death shows London
frolicking with his animals.

London was also an experimental farmer. The 803 acres of his Beauty
Ranch have been purchased by the state. Here you'll see the cottage where
he and Charmian lived and wrote, concrete silos, the distillery, stallion
barn, "pig palace," log bathhouse, and blacksmith's shop. A trail leads to
the still-extant Wolf House ruins and to London's grave. Picnic areas.

❧ Union Hotel Restaurant

Main Street, P.O. Box 4257, Occidental 95465. (707) 874-3555. Daily,
11:30–9. Closed Christmas. Prices range from $8.95 for pasta to $16.95 for
steak. Mangia!

Dining at the Union Hotel, which has been in business since 1879,
is more than just a meal, it's an experience: Italian food—more than you
can possibly eat—is served family style on a plastic red-checked table-
cloth. Regardless of the main course ordered (chicken, duck or steak),
the meal includes salami and cheese, bean vinaigrette, salad, lentil soup,
zucchini fritters, ravioli, vegetables, good sourdough bread and butter,

potatoes, and side dishes. One person in your party could simply order soup and salad, or just the pasta dinner, and you'd still have a bag for tomorrow's lunch. A half-price child's dinner is available. The frequent waits are made bearable by the game room or a walk through the main street of the town.

≫ West County Museum

261 South Main Street, Sebastopol 95472. (707) 829-6711. Thurs.–Sun., 1–4 or by appt. **Ages 8 & up.**

The restored depot of the Petaluma and Santa Rosa Railroad, originally built in 1917 for the electric railroad that served the area, now houses rotating exhibits that reflect the history of Western Sonoma County, from the early Native Americans to the present. There have been exhibits on the apple and on locals' experiences during World War II. The museum also houses the Triggs Reference Room, which contains research materials pertaining to Western Sonoma County history.

≫ Safari West

3115 Porter Creek Road, Santa Rosa 95404. (707) 579-2551. Adults, $48; children, $24. By reservation only. **All ages.**

If you can't go to Africa, this could be the next-best thing. The 2½-hour trek starts with a ramble in the hills in safari vehicles to see the herds living in nature. There are herds of antelope, gazelle, zebra, oryx, eland, aoudad, ibex, and endangered species including birds from all over the world. After a cheese and cracker break, you're introduced to animals on a walking tour and you end up feeding a giraffe.

≫ Redwood Empire Ice Arena

1667 West Steele Lane, Santa Rosa 95403. (707) 546-7147. Daytime hours: Sat. & Sun., year-round: 12:30–2:30 & 3–5. Summer: Mon.–Fri., 2:30–5. Winter: Mon. & Wed., 12:30–2; Tues., Thurs., & Fri., 4–5:30. Nighttime hours: Mon., 8:30–10:30 (adults only); Tues.& Thurs., 7:30–9; Fri. & Sat., 8:30–10:30. Ages 12 & over, $5.50; under 12, $4.50; skate rental, $2. Christmas show tickets: (707) 546-3385. Snoopy's Gallery and Gift Shop: (707) 546-3385. Daily, 10–6. **Ages 3 & up.**

Everyone will enjoy skating in this Alpine wonderland, which Charles Schulz (the creator of Snoopy) built for his family and the community. Hours are complicated because there are frequent shows, so call before setting out. Be sure to make reservations for one of the special events. The gift store boasts the largest collection of Snoopy merchandise in the world. You can even find Snoopy dolls sized from four inches to five feet, as well as a collection of Charlie Schulz's favorite drawings and awards.

❧ Sonoma County Museum

425 Seventh Street, just off Highway 101, Santa Rosa 95401. (707) 579-1500. Wed.–Sun., 11–4. Free. **Ages 7 & up.**

The Sonoma County Museum, located in a beautifully restored 1910 post office building, preserves and honors the rich heritage of Sonoma County. Exhibits change and cover a wide spectrum in both time and subject, from the Native American epoch through the Victorian age to today. Cultural vignettes, special exhibits for children, and the Hart Collection of California landscape art also make the museum worth a visit. One young visitor wrote, "I really liked looking at the pictures of the animals and seeing the carriage."

The nearby **Codding Museum of Natural History** (557 Summerfield Road, Santa Rosa 95405. 707-539-0556. Wed.–Sun., 11–4. Free) focuses on local, regional, and worldwide natural history.

❧ Discovery Center of Sonoma County

1070 Santa Rosa Plaza, P.O. Box 14864, Santa Rosa 95402. (707) 575-1014. Weekends, 12–5; Tues.–Sat., 10–4 in summer. $3. Birthday parties. Storytelling and special programs. **All ages.** *W.*

Discovery Center offers "children of all ages" hands-on fun that engages hands, touches hearts, and challenges minds. An insect zoo, video microscopes, a section for making toys out of kits, an art studio where kids can create with recycled materials, a living butterfly exhibit, and a cross-section of a computer that teaches kids what's inside the machine are just some of the great things to play with, and learn from, here.

❧ Luther Burbank Home & Gardens

Santa Rosa & Sonoma Avenues, Santa Rosa 95401. (707) 524-5445. Gardens free, daily 8–7. Carriage house & shop, Wed.–Sun., 10–4. Home tours Wed.–Sun., 10–3:30. Ages 12 & over, $2. Groups by appt. Gift shop. **Ages 8 & up.**

Luther Burbank, "the father of horticulture," made his charmingly comfortable home here for 50 years. He developed the Santa Rosa plum, the Burbank russet potato, the Shasta daisy, and a spineless edible cactus in these gardens. A walk through the garden will tell you all about his experiments and successes. Try to find the plumcot tree, or the cherry tree with four kinds of cherries growing on it. Burbank furnishings may be seen on tours of the house spring to fall.

❧ The Church of One Tree—Robert L. Ripley Memorial Museum

492 Sonoma Avenue, in Julliard Park at Santa Rosa Avenue, Santa Rosa 95401. (707) 524-5233. Apr.–Oct., Wed.–Sun., 10–4. Adults, $1.50; ages 7–17 and seniors, 75 cents. **Ages 7 & up.**

Nestled in tall redwoods, this little church, built from one tree, houses personal articles and drawings of the Believe-It-or-Not man. A wax figure of Ripley looks out at photos of himself with Will Rogers and Shirley Temple, and at newspaper clippings and samplings of the curiosities he collected. You might hear some of the "Believe-It-or-Not" radio shows or see video clips of his travel films, movies, and TV shows. Rotating displays highlight Santa Rosa's colorful history. The film, *The Incredible Life of Robert L. 'Believe It or Not' Ripley,* is available from the video store.

❧ Jesse Peter Native American Art Museum

Santa Rosa Junior College, 1501 Mendocino Avenue, Santa Rosa 95401. (707) 527-4479. Mon., Tues., Wed., & Fri., 12–4; Thurs., 11–3 and by appt. Closed holidays and school vacations. Call for events schedule. Free. **Ages 7 & up.** *W.*

Native American arts are found in this busy center. Southwest pottery, California basketry, Plains beadwork, Northwest Coast art, sculpture, a Klamath River dugout canoe, and grinding stones are part of a continuing exhibit. There are three permanent house models: a Pomo roundhouse, a Klamath River "xonta," and a Southwest pueblo. Tours include hands-on activities such as grinding acorns, playing Indian gambling games, and using pump drills. Native American drum and dance groups and Native American arts and crafts sales and demonstrations are scheduled regularly. The "Spring Gathering" at A Day Under the Oaks is the first Sunday of May every year.

❧ Windsor Waterworks & Slides

8225 Conde Lane, P.O. Box 69, Windsor 95492. Next to Highway 101, 6 miles north of Santa Rosa. (707) 838-7360. Weekends in May; daily, mid-June through Labor Day. Full Use Plan (waterslides, pool, picnic): Adults, $11.95; ages 4–12, $10.95. Pool and grounds only: adults, $4.95; ages 12 and under, $3.95. Group discounts and events, such as birthday parties and exclusive rental of the park after Labor Day, encouraged. Call for operating schedule. Parking, $2 per car. **All ages.**

Imagine lying down on a foam rubber mat, taking off down a 42-foot drop, speeding 400 feet through tunnels, around spirals, and up and over slips—and finally landing in a pool. This adventure in family parks offers four separate waterslides, picnic grounds, a large swimming pool, Ping-Pong tables, volleyball court, horseshoe pits, a wading pool, video arcade, playground, and splash fountain.

❯❯ Healdsburg Museum

221 Matheson Street, Healdsburg 95448. (707) 431-3325. Tues.–Sun., 11–4. Free. **Ages 7 & up.**

Fine examples of Pomo Indian basketry and crafts, antique firearms, and 19th-century costumes and tools combine with collections of the town newspapers dating back to 1878 and over 5,000 original historic photographs to make this a worthwhile visit.

❯❯ Canoe Trips on the Russian River

The picturesque, winding Russian River is perfect for family canoe trips. It's safe and lovely but can also be fast enough to be exciting. One- and two-hour and also half-day trips are available and there's chicken barbecue on weekends in summer. Swimmers only!

W. C. "Bob" Trowbridge (20 Healdsburg Avenue, Healdsburg 95448. 800-640-1386. Canoes, half-day, $25; full-day, $34. Kayaks, half-day, $14; full-day, $22. Reservations suggested. Call or write for information).

Burke's Canoe Trips (8600 River Road, 1 mile north of Forestville on the banks of the Russian River. (707) 887-1222; $30 a day. Each canoe can accommodate two adults and two children).

❯❯ Fort Ross State Historic Park

Highway 1, 12 curving miles north of Jenner. (Mail: 30 East Spain Street, Sonoma 95476.) (707) 847-3286. Daily, 10–4:30. Cars, $6; senior's car, $5. Living History Day programs. **All ages.**

California history seems especially romantic in this scenic spot. The Russian Chapel, with a bell you can ring in front, is as spare and quiet as it was when the fort was sold by Czarist Russia to John Sutter for $30,000 in 1841. Nine of the wooden buildings have been restored, including the Kuskov house, which was the residence of Fort Ross's founder, Ivan Alexandrovic Kuskov. Visitors can climb up into the eight-sided blockade tower and seven-sided blockhouse to look out over the little beach and inlet where Russian fur merchants used to trade with the Indians. The Visitors Center contains displays and artifacts from the Native American, Russian, and ranch eras. Don't forget to toss a penny into the wishing well!

❖ Duncan's Mills

Moscow Road, off Highway 116, Duncan's Mills 95430. (707) 865-1424.
Ages 7 & up.

The 1880s buildings of this little Victorian Revival village on
the Russian River have been restored to attract visitors to stores, restaurants, delis, and campgrounds. Duncan's Mills was once a vacation destination reached by rail and the restored railroad depot is now a cute little
museum.

It's a handy stop if you're driving from San Francisco to Mendocino.

❖ Anderson Valley Historical Museum

*Highway 128, Boonville 95415. (707) 895-3207. Weekends, 1–4. Closed
in winter. Free.* **Ages 8 & up.**

The 1891 one-room Con Creek Schoolhouse is the center of this
small museum complex that celebrates Anderson Valley's home life and
its lumbering and agricultural history. "Boontling," the valley's unique
folk language, kin to the folk language of the Amish, is star here.

❖ Lake County Museum

*Old Courthouse, 255 North Main Street, Lakeport. (Mail: 255 North Forbes
Street, 95451.) (707) 263-4555. Wed.–Sat., 11–4. Donation. Gift shop.*
Ages 7 & up.

Beautifully woven Pomo baskets and hunting traps are nicely displayed in this country museum, along with arrowheads, spears, and small
tools. Firearms used to tame the West, such as the Kentucky Long and
the Slotterbeck—made in Lakeport in the late 1800s—are also intriguing.
Lillie Langtry, the celebrated English actress who retired to her winery
here (it's still in business), is honored. Other displays include turn-of-the-
century clothing and household items and samples of the semiprecious
gems and minerals found in Lake County. Did you know that the "Lake
County diamond," a natural or faceted quartz crystal, could be pink or
lavender? The museum is also the home of the Lake County Genealogical
Society, which boasts hundreds of books to help you find your roots.

❖ McLaughlin Mine

*Homestake Mining Company, 26775 Morgan Valley Road, Lower Lake
95457. (800) 525-3743; (707) 263-9544. Two-hour tours on the second
and fourth Fri. & Sat. of each month, at 11, by reservation. Free.* **Ages
9 & up.**

California's largest gold mine is still in operation. It's high-tech and
environmentally friendly. The tours really show you how mining is done

today. Kids love to pick through the heap of discarded rocks near the mine entrance in search of gold.

❖ Lower Lake Historical Schoolhouse & Museum

16435 Main Street, Lower Lake 95457. (707) 945-3635. Wed.–Sat., 11–4. Free. **Ages 7 & up.**

This old-fashioned schoolroom has been reconstructed to look as it did a hundred years ago. There are historical exhibits and fine art displays by local artists as well.

❖ Anderson Marsh State Historic Park

P.O. Box 672, Lower Lake 95457. Either take Route 20 to Route 53 or take Highway 29 to Lower Lake, then continue straight on Route 53. (707) 994-0688/279-2267. Farmhouse: Sat.–Sun., 10–4; in summer, 8–5. Parking fee, $2. Park: Wed.–Sun., 10–5. Cultural History Days and Living History Programs. Groups by appt. **Ages 5 & up.**

Costumed docents wander through the old, two-story Anderson ranch house, lost in their roles of yesteryear. The community has worked together to restore the 1855 Anderson farmhouse with authentic antiques augmenting the original cozy furnishings. The ranch house and outbuildings are reminders of California's rich cattle ranching heritage. From an oak-covered ridge above the marsh, you can see a sweeping expanse of grassy lowland. The ridge is also the site of archeological digs. The Cultural Heritage Council conducts a Fieldschool for anyone, from junior high to adult, who wants to learn how to excavate, map, and catalog artifacts and how to make stone tools and shell beads. An Indian Village is under construction. The marsh itself is home for muskrat, mink, otter, deer, and many birds.

�֍ Redwood Country: Mendocino, Humboldt, and Del Norte Counties

Redwood country is one of the most beautiful areas in America. Stately redwoods line the roads "as far as the fog flows," and the Pacific Ocean crashes into the shoreline. Some of the beaches are craggy and surrounded by dangerous currents. Others are calm and protected, with long empty stretches just made for solitary walks.

You can dash up from San Francisco on Highway 101 or you can spend hours winding along the coastline on Highway 1. You can enjoy the Victoriana of Ferndale and Eureka or you can lose yourself in the tiny fishing villages of Rockport and Noyo. Whale watching is a popular pastime from December to April. The waters may be too cold to swim in, but the fish thrive and are there for the catching.

You can get away from it all in the sylvan glens along the Avenue of the Giants, marveling at your smallness next to a 300-foot tree. To show the aims, methods, and benefits of industrial forest management within the redwood region, several firms have made demonstration forests available to the public. Tours are self-guided, and there are restrooms and picnic areas available. You'll learn that only one percent of the tree is living—only the tips of its roots, the leaves, buds, flowers, seed, and a single thin layer of cells sheathing the tree. You'll see Douglas firs, white firs, and redwood residuals—the redwood trees that have sprung up from seeds and sprouts. You'll find the forests along Highway 128, on new and old Highways 101, and on Highway 299.

Redwood country lets you set your own pace—there are many places to see and things to do close to each other, and there are enough parks and beaches for you to relax or picnic in, whenever the mood strikes. It's a great getaway for a weekend or a week.

❧ Point Arena Lighthouse & Museum
P.O. Box 11, Point Arena 95468. (707) 882-2777. Daily, 11–2:30; summer weekends and holidays, 10–3:30. Closed Thanksgiving and Christmas days only. Adults, $2.50; children, 50 cents. **Ages 7 & up.**

If you've ever dreamed about living in history, this is a good way to do it. The lighthouse keepers have restored the lighthouse, museum, and three of the large homes on the lighthouse station to rent to vacationers. Rental fees and fees from whale watching and guided tours help maintain the site. The first Point Arena lighthouse had to be destroyed after the

1906 earthquake; a new 115-foot tower with a Fresnel lens began flashing its guiding beacon in 1908. An automatic rotating beacon was installed in 1977. The museum is housed in the 1869 Fog Signal Building, next to the lighthouse.

➢ Mendocino Headlands State Park and Ford House Visitors Center
Main Street, P.O. Box 1387, Mendocino 95460. (707) 937-5397/937-5804. Mon.–Sat., 10:30–4:30; Sun., 12–4. Videos and headlands walks. Groups by appt.

The Ford House, the second house to be built in the town of Mendocino, was a wedding gift from J. B. Ford to his bride, Martha Hayes Ford of Connecticut, in 1854. Today, it is the Visitors Center, interpreting the natural environment of the area and telling of the history of Mendocino and the surrounding areas. It is also a gallery exhibiting work by local artists. The star of the place is a recently constructed four-by-eight-foot scale model of Mendocino village as it was on December 14, 1890, with its 358 buildings including sheds, outhouses, and 34 water towers, built on a scale of $3/64$ inches to the foot. Buildings were carved by artist Len Peterson of balsa wood and secured to a foam-core terrain that replicates the surface contours of the village. There are tramway tracks for the lumber vehicles, a $3\frac{1}{8}$-inch-tall Presbyterian Church, eight hotels, four boarding houses, a bank, two dressmakers, and a cobbler's store.

Once an old lumber port, Mendocino is now a mecca for driftwood collectors, artists, and tourists. The town has appeared in many movies. (Today, it stars in the *Murder She Wrote* reruns. Jessica Fletcher's home is now the Blair House Inn.) The town has interesting little streets to browse along when it gets too foggy for beachcombing.

Among the highlights are the **Mendocino Art Center** (45200 Little Lake Street, 95460. 707-937-5819), which is open 10 to 5 daily, the **Mendocino Ice Cream Company** (45090 Main. 937-5884), and the **Village Toy Store** (10450 Lansing. 937-4633), the kite and frisbee store.

The old **Masonic Lodge Hall** (Lansing and Ukiah), with its massive redwood sculpture of Father Time and the Maiden, carved from one piece of redwood, is a landmark.

The Kelley House Historical Museum (45007 Albion Street, P.O. Box 922, 95460. 707-937-5791. Daily, 1–4. Donation) is a pleasant step back in time. The nearby **Temple of Kwan Ti,** one of the first buildings in Mendocino, may be seen by appointment.

➤ Mendocino Coast Botanical Gardens

18220 North Highway 1, Fort Bragg 95437. 6 miles north of Mendocino, (707) 964-4352. Mar.–Oct., daily, 9–5; Nov.–Feb., 9–4. Retail nursery and garden store. Adults, $5; seniors, $4; juniors 3–17, $3; children 6–12, $1; student groups and those under 6, free. Group discounts and tours. Complimentary electric cars. **All ages.** *W.*

Forty-seven acres of gardens with a formal perennial garden, coastal pine forest, fern canyons, and ocean bluff explode with multicolored flowers and teem with protected wildlife, including 60 species of birds.

Rhododendrons bloom in April and May; perennials, from May to October. The heather blooms all winter, when you can see gray whale migration. Picnickers are welcome.

One youngster wrote, "That was the most fun place I have ever been. I liked all the flowers that were there. I liked all the trails; I liked all the places, especially the ocean. I liked when we got to eat and played games. We did work and we almost got lost too in The Botanical Gardens."

➤ Guest House Museum

Main Street, c/o City Hall, 416 North Franklin, Fort Bragg 95437. (707) 961-2840. Wed.–Sun., 10–4. Donation. **Ages 7 & up.**

This gift to the city from the Georgia Pacific Company houses historical pictures of the logging industry, a huge bellows, mementos of the loggers, and models of ships. Films and talks contrast the difference between logging's industrial present and its rugged past. Be sure to walk down to the foot of Redwood Avenue to see the huge slice of redwood that was 1,753 years old in 1843.

Nearby, at the foot of Walnut Street, is the **Georgia Pacific Nursery** (Apr.–Nov., weekdays, 9–4), which holds four million trees. A display room explains reforestation and timber management. After visiting the arboretum and nature trails, have a picnic in the picnic area. A free packet of redwood seeds is mailed to each visiting family.

➤ The Skunk Railroad

Skunk Depot, Main and Laurel, Fort Bragg. (707) 964-6371. Call to reserve or write to California Western Railroad, P.O. Box 907, Fort Bragg 95437. Full- and half-day round trips available daily to Northspur and Willits with prices ranging from $10 for children, $21 for adults on the half-day; $12 for kids and $26 for adults on the full-day. Kids under 5 are free. **Ages 5 & up.**

The Skunk Railroad, named for the smell the first gas engines used to cast over the countryside, has been making passenger trips from Fort Bragg to Willits since 1911. During the 40-mile trip, which takes all day, the train crosses 30 trestles and bridges, goes through two tunnels, twists and turns over spectacularly curved track, and travels from the quiet Noyo riverbed to high mountain passes through redwood forests. The half-day jaunt takes you through the redwoods, crossing the meandering Noyo dozens of times, to the midway point for a 30-minute rest stop with picnic tables and snack available. The bouncy diesel Skunk is well worth the price and time. If it's summer, try the open observation car for unforgettable pictures.

There's also a train from Willits to Eureka. **The North Coast Daylight Railway Excursions** (P.O. Box 3666, Eureka 95502-3666. 800-544-3763; 707-442-7705. Call for reservations) sweep from Willits into the Eel River Canyon and the Eel River through redwood forest to Eureka's Old Town, 145 miles away. Tunnel Number 27 at Island Mountain is over 4,300 feet long. Lunch, whether you ride in the "coach" or the Shasta Parlor car, is served in the Diner.

❧ Mendocino County Museum

400 East Commercial Street, Willits 95490. (707) 459-2736. Wed.–Sun., 10–4:30. Free. **Ages 7 & up.** *W.*

The Mendocino County Museum is a storehouse of memories, dreams, and hard-won lessons of survival amid the rugged beauty of California's North Coast. Exhibits use local artifacts to celebrate and explain the life and times of Mendocino County. Oral history interviews capture living memories on tape. Collections of Pomo and Yuki baskets represent the vanished ancestors and today's descendants of the region's Native Americans. The danger and excitement of everyday work in the redwoods is recalled through living history programs featuring restored logging artifacts discovered in the Mendocino woods. Changing exhibits provide fresh experiences for museum visitors.

❧ The Drive-Thru Tree

Old Highway 101, P.O. Box 10, Leggett 95585. (707) 925-6363. Daily, 9–5; in summer, 8 until dark. Each car $3. Gift shop. **All ages.** *W.*

This large, chandelier-shaped, 315-foot redwood was tunneled in 1934. A standard-size contemporary car just fits through. It's 21 feet in diameter and, in spite of the tunnel, is still alive. The winding dirt road leading to the tree takes you right to a gift shop and to the highway. There are 200 acres of nature trails and picnic areas by the side of a lake that is home to geese. There are also logging relics on the grounds. Kids like the log with a hole you can crawl into. One year, everyone in Leggett Valley School had their pictures taken on horseback, in the tree, for the yearbook.

☄ Confusion Hill and Mountain Train Ride

75001 North Highway 101, 15 miles south of Garberville, Piercy 95467. (707) 925-6456. Daily, 11–4; in summer, 8–7. Confusion Hill: Adults, $3; ages 6–12, $2. Mountain Train Ride: Apr.–Sept. Adults, $3; ages 3–12, $2. Gravity house free for kids 5 & under. Petting Farm: $1. **Ages 3 & up.**

When you see six huge bears clowning around, juggling balls—it's the world's largest redwood chainsaw sculpture—you'll know you're in the right place. The miniature Mountain Train follows many switchbacks to take you one and one-quarter miles up to the summit of a redwood mountain, through a tunnel tree, and back down. Try the other experience at Confusion Hill, a spot where gravity is defied. Facing front, you seem to be standing sideways; water runs uphill; your friends shrink or grow taller in front of you. Is seeing really believing?

☄ Avenue of the Giants

Humboldt Redwoods State Park, P.O. Box 100, Weott 95571. (707) 946-2311. Day use, $5; camping, $15 per night, $1 higher in peak season. Reduced senior and winter rates. Visitors Center, on Highway 101 north, next to Burlington Campground, 2 miles south of Weott, has maps of self-guided walks. (707) 946-2263. Daily, 9–5. Special programs. **All ages.**

Standing tall as a nominee for the most spectacular 33 miles anywhere is this bypass road winding leisurely beneath 300-foot trees. One of the few species to have survived from the time of the dinosaurs, the redwoods are majestic, awesome trees to behold. You'll drive through a protected wilderness of soaring trees and moss- and fern-carpeted landscape occasionally spotted with deer. Founder's Grove, Rockefeller Forest, and Children's Forest are some of the best of the special groves. The Chimney Tree near Phillipsville, the Immortal Tree near Redcrest, and the Drive-Thru Tree in Myers Flat are more commercial stopping places. The Visitors Center interprets the redwood enviroment and displays the flora, fauna, and history of the area and has an interesting slide show on request.

☄ Pacific Lumber Company

P.O. Box 37, Scotia 95565. South of Eureka 27 miles. (707) 764-2222. Mill tours: Mon.–Fri., 7:30–10:30 & 11:30–2:30. Mill closed for July

Fourth and Christmas weeks. Museum: Mon.–Fri., in summer, 8–4. Free.
Demonstration Forest open daily, 4¹/₂ miles south of Scotia, just off Highway
101. Free. **Ages 8 & up.**

Scotia is one of the last company-owned towns in the country. The
Pacific Lumber Company was established in 1869, and the present town
of Scotia, originally known as Forestville, was established in 1910. During
the summer, obtain a pass for the mill tour at the Scotia museum. Logging equipment is on display outside, and inside there are historic photographs. You can watch a video about the lumber company. On the mill
tour, you'll see how trees become lumber products. The first step is the
most impressive: a debarker that uses high water pressure to peel the bark
off the log. Signs posted along the catwalk explain the various functions of
the mill. Some sections are noiser than others.

According to Carmen, "It was loud inside and the best part about the
mill was when the debarker blasted the bark off the trees. I also liked it
when the one man sharpened the saws, that must have been hard work."

Don't miss the Scotia fish-rearing exhibit, built by Pacific Lumber to
educate visitors about the company's efforts to enhance the fisheries in the
nearby Eel River. Visitors pass by the exhibit right after leaving the parking lot, before entering the mill.

⇨ Depot Museum

4 Park Street, Fortuna 95540. (707) 725-7645. Daily, 9–4:30 in
summer. Sept.–May, Wed.–Sun., 12–4:30. Donation. **Ages 8 & up.** *W.*

The 1893 train depot is now a small museum housing Fortuna memories of loggers, farmers, Indians, home life and the railroad. The newly
restored first room tells a story about the railroad and trains; George, the
teletyper, is at the ready; fancy dresses and shoes wait for the next dance;
fishing poles and tackle stand waiting for the next fishing trip; and pictures, school books, railroad memorabilia, and farmers' barbed wire round
out the collection. The three old marriage certificates are lovely. The museum is located in Rohner Park, a lovely family park with picnic tables
and playground equipment.

Visitors in autumn may want to stop by **Clendenen's Cider**
Works (Twelfth Street and Newburg Road. 707-725-2123, most Mondays and Thursdays) to see the mill in action and buy fresh cider. A bakery has also been added, for pies, scones, and cookies, and you can watch
the baker work, too.

⇨ Ferndale Museum

Shaw and Third streets, P.O. Box 431, Ferndale 95536. (707) 786-4466.
Feb.–May & Oct.–Dec., Wed.–Sat., 11–4; Sun., 1–4. June–Sept., Tues.–

Sat., 11–4; Sun., 1–4. Closed Jan. Adults, $1; ages 16 and under, 50 cents; ages 6 and under, free, when accompanying an adult. **Ages 8 & up.**

A blacksmith shop with a working forge, antique farming and logging equipment, and a working seismograph are permanent exhibits, along with rotating collections that show the lifestyles, work habits, and activities of Ferndale's ancestors. Since most of the successful businessmen made their money with farms, their Victorian homes were called "Butterfat Palaces" and the town was called "Cream City." Ferndale, a restored and repainted Victorian town, is a wonderful place to spend time.

❯❯ Kinetic Sculpture Race Museum
580 Main Street, P.O. Box 916, Ferndale 95536. Daily, 10–5. Free.
Ages 7 & up.

Ferndale's Kinetic Sculpture Race takes place over Memorial Day weekend from Arcata to Ferndale, when 50 or more entrants power their wildly decorated motorless vehicles over choppy water, slippery mud flats, sand dunes, and city streets. This warehouse museum is crammed with dozens of racing chariots. These past winners show the artistry and occasional foolhardiness of their creators.

❯❯ Fort Humboldt State Historic Park
3431 Fort Avenue, off Highway 101, Eureka 95501. (707) 445-6567. Daily, 9–5. Free. **Ages 7 & up.** *W.*

High on a windy hill, Fort Humboldt is primarily an outdoor museum of the logging industry. Old machinery is accompanied by large display boards telling what it was like to be a logger in the 19th century. A logger's cabin is furnished with a stove, a bed, a shelf of cans of beans, and a "pin-up" calendar. You learn how to "fall" a tree (the falling branches are called widow makers) and then see how it is dragged out of the forest and cut up. One logger notes that it's "a shame to wash clothes while they can still bend." An 1884 Falk locomotive and an 1892 Andersonia locomotive are on view. Old Fort Humboldt, where U. S. Grant served as a staff officer in the 1850s, is nearby. Fort Humboldt was retired as a military post in August 1870. The land and the one remaining building, the hospital, completed in 1863, were sold to W. S. Cooper in 1893 for $6,500. Today the hospital has been restored and is used as a museum.

A short drive away are the only two covered bridges in the area. Take Highway 101 south to Elk River Road and follow it along to either Zane or Berta Road. The bridges are covered not to protect them from snow but to protect the wood from rain. Boarding up the bridges preserves the wood longer and is less expensive than constant repainting.

➤ Clarke Memorial Museum

240 E Street, at Third, Eureka 95501. (707) 443-1947. Tues.–Sat., 12–4. Free. **Ages 6 & up.** *W.*

This large regional history museum is housed in a palatial 1912 bank. A recent addition is devoted to the Native American Indian culture of northwestern California. The world's largest and most complete collections of Hoopa, Yurok, and Karuk regalia and basketry are at the Clarke, with over 1,200 artifacts displayed. There are also extensive collections on the development of Humboldt County: shipbuilding, logging, milling, firearms, furniture, textiles, and Victorian decorative arts.

Alyssa and Courtney of Scotia noted, "We had a blast looking at all the things in the museum. Some of the baskets were really rad. We loved the children's corner. We especially liked the 3-D thing. It was cool. Altogether it was fun."

The Clarke Museum is located in Eureka's Old Town, the original, restored, commercial district on the shore of Humboldt Bay. This district of Victorian commercial and residential buildings, crowned by the remarkable Carson Mansion (on Second and M Streets, not open to the public), the greatest Victorian in California, includes many bookstores and boutiques. Be sure to visit the crafts shop of the Northern California Indian Development Council on F Street, next to the ice cream parlor. There's a self-guided tour of the town's Victorians.

➤ Blue Ox Millworks Historical Park

Foot of X Street, Eureka 95501. (707) 444-3437; (800) 248-4259. Winter: daily, 9–5; summer: Mon.–Sat., 9–5; Sun. 11–4. Adults, $5; seniors & teens, $4; ages 6–12, $2.50. Group discounts. **Ages 6 & up.**

Real live Blue oxen are part of the family in this working museum of Victorian era machinery manufacturers of "gingerbread," ornamental wood, plaster, and iron work. A wood-fired kiln shows how pottery is fired. Guided and self-guided tours are available. Call for the schedule of workshops on traditional arts such as candle making, basket weaving, blacksmithing, and pottery. Kids will enjoy the kids camp, and the 1800s farm with some petting animals.

Demonstrations include making varnish from tree sap, making stains from red adder bark or Spanish moss, and how to make an 1852-design picket pointer or a pedal bower shaper.

➤ Humboldt Bay Maritime Museum

1410 Second Street, Eureka 95501. (707) 444-9440. Daily, 11–4. Donation. **Ages 7 & up.** *W.*

Nautical displays are housed in a replica of the McFarlan House, built in 1852, the oldest home in Eureka. A Fresnel lighthouse lens, a hand-operated bilge pump, a salmon gear pulley, old navigation instruments, a fathometer, an early radar unit, cork and glass floats, and a porthole from the cruiser USS *Milwaukee*, which was wrecked on the Samoa peninsula in 1917, are shown. There have been hundreds of wrecks off the entrance to Humboldt Bay. The museum's dedicated volunteers continuously dive for and salvage remains of these relics for display.

❧ Humboldt Bay Harbor Cruise, M/V Madaket Bay Tour

Foot of C Street, Eureka 95501. (707) 445-1910 for times and prices. Reserve for Saturday night dinner cruise, Sunday brunch cruise, or special holiday cruises. **Ages 5 & up.**

The 75-minute cruise aboard this venerable vessel, a 1910 ferry, takes in the oyster beds, pelican roosts, saw mills, egret rookery, and a former Indian village, and includes history of the area. There are daily trips, depending on the weather.

❧ Sequoia Park Zoo

3414 W Street, at Glatt, Eureka 95501. (707) 442-6552. Tues.–Sun., 10–5; until 7 in summer. Children's Petting Zoo (only in summer): Tues.–Sun., 11:30–3:30. Free. **All ages.** *W.*

Located in the heart of the redwoods, the Sequoia Park Zoo houses an excellent variety of both local and exotic animals including the gibbon, otter, emu, prairie dog, reticulated python, black bear, and Pacific giant salamander. The zoo is part of Sequoia Park, which encompasses picnic areas, a playground, flower gardens, a duck pond, and 54 acres of North Coast redwoods.

❧ Samoa Cookhouse

Samoa Road (445 West Washington), Eureka 95501. (707) 442-1659. Breakfast: ages 3–6, $2.95; ages 7–11, $4.85; adults, $6.25. Lunch: $3.50, $4.95, & $6.95. Dinner: $4.50, $6.95, $11.95.

Delicious, large, affordable family-style meals are served seven days a week in this old lumber-camp cookhouse that once served as relief quarters for shipwreck victims. Today, it's the last surviving cookhouse in the West. The long tables are set as they were in 1885, with red and white checked cloths and large bottles of catsup. Our breakfast consisted of huge amounts of orange juice, coffee, delicious French toast, and sausage. Dinner the night before included thick cuts of ham and sole with all the fixings, and peach pie. Before or after the meal, wander through the adjoining rooms to see an assemblage of logger's boots, photographs of shipwrecks, dinner bells, kitchen utensils, and a steam coffeemaker that once served 500 men three times a day.

➤ Hoopa Tribal Museum

Hoopa Valley Indian Reservation, General Delivery, Hoopa 95546. Highway 96, off Highway 299 West. In the Hoopa Shopping Center across Trinity River Bridge. (916) 625-4110. Weekdays, 9–5; also Sat. in summer. Free.
Ages 7 & up.

California's largest Native American Reservation is nested in the mountains of Northern Humboldt. Stone implements, dishes, tools, baskets, and dance regalia of the Hoopa Indians—"the people who live up the river," as named by Jedediah Smith's Yurok guide—are shown here, along with items from other tribes, such as the Yurok and Karuk, the Dakotas, and Alaskan tribes. Many of the Hoopa items are on loan from local residents, for this is a living museum, run by members of the Hoopa tribe. The artifacts are still used regularly in traditional tribal ceremonies in this "Land of the Natinixwe." *Where the Trails Return*, a documentary video explaining the Hoopa culture, tradition, and government, can be viewed at the museum, which will also arrange tours of the reservation. The ruins of Fort Gaston, built in 1851, include a dwelling once occupied by Ulysses S. Grant.

➤ Humboldt State University Natural History Museum

1315 G Street, at 13th Street, Arcata 95521. Wells Fargo Hall. (707) 826-4479. Tues.–Sat., 10–4. Donation. Groups by appt. Gift shop. **Ages 8 & up.** *W.*

Insects fossilized in amber, trilobites and ammonites, and an extensive international fossil collection are headliners in this revitalized museum. Displays include regional natural history exhibits with six live animal families. Butterflies, shells, sponges, crabs, and corals are featured. Hands-on exhibits include a dinosaur fossil touch table, a Discover Box Center, an earthquake simulator, plate tectonics models, and two computer terminals with interactive natural science programs. "Nature Adventures" programs, field trips, and workshops are offered almost every weekend and all summer.

The nearby **Arcata Museum** (Phillips House, 7th & Union Streets. (707) 822-4722. Sunday, 12–4. Donation) offers guided tours of one of Arcata's earliest houses. Its rooms recall the late 1800s and early 1900s.

⇝ Humboldt State University Marine Laboratory

*P.O. Box 690, Trinidad 95570. Off Highway 101 at Edwards & Ewing.
(707) 826-3671. Mon.–Fri., 8–12 & 1–4, until 5 in summer. Free.* **Ages
8 & up.** *W.*

Located near Land's End, in the picturesque fishing village of
Trinidad, this working laboratory is open to the public for self-guided
tours. Hallway aquariums hold rare and common mollusks and crusta-
ceans, and fresh- and saltwater fish. Varicolored anemones, walleye surf
perches, Siamese tigerfish, and shovel-nose catfish were there for our visit,
along with a tame wolf eel and a small black octopus. Exhibits change
regularly. Special school programs.

Stop at the **Trinidad Lighthouse** on your way to the lab. This is the
spot where the Spaniards landed on Trinity Sunday in 1775. The original
gear system of descending weights still works to turn the light, but the
original two-ton bell is for display only.

Patrick's Point State Park (707-677-3570. Each car, $5. W), five
miles north of Humboldt State University Marine Laboratory along the
shore, has natural history displays at park headquarters. This is a 632-acre
outdoor museum of natural and area history and a sea lion overlook with
plaques in braille. You'll want to see Sumeg, a Yurok village constructed
to look as it might have a century ago. It's a unique, realistic setting for
the presentation and preservation of authentic Yurok Indian traditions
and skills.

⇝ Simpson Korbel Forest Nursery

*P.O. Box 1169, Arcata 95521. Highway 299 near Blue Lake in Korbel.
(707) 688-4464. Free.* **Ages 8 & up.**

Tours by appointment only, to see the care and nurturing of our
forests.

⇝ Mad River State Fish Hatchery

*1660 Hatchery Road, Blue Lake. (Mail: 1660 Hatchery Road, Arcata
95521.) (707) 822-0592. Daylight hours. Groups by appt. only. Free.
Picnic areas.* **All ages.** *W.*

Baby salmon, steelhead, and trout can be seen and fed here. There is
fishing (also wheelchair accessible) adjacent to the hatchery. By the way,
the river is not ferocious. It was named for a fight between Joe Greek and
L. K. Wood, two explorers of the region, in 1849. One Headstarter named
Nathan wrote, "It was nice feeding the fish. I liked when the fish jumped.
It was nice letting the fish free."

❖ Blue Lake Museum
330 Railroad Avenue, Blue Lake 95525. (707) 668-5576. Tues. & Wed., 1–4; Sun., 12–4. Free. **Ages 8 & up.** *W.*

This diminutive museum presents historical displays of the Mad River Railroad and logging operations, along with a collection of local Native American basketry.

❖ Orleans Mining Company Museum
Highway 96, Orleans 95556. (916) 627-3213. Daily, 6 A.M.–11 P.M.; Sunday from 7 A.M. Free. **Ages 8 & up.** *W.*

An old ghost town, once the county seat, is coming to life again in Orleans, with dining hall, motel, bunk house for rafters, and gas station. There's also a museum being remodeled. Visitors will be able to see an old doctor's office, an old kitchen, a bar scene with mannequins in place, and a working generator with logging tools and equipment dating back to the first days of logging. The owner is most proud of his cast-iron frying pans—he's going for the *Guinness Book of World Records.*

❖ Pomo Visitors Center
Coyote Valley Band of Pomo Indians, P.O. Box 39, Redwood Valley 95470. (707) 485-8723. **Ages 8 & up.**

The Visitors Center has displays and video presentations of Native American culture and an art gallery of art and baskets by the Pomos.

❖ Prairie Creek Redwoods State Park
Highway 101 North, 127011 Newton Drury Parkway, Orick 95555. North of Orick 6 miles. (707) 464-6101. Day-use fee, $5. Camping: Memorial Day to Labor Day; weeknights, $15; weekends, $16; the rest of the year, $12 per night. Junior ranger programs for children 7–12. Call for times and topics. **Ages 7 & up.** *W.*

Roosevelt elk roam this state park and can be seen grazing on the meadow outside the Visitors Center. Inside the center you'll see an interesting exhibit on the elk and the trees, ferns, flowers, and animals in the area. Fine nature trails lead from the center. On one is a redwood hollowed out by fire that is still living. One hundred and twelve school children have been inside it at one time.

❖ Trees of Mystery & End of the Trail Museum
15500 Highway 101 South, P.O. Box 96, Klamath 95548. South of Crescent City 16 miles. (707) 482-2251/(800) 638-3389. Open daylight hours year around except Thanksgiving and Christmas. Adults, $6; seniors, $5; ages 6–12, $3. Group discounts. Gift shop. **All ages.** *W.*

A talking 49-foot-tall Paul Bunyan greets you at the entrance, and then you walk through a hollowed redwood log into a forest of unusual tree formations, where recorded music and explanations take you past trees such as the "Fallen Giant" and the "Elephant Tree," and the immense and moving "Cathedral Tree." Back down the hill is our favorite section—Paul Bunyan's "Trail of Tall Tales"—where you hear how Babe the Blue Ox was found, how the Grand Canyon was dug, and how Sourdough Sam makes his pancakes. (His recipe includes the lard from one summer-fatted bear.) Indians called this "a place of spirits," and the End of the Trail Museum in the gift shop offers an extensive array of clothes and an excellent museum of artifacts of tribes ranging from the Mississippi to the Pacific and north to the Aleutians.

The **Drive-Through Tree** five miles south, on Highway 101 at the north end of the Klamath River Bridge (known for its decorative golden bears), is worth a short visit.

➤ Undersea World

Highway 101 South, Crescent City 95531. South of the Oregon border 20 miles. (707) 464-3522. Daily: 8–8 in summer; 9–5 in winter. Adults, $5.95; ages 3–10, $2.95. Group rates. Gift shop. **Ages 3 & up.**

Thousands of marine specimens live in this interactive sea environment. At the touchable tide pool you can pick up a starfish, tickle sea anemones, and touch many types of sea critters. You can look a shark in the eye, see bat rays flying through the water, pet an octopus, and see sea lions perform.

➤ Del Norte Historical Society Museum

577 H Street, Crescent City 95531. (707) 464-3922. Mon.–Sat., 10–4. Adults, $1.50; children under 12, 50 cents. **Ages 7 & up.**

The 1935 version of *Last of the Mohicans* was filmed in Crescent City, and this museum, once a county jail, has a photo of the Indian who appeared in it. A replica Yurok bark house and stick games, headdresses, beads, dolls, and baskets of the Tolowa, Pomo, Hoopa, and Yurok tribes are shown, as are photos of Crescent City since its beginnings, with lots of "before and after" shots of the 1964 tidal wave. Unicycles, jail cells, a moonshine still, pioneer clothing, the Fresnel lens from the St. George Reef Lighthouse, and other collections by local residents bring new life to local history.

➤ Northcoast Marine Mammal Center

424 Howe Drive, near Beachfront Park, Crescent City 95531. (707) 465-6265. Free. **Ages 6 & up.**

To learn about the effects of illness and predators on seals, visit these animals, caged out-of-doors, so they can be seen anytime during daylight hours. There are also seal pups "rescued" by people who thought they were abandoned. Since their mothers won't come near them if they smell of humans, they have to be raised here until they are old enough to be released back into the ocean. A brief description of each animal is posted by its cage.

≫ Battery Point Lighthouse

Foot of "A" Street, P.O. Box 396, Crescent City 95531. (707) 464-3089. Apr.–Sept., Wed.–Sun., 10–4, tide permitting. Adults, $2; under 12, 50 cents. **Ages 7 & up.**

Battery Point Lighthouse is located offshore from Crescent City on a little island accessible only at low tide. The guided tour covers most of the lighthouse and most of its history. The beacon on display is the fourth one used in this lighthouse. The fifth beacon is in use now, as the lighthouse is active as a private aid to navigation. Visitors can see an old log book, banjo clock, shipwreck photos, and nautical mementos. Although many have hopes of being stranded by the tide, along with the resident ghost, the wealth of native plants and view of the ocean from the tower will make up for their disappointment in finding themselves safely back on the mainland.

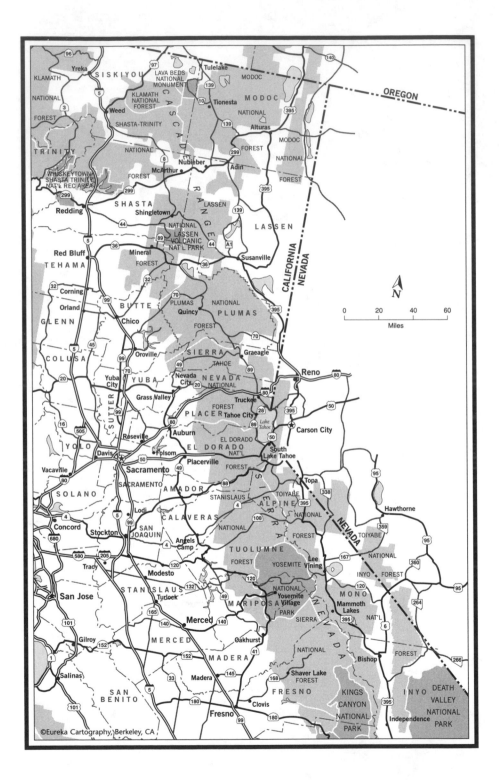

©Eureka Cartography, Berkeley, CA

The Big Valley

Solano, Sacramento, and San Joaquin Counties

Today, the Sacramento area is the political heartland of the state of California. Two hours away from San Francisco, the city of Sacramento is worth a visit to get a feeling for how the world's eighth largest economy functions.

At different times, the capital of California has been Benicia, Vallejo, and San Jose. The state capitol is now firmly ensconced under the beautifully restored dome in Sacramento. The rich farmland surrounding the city is reflected in the 40-acre Capital Park in the city. You will appreciate the mix of urban, suburban, and rural settings, which symbolize the variety of California's lifestyles.

Stockton, south of Sacramento, is one entrance to the Gold Country. Visitors will find rolling hills and farmland dotted by small towns. Stockton is named in honor of Commodore Robert Stockton, who led the forces that took over California for the United States in 1847. The lakes and peaceful atmosphere of the San Joaquin Valley add to the ambience of the area, and water-sports lovers will find ample opportunities for houseboating, skiing, fishing, and every kind of boating.

Marine World Africa USA

Marine World Parkway, Vallejo 94589. Located at the intersection of Highways 80 and 37. (707) 643-ORCA/644-4000. Open daily Memorial Day to Labor Day, Wed.–Sun. and holidays the rest of the year. Winter, 9:30–5; summer, 9:30–6; spring and fall, 9:30–5:30. Adults, $25.95; over 60, $21.95; ages 4–12, $17.95; tots 3 & under, free. Prices cover everything except elephant rides and giraffe and lorikeet feedings. Parking, $4. Gift shops. Dolphin strollers and wheelchairs for rent. Picnic areas. Blue & Gold Ferry from San Francisco's Pier 39: (415) 705-5444 or (707) 64-FERRY. BARTLINK: (707) 648-4666. Yearly memberships, group discounts available. **All ages.**

Dancing dolphins, killer whales, waterskiing extravaganzas, birds and butterflies, an Australian "walkabout," and a "Gentle Jungle" petting area are just some of the many attractions in this remarkable wildlife park and "oceanarium." For a real experience, come eye to eye with 15 different species of sharks as you move down a crystal-clear tunnel swirling with other fish in coral caves. Let a walrus wink at you. When the kids tire of looking at the aquarium and other exhibits, they can sit and watch one of eight exciting shows or let off steam at the Whale-of-a-Time Playground. There are elephant rides, giraffe feedings, animal encounters, and dozens of ways to have a wonderful day.

⇒ Vallejo Naval & Historical Museum

734 Marin Street, Vallejo 94590. (707) 643-0077. Tues.–Sat., 10–4:30.
Adults, $1.50; children, 75 cents. Children under 12 admitted free with an
adult. Gift shop. Research libarary. Tours, special events. **Ages 7 & up.**

Ship models, murals, naval memorabilia, and the periscope from the
U.S.S. *Baya* attract naval buffs to this community museum, where revolving exhibits focus on community and naval history. A working periscope
installed through the roof gives an excellent view of San Francisco and
Mare Island.

⇒ Herman Goelitz Candy Company

2400 North Watney Way, Fairfield 94533. (707) 428-2838. From
Highway 80, take West Texas to Beck Avenue, right to Courage Drive, right
on North Watney. Store open Mon.–Sat., 9–5. Tours, Mon.–Fri., 9–2. No
open-toed shoes; shoes with soft soles recommended. An informative video begins
the 30-minute tour. Free. **All ages.**

"The day I went to the Jelly Belly factory I fell in love. You could
see how they make the candy and how they put the chocolate on the raisins. They put the raisins in a barrel and the barrel turned. You'll get
samples of candy. You will enjoy it. I did. They have jelly beans in 40
flavors which are very good. The Jelly Belly is an interesting place to go
and see how candy is made. You should go. You will have a blast." So
gushed Tina Miranda, a fourth grader at David A. Weir School, Fairfield.

The Goelitz Candy Company has been in business since 1898. Its
candy makers invented the jelly bean, after inventing candy corn, in 1926.
Gummi products are a recent addition. There are only four calories per
jelly bean—and it takes 7 to 10 days to make one.

⇒ Vacaville Museum

213 Buck Avenue, Vacaville 95688. (707) 447-4513. Wed.–Sun., 1–
4:30. Adults, $1; students, 50 cents. Wed. free. Gift shop. Video theater
and special programs. **Ages 8 & up.** *W.*

This Center for Solano County History honors the city's heritage,
its founders, and the farmers who settled Solano County. Changing exhibits such as the Vaca Valley Doll Club's collection and a Victorian dining
room will interest the whole family.

After remodeling, the **Pena Adobe,** on Highway 80, five miles south
of Vacaville, will be open to visitors who want to see what rancho life was
like. The Pena Adobe is the original adobe built here, on an ancient Indian site, and some of the Wintu artifacts found during restoration are
displayed. There are picnic tables on the grounds.

✈ Travis Air Force Base Museum

Building 80, East Bergen Street (Mail: 400 Brennan Circle, Travis Air Force Base 94535). (707) 424-5605. Mon.–Fri., 9–4; until 5 on Sat.; Sun., 12–5. Free. Stop at the main gate or visitor's center for a pass. Gift shop. **Ages 8 & up.**

A B-29 Superfortress bomber is just one of the 30 vintage airplanes on display outside this cavernous museum. There are fighters and transports and helicopters from World War II, the Korean War, and Vietnam, as well as the 192-pound biplane made by California's little known pioneer aviators, Arthur and Willie Gonzales. Inside you'll find engines, flight uniforms, photographic exhibits, and a few planes from Desert Storm. Airplane buffs will love it.

✈ Suisun Valley Harvest Trails

Farmers and farm stores have put together a map and guide to producers who are open to the public. An afternoon outing to see where our food comes from can be educational as well as entertaining. Youngsters will particularly want to visit the **Suisun Valley Fisheries** (5114 Suisun Valley Road, Suisun Valley. 707-426-1422).

The Environmental Education Farm Foundation (25344 County Road 95, 0.6 miles north of Road 31, Davis 95616. 916-758-1387; by appointment) arranges for farm tours and teaches environmentally sound agricultural and aquacultural practices either on site or in schools. You may call the same number to arrange for special free interpretive walks in the Quail Ridge Reserve on Lake Berryessa in the Vaca Mountains. The Reserve is noted for the native California oak stands and rare bunch grasses, as well as a plethora of protected fauna. To receive your map, send a stamped, self-addressed envelope to Suisun Valley Harvest Trails, 200 West Texas Street, Fairfield 94533. 707-421-6790.

✈ Western Railway Museum

Rio Vista Junction, 10 miles east of Fairfield at 5848 State Highway 12 (Mail: 5848 State Highway 12, Suisun City 94585-9641). (707) 374-2978/(800) 900-RAIL. Wed.–Sun. in summer, weekends in winter, 11–5. All day passes: Adults, $6; seniors, $5; children, $3; families (2 adults and up to 6 children), $18. Charters and groups by appt., call (415) 673-7774. Picnic areas. Gift shop. **Ages 4 & up.**

The Western Railway Museum was put together by a nonprofit organization of people who love trains. A major museum is in the works. Meanwhile, visitors can ride on or walk through and around the more than 120 retired trolleys and steam locomotives or just watch the railroad buffs at work. Our favorite is the old-fashioned Salt Lake Utah observation car (remember Judy Garland in *The Harvey Girls?*). The Birney "dinkey" streetcars, the New York City "el," the Pullman ready for sleep, the Toonerville trolley from the Key System, and Oakland and San Francisco streetcars will spur youngsters' imaginations. The gift shop holds the largest collection of railroad books in the West, along with cards, old ads, tickets, and badges.

On weekends, mid-March to mid-May, the **Prairie Train Wildflower Express** makes special excursions through the Jepson Prairie at the height of the wildflower blooming season.

In December, the **Santa Claus Express** allows kids a chance to talk to Santa Claus. Both trains recall the best of the railroad travel era, with complimentary hors d'oeuvres and beverages and entertaining guides. (800-900-RAIL. Adults, $12 to $35; children, $8 to $20. All fares include admission to the museum.)

❖ Rio Vista Museum

16 North Front Street, Rio Vista 95471. (707) 374-5169. Weekends, 1:30–4:30 and by appt. Free. **Ages 8 & up.**

All of the treasures in this little museum have been donated by local residents. There are antique etchings and photos; newspapers and books; and farm implements such as tools, plows, a buggy, a wagon, a forge, and a foundry, typewriters, a wine press, Chinese hats, and local birds' eggs. The museum was created during the Bicentennial, "so we won't forget all about the past."

❖ Explorit Science Center

3141 Fifth Street, P.O. Box 1288, Davis 95617. (916) 756-0191. Tues.– Fri., 2–4:30; Sat., 11–4:30; Sun., 1–4:30. General admission, $3; under 4, free. **Ages 2 to 12.**

This small, entertaining, hands-on science museum offers fun for even the youngest child. Winston the iguana and his three snake buddies rule over a collection of changing exhibits such as an international sand sample collection and a take-apart center, where kids can look at the insides of things such as microscopes and solar energy panels. The sand pool in the back is also fun.

A new carousel is being built in a pavillion in Davis's Central Park, between 4th & 5th and B & C Streets, so be on the lookout for it.

❖ Yolo County Historical Museum

512 Gibson Road, Woodland 95695. Highway 80 to Highway 113. (916) 666-1045. Mon. & Tues., 10–4; weekends, 12–4, and by appt. Adults, $2; ages 12 & under, free. Picnic areas. **Ages 8 & up.**

Housed in the Greek Revival style mansion built by William Gibson to remind himself of his Virginia home, this museum records area history as seen through the lives of one family. Each room represents a different era and furnishing style, from 1850 to 1940. Visitors will see the dairy, root cellar, and washroom, along with antique farm equipment, an exhibit of local agriculture in the barn, a blacksmith shop and an herb garden. Little Melissa wrote, "I really enjoyed Gibson House a lot. The steriopti-scope [sic] was neat! The commode must have been very handy. The hog oiler looked handy too. The hair pictures were very neat. The sad iron was pretty heavy. Those wringers were dangerous! Gibson House was fun!"

⇻ Yolo Short Line Railroad

East Main at Hollis, Woodland 95776. (916) 372-9777. Weekends & holidays, May–October, 10 & 2 P.M. Adults, $13; seniors, $11; ages 4–14, $8. **Ages 4 & up.**

The YSL is an old-fashioned excursion railroad that rolls along the original 1912 Sacramento Northern route, through farmland, along the Sacramento River, and over an 8,000-foot-long wooden trestle to West Sacramento. The roundtrips take two hours and 20 minutes. You can buy snacks or take picnics and eat at one of the tables on the "open-air" bag-gage car. There are closed cars, too. Your five-car train will be pulled by a diesel engine or #1233, a World War I–vintage steam locomotive.

⇻ Hays Antique Truck Museum

2000 East Main Street, Woodland 95776. (916) 666-1044. At Interstate 5 and Road 102. Daily, 10–4. Closed holidays. Adults, $5; children 6–14, $2. Group rates available. Gift Shop carries teacher information packet. **Ages 7 & up.** *W.*

Junior (and senior) mechanics will find this a must-stop. There are nearly 200 vintage trucks, in 132 different makes and models, from the solid turn-of-the-century truck with solid rubber tires to the gorgeous '50s vintage hauler. The Hays Antique Truck Museum is one of the larg-est collections of antique trucks in the world.

⇻ Old Sacramento

Sacramento was the major transportation hub for north-central California, providing a convenient location where water and land trans-portation systems could meet. Today, along the Sacramento River where Captain John Sutter established his Embarcadero in 1839, an important part of Sacramento's history has been restored to its former glory. Fifty-three structures built during the Gold Rush, including restaurants, stores, offices, and museums, stand as living memorials to their past. For tour information, call the visitors' center, (916) 442-7644. It's open daily, 9–5, at 1104 Front Street at K Street, and offers maps for walking tours. Horse-and-buggy and covered-wagon rides are available.

The **Old Eagle Theater** (box office: 916-381-3263) at Front and J streets, which first opened in 1949, presents old melodramas and plays. School tours, by appointment (916-445-4209), see "Sacramento Illustrated," a 15-projector multimedia portrayal of Sacramento's history.

The **Central Pacific Passenger Station** (10–5 daily; free with Railroad Museum ticket) at Front and J streets is a reconstruction of a station that was built in 1876. Waiting rooms, ticket offices, baggage rooms, and railroad cars tell their stories. This is where passengers board the hourly excursion trains on summer weekends.

The **Old Sacramento Schoolhouse** at Front and L looks just as it did in the 1880s. In winter, you can go inside when there are docents; otherwise, just peek in the windows.

The **B. F. Hastings Museum** at Second and J streets was the first western terminus of the Pony Express and the Sacramento office of Wells Fargo. Hours can be limited because of state budget cutbacks, but when open, Wells Fargo and Pony Express exhibits beguile, as do the reconstructed Supreme Court rooms, the Grass Valley stage, and posters on the early post office system. You can tap out Morse Code or write with a quill pen.

The **Huntington-Hopkins Hardware Store** (1111 I Street. Daily, 10–5. Free), a reconstruction of one of the West's more historic hardware stores, shows off old tools and supplies in a surprisingly appealing display. Merchandise that could have been sold in the 1880s, such as spinning tops and enamel coffee pots, is for sale.

The **California Military Museum** (1119 Second Street. 916-442-2883. Tues.–Sun., 10–5. Adults, $3; seniors, $1.50; under 17, $1) is located right next to the original California Militia Headquarters. It glorifies California's military history from Mexican skirmishes in the 1770s to Operation Desert Storm with uniforms, flags, pictures, medals, newspaper articles, and lots of firearms.

�֍ Discovery Museum

101 I Street, Old Sacramento 95814. (916) 264-7057. Tues.–Fri., 12–5; Sat. & Sun., 10–5 in winter; Tues.–Sun., 10–5 in summer. Adults, $3.50; ages 6–17, $2. **Ages 4–15.**

Located in a replica of the 1854 City Hall, Sacramento's museum of history, science, and technology offers hands-on, interactive exhibitions

and activity stations to bring the past, present, and future alive. A working 1890s print shop and exhibits such as "Computers: Bits and Pieces" and "Treasures from the Trash" vie with the Gold Gallery, where you can pan for gold, and the photo scanner for youngsters' attention.

❥ California State Railroad Museum

Second and I streets, Old Sacramento 95814. (916) 445-7387/448-4466. Daily except holidays, 10–5. Adults, $6; ages 6–12, $3. Groups by appt., (916) 445-4209. Gift store and research library. **Ages 5 & up.** *W.*

This state-of-the-art museum combines slide shows, theater presentations, panel exhibits, dioramas, interpretive exhibits, shiny locomotives, and historic railroad cars to walk in, around, and through so you can see how railroads have affected our history and culture. You start your self-guided tour with a movie—and then walk through the back wall of the theater into Gold Rush California. There, wander through Lucius Beebe's elegant private car; the Railway Post Office Car, where you can sort mail; and the St. Hyacinthe Sleeping Car, which really rocks; these three are highlights of the 21-car collection. The museum is justifyingly proud of its shiningly restored "Cochiti," the 1940s dining car from the Santa Fe Super Chief, with its 37 place settings of rare silver, china, and glassware, sample menus, and full galley. Don't forget to see the toy and miniature train collection upstairs.

In summer, the California State Railroad Museum's Sacramento Southern Excursion Train offers special hourly steam train excursions along the Sacramento River from the Central Pacific Freight Depot at Front and K streets. October's "Goosebumps Express" is also a great hit. (Call 916-552-5252 for schedule. Adults, $5; ages 6–12, $2.)

❥ "Matthew McKinley" & "Spirit of Sacramento" Paddlewheeler Excursion Boats

110 L Street, Old Sacramento 95814. (916) 552-2933/(800) 433-0263. Call for prices and schedule.

Cruise and dine aboard elegantly refurbished Victorian paddleboats year-round. Call for information on brunch, dinner, and special events.

❥ Crocker Art Museum

216 O Street, at Third, Sacramento 95814. (916) 264-5423. Wed.–Sun., 10–5; Thurs. until 9. Closed holidays. Adults, $4.50; ages 7–17, $2. Tours for hearing or visually impaired. **Ages 7 & up.** *W.*

The oldest art museum in the West was built around 1873 to house the paintings and prints collected by Judge Edwin Bryant Crocker. The collection includes pottery from the fifth century B.C. through contemporary works of art. Rococo mirrors, frescoed ceilings, and curving staircases make the building itself a work of art. The stars are the Gold Rush-era paintings by Charles C. Nahl, "Fandango," and "Sunday Morning Life in the Mines." Concerts, lectures, and other special demonstrations and events are scheduled throughout the year.

❦ Leland Stanford Mansion
802 N Street, Sacramento 95814. (916) 324-0575. Tours Tues. & Thurs., 12:15; Sat., 12:15 & 1:30 and by appt. Free. **Ages 8 & up.**

The century-old home of former California governor, senator, and railroad baron Leland Stanford is in the process of restoration. Pre-restoration tours, often in hard-hat, focus on the archaeological search for clues to the house's past and the upcoming re-creation of its 19th-century splendor. We've found that looking at work in progress can often be more intriguing for youngsters than the finished product.

❦ California State Capitol
10th and Capitol, Capitol Mall, Room B 27, Sacramento 95814. (916) 324-0333. Daily, 9–5. Free. Guided tours on the hour. **Ages 7 & up.** *W.*

After 13 years of construction, the State Capitol building was completed in 1874. It has recently been restored to its historic 19th-century dignity and beauty, with a mural of Columbus expounding on the earth to Queen Isabella beneath the capitol dome. It's fun to wander the halls, to see the county window displays and the restored offices and to hear the rustle of politics in action. A tiny museum in the basement chronicles the building's history and offers films and tours.

❦ Old Governor's Mansion
1526 H Street, at 16th, Sacramento 95816. (916) 323-3047. Daily, 10–4, with tours on the hour. Adults, $2; ages 6–12, $1. **Ages 7 & up.**

The official residence of California's 13 governors from 1903 to 1967 is now a handsome Victorian museum that captures the history of the state. The melange of furnishing styles, including 14-foot ceilings, Italian marble fireplaces, chandeliers, and French mirrors reflects the different inhabitants. The old carriage house has been converted to a museum where you may view photographs of the governors and their families.

❦ Towe Ford Museum of Automotive History
2200 Front Street, Sacramento 95818. (916) 442-6802. Daily, 10–6 except major holidays. Adults, $5; seniors, $4.50; high schoolers, $2.50;

elementary school students, $1. School groups, half price. Groups by appt.
Guided tours. Special events. Gift shop. **Ages 5 & up.** *W.*

The world's most complete antique Ford museum will be a dream
come true to some youngsters. There are 170 cars and trucks on display,
with Fords dating *before* the Model T. Kids can sit in a Model T, a Model
A, or Governor Earl Warren's Cadillac limousine or Governor Jerry
Brown's 1974 blue Plymouth. There's one of every Ford model made from
1918 to 1953. Our favorite is the 1955 Thunderbird.

One little girl wrote, "We liked your car that you sawed and we
like the limousine and the ambulance rescue and the police car and the
starcruiser."

⇢ Sutter's Fort State Historic Park

2701 L Street, at 28th Street, Sacramento 95816. (916) 445-4422. Daily
except Thanksgiving, Christmas & New Year's Day, 10–5. Summer fees: Over
12, $5; ages 6–12, $2. In winter: $2 and $1. Information wand free. Tours,
groups, Environmental Living Programs, and demonstrations by appt. (916-
445-4209). Living History Days or Pioneer Demonstrations Days monthly.
Ages 6 & up. *W.*

Monica from Bitterwater Tally School wrote, "Dear Sutter's Fort,
Thank you for giving us the opportunity to participate in the ELP. It was
fun looking at the rooms like the bakery, the kitchen, and the others. It
was fun working there, too. I enjoyed it." Sutter's Fort is one of the best
places to relive California history. The fort and its buildings and stables
have been well reconstructed, and the cooperage, doctor's office, candle-
making room, kitchen, blacksmith shop, immigrant room, blanket factory, carpentry shop, guard room, bunk room, and Sutter's bedroom are
as they once were.

The information provided through audio wands is clear, helpful, and
entertaining. For example, while facing a model of James Marshall showing Sutter the gold he found at the mill, you hear their conversation and
Sutter's German-Swiss accent. Knowing that this is the actual room where
James Marshall's gold from Coloma was tested makes it more exciting.

An orientation room in the museum relates Sutter's biography and
the life of the California pioneers. A doll that survived the Donner party
tragedy is on display. ELP enables fourth- to sixth graders to actually
spend a night at the fort, spinning wool, weaving baskets, and preparing
their evening meal over fireplaces and in the beehive ovens. Living History Programs also allow youngsters of all ages to step back into the
Wild West.

⇛ State Indian Museum

2618 K Street, between 26th and 28th streets, Sacramento 95816.
(916) 324-0971. Daily except holidays, 10–5. Adults, $2; ages 6–12,
$1. Films by request. Groups by appt. Teacher's Guide available. **Ages**
6 & up. *W.*

This mesmerizing museum is a treasure house of the Native American world. Dioramas and well-labeled exhibits display Maidus grinding acorns, the healing child dance, headdresses, maps, minerals, musical instruments, games, jewelry, household goods, baskets, and featherwork. Ishi, last of his California tribe, shows his Yahi way of life in photographs, in film, and on tape. Hands-on areas, such as a place to touch different pelts and a table for use of a mortar and pestle, add spice to the exhibits. Many Native Americans volunteer for special events, especially in the outdoor demonstration area, which contains a tule house, bark house, acorn leaching pit, acorn granary, and a hand-game house.

⇛ Fairytale Town

William Land Park, 1501 Sutterville Road, off Interstate 5, Sacramento
95822. (916) 264-5233. Daily, 10–4:30, except rainy days and Christ-
mas. Adults: $2.75 weekdays, $3 weekends; ages 3–12, $2:25 and $2.50.
Combination Ticket with Zoo: Adults, $5.25; children, $3.50; ages 13–64,
$2.50; over 65, $1. Combination tickets to Fairytale Town and the Sacra-
mento Zoo are available at either gate. **Ages 3–12.**

Nursery rhymes and favorite stories come to life as children crawl through the Holes in the Cheese, sit in Cinderella's Pumpkin Coach, and slide down the circular slide after visiting Owl's House. You can visit the Three Little Pigs and Farmer Brown's Barn.

Children's birthday parties can be held in King Arthur's Castle (916-264-7061) and in Sherwood Forest daily. Special events, such as Farmer Brown's hoedown or a scarecrow-stuffing contest, are held monthly. Fairytale Town's motto: "Find Mother Goose, the Crooked Mile, a puppet show to make you smile, a pirate ship, a castle moat. Mary's lamb and a billy goat."

⇛ Sacramento Zoo

William Land Park, 3930 West Land Park Drive at Sutterville Road,
Sacramento 95822. (916) 264-5885/264-5166. Daily except Christmas,
10–4, in summer, 9–4. Adults, $4, weekdays, $4.50 weekends; ages 3–12,
$2.50 and $3. Combination ticket with Fairyland: Adults, $5.25; children,
$3.50. There are strollers to rent. Gift shop. **All ages.** *W.*

Who would imagine that there would be a Lake Victoria in California? This 200,000-gallon freshwater lake is home for African and South American waterfowl including Argentine ruddy ducks and crested screamers.

Over 400 animals live in this tree-shaded garden and zoo. Any inhabitant of the reptile house is a favorite; others are the wallaroos, flamingos, giraffes, and the hippo. Orangutan, tiger, lion, and chimpanzee exhibits show these beautiful animals in natural settings. The Rare Feline Center houses a Geoffroy's cat, jaguar, and margay.

❖ Discovery Museum Learning Center

3615 Auburn Boulevard, Sacramento 95821. (916) 277-6181. Open the first weekend of the month. Adults, $3.50; ages 6–17, $2. **Ages 4–14.**

The center specializes in classes, tours, and outreach programs. It has the only planetarium in the region, an outside Discovery Trail, and hands-on activity stations. By the end of 1997 it will include the Challenger Learning Center. Using space explorations as a theme, the center's computer-simulated space science flight center will enable students to experience the hands-on application of science and math principles. That's one way to get to the moon!

❖ Waterworld USA Sacramento

1600 Exposition Boulevard, Cal Expo, Sacramento 95815. (916) 924-0556. Daily late spring to late fall, 10:30–6. Adults, $14.99; children under 48 inches high, $9.99. Season passes, group, and party rates. **Ages 4 & up.**

There are 20 ways to get wet and wild at this Waterworld, including the Cannonball Falls, where you plummet over six feet. There's also the Cobra, an intertwined double flume that is twice as much fun to race with a friend. The Hurricane and the Cliffhanger aren't for sissies, either. Parents can relax instead in the Calypso Cooler with its gentle current. Don't forget big towels, snacks, and sunscreen.

❖ Effie Yeaw Nature Center

Back gate of Ancil Hoffman County Park, Tarshes Drive, P.O. Box 579, Carmichael 95609. (916) 489-4918. Mon.–Fri., 9–3; weekends, 10–5. Closed Thanksgiving, Christmas, and New Year's Day. School programs, guided walks. Gift shop. **Ages 6–14.**

Sacramento teacher Effie Yeaw always dreamed of "A Place for Children to Discover Nature" and volunteers have made sure that such a place exists. The center is more "out" than "in," offering outreach programs about nature in schools and other centers. The Nature Center will give you three self-guided trails through the 77-acre nature study area along the American River. They'll even loan you the binoculars to see wild turkeys, deer, and other wildlife. There are Cultural Heritage programs such as Frontier Ranch Life, Pioneer Children, or "Maidu Indian Day," which makes use of the replica structures of a Maidu summer village on the property. Inside there's a mountain lion exhibit, live animal wild kingdom, and other exhibits that change regularly.

⇒ McClellan Aviation Museum
McClellan Air Force Base, P.O. Box 553, North Highlands 95660-0553. Enter at the Palm Gate. Mon.–Sat., 9–3; Sun., 12–3. Free. Gift shop. **Ages 7 & up.**

A work in progress, the McClellan Aviation Museam aims to be one of the best collections of aircraft and aviation memorabilia in the West. Museum programs will include guided tours, lectures, oral and visual history programs, and a large screen video theater presenting a wide selection of aviation subjects during normal operating hours. The Gallery takes the visitor from the genesis of the McClellan era to the present-day high tech "revolution in Air Logistics." You can see a 1943 L-2M Grasshopper, a P-80B Shooting Star, a C-119G Flying Boxcar, an F-101B Voodoo, and dozens more, along with engines, an O-11A La France fire/crash rescue truck, and "Birth of the Blues," a look at the evolution of the Air Force uniform.

⇒ Nimbus Fish Hatchery
2001 Nimbus Road, Rancho Cordova 95670. On the American River. (916) 355-2820. Daily, 7:30–3. Free. **Ages 7 & up.** *W.*

After fighting their way from the Pacific Ocean, salmon and steelhead spawn here each fall and winter. The hatchery has a capacity of 20 million salmon eggs and accounts for 60 to 70 percent of the commercial catch off the California coast. Visitors can see raceway ponds, the fish weir and ladder entrance, a holding pond, the sorting and spawning area, nursery ponds, and the hatchery building.

⇒ Gibson Ranch County Park
8444 El Modena, P.O. Box 130, Elverta 95626. Take Watt Avenue north to Elverta Road, left on Elverta, right on El Modena to Gibson Ranch. (916) 991-9500/991-2066. Groups and tours and individual visits by reservation. **All ages.**

This is really a working farm. There are cows, hens, and horses to feed, and muskrats, ducks, and geese swim in the lake, which you can fish or swim in. There are ponies and horses to ride, old buggies, a blacksmith shop to play with, and hayrides to enjoy.

✦ Folsom Project Dam and Powerplant

7794 Folsom Dam Road, U. S. Bureau of Reclamation, Folsom 95630. (916) 989-7275. Mon.–Sat., at 10 & 1. Free. **Ages 8 & up.**

Drive on top of the dam and past the gorgeous lake, which is about the size of the state of Rhode Island, to get to the powerhouse. The tour ventures through the Power Plant, where you will get an up close and personal view of the generator area. The generators have capacities of 66,240 kilowatts each. From there, you head out to the dam. Once inside, you will get a lot of information while taking the elevator ride 40 stories up.

✦ Folsom City Park and Zoo

50 Natoma Street, Folsom 95630. (916) 355-7200. Daily except Mon., 10–4. Adult, $2. **All ages.**

This small zoo specializes in North American native animals. Many of the animals were raised as pets; some are disabled. None can live in the wild. The zoo is located in City Park, which offers shaded picnic and barbecue areas and an extensive area of new playground equipment for both preschool and older children. A one-third scale steam train runs in summer and fall (916-985-7347).

Downtown, historic Sutter Street has been restored to old buildings and shops that remind visitors of early times. The Historical Society has opened the **Folsom History Museum** in the 1850s Wells Fargo Assay Office. The museum offers a slide show of local Indian and Gold Rush history and important local sites (916-985-2707). At Sutter and Wool streets, the reconstructed Southern Pacific Depot displays historical treaures.

Further out of town, the **Folsom Powerhouse,** on Riley Street, relayed electricity to Sacramento from 1895 to 1952. For tours, call (916) 985-0205.

A new addition to the area is the **Folsom Prison Museum** (Daily, 10–4. $1. 916-985-2561, ext. 4589) at the visitor's gate, where you can experience a little of the prison's "end of the world" atmosphere. Gatling guns, prisoners' made-up weapons, a video presentation, and an 1880 cell complete with re-created 1880 inmate tell the tale. Buy a postcard with Black Bart's rap sheet on it at the museum store.

✢ Micke Grove Park and Zoo and San Joaquin County Historical Museum

11793 North Micke Grove Road, Lodi 95240. South of Lodi 3 miles, on Highway 99 and on Highway 5. Park: (209) 953-8800. Daily, dawn to dusk. On weekends and holidays, $4 per car. Rental facility reservations: (209) 953-8800/331-7400. Zoo: (209) 331-7270. Daily, 10–5. Adults, $1.50; children and seniors, 50 cents. Museum: P.O. Box 21, Lodi 95241. (209) 368-9154. Wed.–Sun., 1–5, and by appt. Adults, $2; ages 6–12 & seniors, $1. Japanese Garden: daily, 9–2. Free. **All ages.** *W.*

This bustling community park offers picnic and play areas, a full range of water sports, a rose garden, a Japanese garden, horseback riding, nature trails, and party facilities. The museum, zoo, and amusement park are all near the main north entrance parking lot.

"Man and Nature Hand in Hand" is the theme for the remarkable multibuilding museum. In the main building, changing exhibits are always based on memories of the pioneer people, including a millinery shop and Victorian sitting room, both meticulously furnished.

On the grounds, you can visit the Tree & Vine building, the Delta building, an 1800s Calaveras schoolhouse, a 1920s kitchen, a harness shop, a ranch blacksmith shop, a farm tools and tractor collection, a model of a dairy, and the Sunshine Trail Garden for the Blind. "Earth is so kind, that just tickle her with a hoe and she laughs up a harvest," is what one Delta farmer wrote, while another prophesied, "We will dig gold with a plow."

Lions, bobcats, gray foxes, kinkajous, pumas, and black leopards are some of the animals in this little zoo, now being refurbished. There are daily public feedings of the animals. The seal pool and tropical forest canopy always draw crowds.

✢ Pixie Woods

Louis Park, Stockton. (Mail: City Hall, 415 North El Dorado, Stockton 95202.) (209) 466-9890/944-8220. Fall and spring: weekends, 12–5. Summer: Wed.–Fri., 11–5; until 6 on weekends. Closed from Halloween to mid-February. Ages 12 and over, $1.50; under 12, $1. Train, boat, and merry-go-round, 60 cents. Parties by appt. **Ages 2 to 12.** *W.*

Stockton's fairyland is for the "young in age and young in heart." You enter the Rainbow Gates to a magical forest and enchanted lagoons and begin a journey that will take you through some of your favorite fairytale settings. Ride the Pixie Express or take a trip on the *Pixie Queen*, a replica of the paddle-wheel steamers that long ago graced the Delta waterways. And be sure to visit Pirates' Cove and the magical volcano. See a puppet show in the Toadstool Theater. Have an adventure in Frontier Town and pet the animals in McDonald's Farm.

➤ The Haggin Museum

Victory Park, 1201 North Pershing Avenue, Stockton 95203. Off Interstate 5. (209) 462-4116. Daily, except Mon. & holidays, 1:30–5. Donation. Groups by appt. **Ages 6 & up.** *W.*

Three floors of history and art fill this handsome brick building. The "Pioneer Room" boasts of interactive video programs and other displays dealing with the history of Stockton. Interpretive displays of California include an arcade of 19th-century storefronts, arms, a firefighters' gallery, and an American Indian Gallery. The Holt Hall of Agriculture includes a fully restored 1919 Holt 75 caterpillar tractor and a 1904 combine harvester. The art galleries include work by American artists such as Albert Bierstadt and William Keith. The letter by Daniel Boone, the 1927 Stephans Brothers speedboat, and the display of 100-year-old dolls are of special interest to kids.

➤ Stockton Children's Museum

402 West Weber Avenue, Stockton 95203. (209) 456-4386, Mon.–Sat., 9–4. Adults, $4; ages under 2, free. Groups, school programs, summer camp. **Ages 2–12.**

This wonderful, hands-on, interactive museum encourages kids to climb on a fire engine, "work" in a cannery or a grocer store, explore the arts and crafts station, and check out the hospital, firehouse, TV station and art center. In the Kids World mini-city, kids can play at shopping for groceries, swinging by the post office, stopping at the bank, or visiting the optometrist, just the way their parents do.

Youngsters will also enjoy a visit to the **Clever Planetarium** (209-474-5110) at the San Joaquin Delta College, 5151 Pacific Avenue in Stockton.

➤ McHenry Museum

1401 I Street, Modesto 95354. (209) 577-5366. Tues.–Sun., 12–4. Free. Tours by appt. (577-5344). **Ages 7 & up.** *W.*

"Not to know what happened before one was born is to remain a child," said Cicero. And that is the credo of this historical museum, which aims to appreciate the past and the people who pioneered this area. A complete doctor's office, a general store, a recreated blacksmith shop, gold mining paraphernalia, firefighting equipment, and a collection of guns and cattle brands are permanent exhibits. Changing displays focus on families, ethnic and religious groups, quilts, fans, dolls, and other areas of interest. Slide shows, movies, and musical events are held in the auditorium. And there are traveling exhibits to schools and groups.

Down the block, history buffs will want to visit **The McHenry Mansion**, which was built in 1883 and is one of the few surviving reminders of Modesto's past. Today the Italianate mansion has been completely restored and refurbished, right down to the William Morris-designed wallpaper, the rose brass gas chandelier in the front parlor, the 19th-century English wall-to-wall carpeting, and the milled redwood columns on the front veranda. (906 15th Street at I, Modesto. 209-577-5341. Sun., Tues., Wed., Thurs., 1–4; Fri., 12–3; group and individual tours and party rentals available.)

✦ Newman Museum

1209 Main Street, Newman 95360. 30 miles southwest of Modesto on Highway 33. (209) 862-0239. Mon.–Fri., 1–4; third Sun., 1–4; closed third Thurs. Free. **Ages 6 & up.**

The Newman Historical Society has banded together to help Barbara and Tom Powell restore and re-open their little museum. The changing exhibits are community work-togethers, such as the one on Wedding Attire of the 20th Century or the one on Hills Ferry, a town on the San Joaquin River that was passed by when the railroad founded Newman in the late 1880s. Farming tools, pioneer tools, Chinese artifacts, and a collection of 29 branding irons dating to 1864 are also on display.

✦ Castle Air Museum

Castle Air Force Base, P.O. Box 488, Atwater 95301. Off Highway 99 near Merced. (209) 723-2178. Daily except holidays, 9–5. Free. Shop and restaurant. **Ages 7 & up.** *W.*

This is an airplane lover's dream. A B-24 Liberator bomber, its plexiglass bubbles bristling with machine guns and the bombs painted on its side numbering its World War II missions, greets you when you drive through Castle's gate. Volunteer enthusiasts refurbished this plane, along with the over three dozen military aircraft on view at the museum. There are bombers of all ages; jets; an up-to-date SR-71 spy plane; a plane so small a pilot can't fit in it; and one, a KC-97 Stratotanker, impossibly large. Air Force memorabilia in the indoor display such as a World War I machine gun, a World War II Norden bombsight, and a special display of NASA shuttle flights, add to little flyers' interest.

✥ Hershey Chocolate U.S.A.

120 South Sierra Avenue, Oakdale 95361. (209) 848-8126. Mon.–Fri., 8:30–3, Closed major holidays. Visitors Center on G Street next to the park: weekdays, 8–5. Groups by appt. Free. Gift store. **All ages.**

Once you register at the Visitors Center, inhale and wait for the next available tour while watching a chocolate-making video and checking out the historic displays. Each visitor gets a coupon for a free chocolate bar. Then you're shuttled to the factory to see candy bars, chocolate kisses, and chocolate syrups made, weighed, packaged, and labeled in the course of a 30-minute tour. Follow the cocoa bean to the candy bar, passing huge chocolate vats, candy-bar molds in action, and rooms for the processing of instant cocoa and chocolate syrup. Then it's back to the Visitors Center for the fateful chocolate choice.

✳ The Gold Country

To drive along Highway 49 is to relive California's history and legends. This is the Gold Country—the land of writers such as Mark Twain, Bret Harte, and Joaquin Miller, the bandits Black Bart and Joaquin Murietta, and heroes such as Ulysses S. Grant and Horatio Alger.

Passing through little towns named Copperopolis and Jenny Lind, visitors who look carefully will see the traces of the hundreds of thousands of people—Cornish, Welsh, English, German, French, Italian, Mexican, Peruvian, Australian, Chinese, and African—who migrated to this place seeking fame and fortune from the "tears from the sun." The town of Volcano still has an old Chinese store and a Jewish cemetery.

In the Gold Country, you'll find the only town in the United States ever to name itself a nation: Rough and Ready seceded from the Union in April 1850, to become a republic with its own president, constitution, and flag; by the Fourth of July, it had slipped quietly back into the Union.

The many parks and campgrounds are mostly near quiet streams that once teemed with gold panners. Although there are mining, river rafting, ballooning, and kayaking expeditions available, to me, the best thing to do in the Gold Country is just explore, get a little lost. You'll have memorable experiences you couldn't possibly find listed in a book and you'll hear about towns that exist now only in history books. On the other hand, you could pick up a pan and start sifting.

✨ Railtown 1897—The Sierra Railway Company of California State Historic Park

Sierra Railway, P.O. Box 1250, Jamestown 95327. Off Highways 49 and 108 on Fifth Avenue, Jamestown. (Mail: California State Railroad Museum, 111 "I" Street, Old Sacramento 95814-2265.) (209) 984-3953. Self-guided tours of the Historic Sierra Railroad shops, 10–4 daily except Thanksgiving, Christmas, and New Year's Day. Adults, $2; ages 6–12, $1. Train rides daily in summer, and on fall and spring weekends, 10–4. Adults, $6; youngsters, $3. Group rates. Varying times and prices for special train rides. Museum gift store, 10–5 daily. Picnic areas. **Ages 3 & up.** *W.*

The Sierra Railway has been working since 1897. It has been starring in movies since the Marx Brothers went west. You can walk through working turn-of-the-century machine shops, the historic Sierra Railroad Shops. After a short film, you'll be guided through the roundhouse to see rolling stock that's starred in over 200 movies and TV shows, from *High*

Noon, Petticoat Junction, and *Wild Wild West* to *Mother Lode Cannonball* and *Butch Cassidy & The Sundance Kid* and *Back to the Future III.*

➤ Gold Prospecting Expeditions

Old Livery Stable, 18170 Main Street, P.O. Box 1040, Jamestown 95327-4653. (209) 984-GOLD. Reservations: (800) 596-0009. http://www.goldprospecting.com. Call for details. **Ages 5 & up.**

Every day, a tape showing Jamestown's history and how to prospect for gold is shown free. It includes scenes about a couple who walked into Ralph Shock's store in January 1895, carrying a shopping bag with 11 pounds of gold nuggets valued at $140,000. There's a "slough" right on the main street of Jamestown for an instant panning experience. Families and groups can go on expeditions that take an hour or two days, by foot, river raft, train, or helicopter. Harlan of Modesto wrote, "Thank you so much for teaching me how to pan for gold. It could come in handy sometime. I enjoyed your explaining about gold and its uses. I also enjoyed panning for gold. . . ."

Gold panning expert Ralph Shock has these suggestions for gold panning: "At a bend in a creek with a light flow of water, dig behind rocks, fallen limbs and uprooted trees. Use an 8- to 10-inch pan and dig a deep hole for material for your pan. Fill it three-quarters full, then stir lightly, underwater, so the lighter material floats out. Pick out the big rocks and shake the pan back and forth at least 20 times. Dip the pan's rim into the water, again sweeping so the lighter material floats out. Shake and sweep until you have a tablespoon of dirt left. Tip so sand and gravel is at the top and gently swirl water across the material to uncover the gold left in your pan. Using a dry fingertip, transfer your gold to a water-filled vial."

The California Gold Country Visitors Association (800-225-3764. P.O. Box 596, Jackson 95642) can tell you where to pan for gold, raft the rivers, explore the redwood groves, dine, sleep, shop, and enjoy Yosemite and Tahoe.

➤ Tuolumne County Museum and History Center

158 West Bradford, P.O. Box 299, Sonora 95370. (209) 532-1317. Sun.–Fri., 10–4; Sat., 10–3:30. Group tours by appt. Picnic tables in the courtyard, once the former prisoners' exercise yard. Free. **Ages 7 & up.**

This thriving museum is proud of its Gold Exhibit, which features the Tuolumne County Gold Collection—44 specimens, including two solid gold nuggets. Information about the three gold rushes (in 1849, at the turn of the century, and modern open pit mining) is found in photos, lithographs of early mining scenes, and a large map showing where all the gold camps were located. Mark Twain has a corner to himself. Over 160 pictures, vignettes, and historical items tell the exciting story of Tuolumne County and its six geographical regions. The museum is in the 1857 county jail. The cellblock in back has exhibits of pioneer crossings of the Sierra Nevada mountains between 1841 and 1860 and an extensive gun collection in a jail cell, with fascinating tales of the stalwart, independent men who used them. Visitors can walk into the cell to see the guns in their cases. Another cell has a display vignette of an old-time gun shop.

Two blocks west on Bradford and Highway 49 (West Stockton Road) is **Prospector's Park,** with a five-stamp mill, an authentic *arrastre,* or gold-mining platform, and a waterwheel that works on an impulse method, along with information plaques.

❧ Sonora Fire Department Museum

City Hall, 94 North Washington Street, Sonora 95370. (209) 532-7432. Daily, 9–5. Free. **Ages 5 & up.**

Speaking trumpets from the 1850s, handmade uniforms from the 1870s, and leather firemen's helmets are displayed along with trophies and hand-operated firefighting equipment, including the Eureka No. 1 hand pumper, which was shipped around the Horn from New York in 1876.

Sonora, once called the Queen of the Southern Mines, is a well-preserved town. Visitors may be interested in stopping by the Archaeology and History Display in the **A. N. Francisco Building** (48 West Yaney Street. Weekdays, 9–4. Free) to see bottles, fragments, and objects found on the site of the building during construction. Another display case contains memorabilia from the 1854 *Union Democrat*, including old type, photos, headlines, and old editions.

❧ Columbia State Historic Park

P.O. Box 151, Columbia District 95310. Highway 49, north of Sonora. (209) 532-4301. Daily except Christmas and Thanksgiving, 10–4:30. Free. **All ages.** *W.*

Columbia, "The Gem of the Southern Mines," is the best of the restored gold-mining towns. The streets and wooden sidewalks lead you to buildings, stores, and eateries outfitted as they were in the town's heyday.

The Columbia Gazette office still prints a small newspaper; the **Columbia Candy Kitchen** still sells hand-dipped candy; the 1857 **Douglas's Saloon** still dispenses an occasional draft beer along with sarsaparilla.

Peek into the carpenter's shop and the schoolhouse, which has a bell tower, pump organ, desk, and potbellied stove. The Chinese herb shop, the town jail, firehouse, blacksmith shop, and drugstore are other main attractions. The gold scales in the Wells Fargo Office weighed out over $55 million in dust and nuggets of the $87 million mined here. You can also ride a stagecoach and pan for gold!

Fallon House, a Victorian-era hotel, houses an ice cream parlor and the Columbia Actors' Repertory theater, which has given continuous performances for over 30 years. The City Hotel has been restored to Victorian glory and is also justly proud of its dining room.

During a **Hidden Treasure Gold Mine Tour** (209-532-9693; $7) visitors see the quartz vein that gold formed millions of years ago and discover what "side drifts" and "glory holes" are all about. You can also have gold panning lessons in the Matelot Gulch Mine Store.

The park museum offers slide shows and exhibits on the Indians, the Chinese (once one-sixth of Columbia's population), and the gold miners. Your family could happily spend a day—or a weekend—in this thriving town of yesteryear.

⇛ Moaning Cave

5350 Moaning Cave Road, Vallecito 95251. Off Parrots Ferry Road, between Columbia and Highway 4. (209) 736-2708. Daily 45-minute tours: winter, 10–5; summer, 9–6. Adults, $6.75; ages 6–11, $3.50; under 5, free. **Ages 7 & up.**

You can count the 144 winding steps that lead you 165 feet down to a graveyard of prehistoric bones and moaning sounds. You'll see fantastic rock formations, such as Elephant's Ears and the Little Girl's Face, that add to the eerie feeling you're intruding on unknown spirits. The main chamber is tall enough to hold the Statue of Liberty. Stalactites hang "tight" from the ceiling and stalagmites are "mighty mounds" in the floor. Moaning Cave also offers a three-hour-long "Adventure Tour," with a 180-foot rappel, or rope descent, for ages 12 and up. Picnic tables with a view of the hills offer a pleasant spot to wait, as does the exhibit-filled waiting room.

⇛ California Caverns

Cave City, Box 78, Vallecito 95251. Mountain Ranch Road, 9 miles east of San Andreas. Daily, 10–5, but not open if there's snow or rain. Hours depend on water level inside the cavern. (209) 736-2708. Adults, $7; ages 6–12, $3.50. **Ages 7 & up.**

"When we emerged into the bright landscapes of the sun everything looked brighter, and we felt our faith in Nature's beauty strengthened, and saw more clearly that beauty is universal and immortal, above, beneath, on land and sea, mountain and plains in heat and cold, light and darkness." John Muir wrote this after wandering through the 200-foot-deep crystalline jungles. California Caverns offers an 80-minute "Trail of Light" tour and "Wild Cave" expedition tours for the adventurous.

The same company controls the **Boyden Cavern** in Kings River Canyon, Sequoia National Forest, on Highway 180, east of Fresno (209-736-2708).

❧ Mercer Caverns

P.O. Box 509, Murphys 95247. Ebbetts Pass Highway, 1 mile from Murphys. (209) 781-2101. Daily, in summer, 9–5; in winter, weekends and holidays, 11–4. Last tour at 3:15. Adults, $5; ages 5–11, $2.50, subject to change. School tours by appt. **Ages 6 & up.**

This 45- to 50-minute tour past stalactites and stalagmites, aragonites and helictites, takes you into a subterranean wonderland. Eerie rock formations like the Organ Loft, Angel Wings, and the Chinese Meat Market are dazzling examples of the artistry of nature. Mercer Caverns was discovered in 1885 by a tired, thirsty prospector, Walter J. Mercer, who noticed bay bushes growing near a limestone bluff and thought he had found a well. Stacey loved the story about Mr. Mercer, but "my favorite part was the beautiful formations that you turned into very wild fairy tales. I especially liked the Rapunzel story. It was so fantastic the way the limestone shaped itself into the shape of a girl with long hair. The little frog prince that was so embarrassed it turned around all the time was cute too."

❧ Angels Camp Museum

753 Main Street, Angels Camp 95222. (209) 736-2963. Daily, 10–3. Adults, $1; children, 25 cents. **Ages 6 & up.** *W.*

A sulky, phaeton, surrey, hearse, steam tractors, and a mail stage are part of this extensive collection of antiques, clocks, old wagons, and rolling stock. Old mining equipment and the working stamp mill are especially fascinating. Indian artifacts and memorabilia of the county's past are nicely presented. Homage is paid to Mark Twain and the annual Jumping Frog Contest.

North of Columbia on Highway 49, before you reach New Melones Reservoir, you'll come to a turnoff leading to the **Mark Twain Cabin** on

Jackass Hill. This is a replica built around the chimney of the original cabin, which burned down many years ago. While living here in 1864 and 1865, Twain wrote his book *Roughing It* and gathered material that inspired later stories such as the famous "Jumping Frog of Calaveras County."

✦ Calaveras County Historical Museum

30 Main Street, P.O. Box 721, San Andreas 95249. (209) 754-6579. Daily, 10–4. Adults, 50 cents; children, 25 cents. Gift shop. **Ages 7 & up.** *W.*

The Hall of Records Building in the County Courthouse and Jail has been transformed into a beautifully designed treasure house. You can walk through the judge's chambers and then go downstairs to see the cell where Black Bart awaited trial. The museum focuses on the Miwok way of life and on the people living in San Andreas during the 1880s, with representative rooms and exhibits. There's a full-size bark teepee. The upper floor displays the geologic history of the gold country. I liked Jenny Lind's practice piano. One fourth grader from Fairfield wrote, "I liked it a lot— and it helped me with my term paper." An Italian stone oven in the Jail Yard is used to bake bread for meetings and social events.

✦ Amador County Museum

108 Church Street, Jackson 95642. (209) 223-6386. Wed.–Sun., 10–4. Donation. **Ages 7 & up.** *Model mine tour for those 8 & over, $1.*

Working scale models of the Kennedy Mine Tailing Wheel No. 2, the Kennedy Mine head frame, and a stamp mill, along with a gold room tracing the history of the area from the discovery of gold to the advent of the hard-rock machinery, and a "Congress of Curiosities"—almost an old-fashioned Sears Roebuck catalog come to life—make this cheerful museum a pleasant stop. The children's bedroom and the chair used by a woman while driving her own covered wagon west are personal favorites. A tape and live narration show one-half-hour long shows how gold was mined.

One mile out of town on North Main Street there are two wheels on each side of the road, 58 feet in diameter. They were used to transport waste from the mine to a reservoir a half-mile away. Almost lost in history, the huge wheels are still impressive.

✦ Chaw'se Indian Grinding Rock State Historic Park

14881 Pine Grove-Volcano Road, Jackson 95689. East of Jackson 9 miles. (209) 296-7488. Day use: $5 per car; senior's car, $4; $20–40 per bus.

Museum open daily, Mon–Fri., 11–3; Sat. & Sun., 10–4; longer in summer. Camping available. Picnic areas. Gift shop. **Ages 6 & up.** *W.*

An 18-minute orientation video is shown in the museum, along with one of the finest collections of Native American artifacts in the state. Rangers offer demonstrations with artifact reproductions.

At first, the huge flat limestone bedrock, 173 feet long by 82 feet wide, looks empty. But then you look closer and discover the petroglyphs scratched in by the Miwok Indians to commemorate their hunting and fishing tales. You'll also see the 1,185 mortar cups where the women ground the seeds, bulbs, fungi, and acorns that served as the staples of their diet. The acorn meal was sifted and washed many times to remove bitterness, then the meal was mixed with water in a basket and heated by hot rocks dropped into the mush. One family would consume 2,000 pounds of acorn a year. This is the largest bedrock mortar in North America. Visitors may also see restorations of a ceremonial roundhouse, a granary, eight bark dwelling houses, and a hand-game house. One of the self-guided trails shows you how plants were used by the North Sierra Miwoks.

❯❯ Chew Kee Store

Fiddletown 95629. 6 miles east of Highway 49 and Plymouth on Fiddletown Road on the way to Volcano. Saturdays, Apr.–Oct., 12–4, and by appt. Free. **Ages 10 & up.**

Built in the 1850s, the Chew Kee Store is believed to be California's only surviving rammed-earth structure of the Gold Rush era. Originally operated as an herb store catering to Chinese miners, it later provided groceries and supplies to Chinese railroad workers. Left to Chew Kee's "adopted" son, Jimmy Chow, in 1913, the store was his home until his death in 1965. With its herb drawers, ceramic rice crocks, prayers, gambling hall receipts, old photos, examining room, living quarters and numerous artifacts of a bygone era, the story remains largely intact as the only remnant of the once thriving Chinese community in Fiddletown. The small store is a remarkable example of history frozen in time, "a fly in amber," since Jimmy Yee lived there from 1913 to 1965 and didn't change a thing.

❯❯ Daffodil Hill

From Fiddletown, take Shake Ridge Road 3 miles north of Volcano. (209) 223-0350/ 296-7048. Daily, mid-Mar.–mid-Apr., 10–5, weather permitting. Free. **All ages.**

Although the hill is open only when the daffodils are in bloom around Easter, this is worth planning for. The McLaughlins, who have owned the farm since 1887, have planted about 300,000 daffodils in many varieties and colors, and, between the flowers and the 11 peacocks walking around, have created an enchanted hillside.

⇢ El Dorado County Historical Museum

104 Placerville Drive, El Dorado County Fairgrounds, P.O. Box 104, Placerville 95667. (916) 621-5865. Wed.–Sat., 10–4; Sun., 12–4. Donation. **Ages 7 & up.** *W.*

"Smokers and chewers will please spit on each other and not on the stove or the floor." This sign is one of many in this big old barn of a museum staffed by caring volunteers. There's an old cash register run by steel balls, lots of dolls, a Civil War viewing casket, two well-stocked country stores, a surrey with a fringe on top, and lots more. Snowshoe Thompson, one of California's pioneering heroes, used to walk all over the Gold Country delivering mail and packages, even in winter. He stored a pair of his extra-long nine-foot skis and a cache of food every five miles along his 80-mile route, so he'd always have a way to keep going "in case." This museum is the proud owner of one set.

Right outside the door a mammoth shaking table, for separating gold from ore, and a walk-in Shay engine No. 4 grab the kids' attention. There are also three locomotives and about 20 pieces of narrow-gauge rolling stock—cabooses and passenger cars.

In town, check out the 1852 **Fountain-Tallman Soda Factory Museum** (524 Main Street. 916-626-0773. Fri., Sat., and Sun., 12–4. Free). The factory made baking soda, not ice cream sodas. Pieces of history of the area are presented in one of the original buildings of the town. You'll find another pair of Snowshoe Thompson's skis here.

⇢ Hangtown's Gold Bug Mine Park

549 Main Street, Placerville 95667. North of downtown Placerville 1 mile, at the end of Bedford Avenue. (916) 642-5238. Apr. 6–May 5 & Nov. 1–Mar. 1, 10–4, weekends. May 6–Oct. 31, 10–4, daily. Adults, $2; ages 12–16, $1 (without the hand-held cassette). Guided tours of the Gold Bug Mine, the Priest Mine, and the Stamp Mill building weekdays, 9–5 by appt. Picnic areas. **Ages 8 & up.**

A ghost of an old gold miner narrates the entertaining, educational audio tour of Gold Bug, the only municipally owned, open-to-the-public gold mine in the world. It was worked as recently as 1947. The longer shaft (a 362-foot-long tunnel) of the mine ends at an exposed gold-bearing quartz vein. The occasional drip of water rings in the cool, eerie silence of the tunnel.

Placerville was originally called Old Hangtown after the Hanging Tree in the center of town. In one week, two Englishmen found $17,000 worth of gold on the main street of town. It is said that the legendary "Hangtown Fry" originated here when a miner walked into a restaurant and demanded a meal that used the three most expensive ingredients at once: eggs, bacon, and oysters.

❖ Marshall Gold Discovery State Historic Park
Highway 49, P.O. Box 265, Coloma 95613. (916) 622-3470. Museum: daily, 10–5, except holidays; shorter in winter. Adults, $1. Park: 8–sunset. Park entry: $5 per car. **Ages 7 & up.** *Partially W.*

"This day some kind of mettle found in the tailrace . . . looks like goald." A millworker noted this in his diary in January 1848. The gold found changed the face of California—and America.

Sutter's Mill has risen again on the American River. Across the highway, a modern museum is dedicated to the discovery of gold and the lives of the gold miners. Maps, tools, mementos, and pictures are displayed against informational panels and dioramas. On the grounds, follow a self-guiding trail to see the mill; a Chinese store; a mine; a monument to James Marshall, the discoverer; a miner's cabin furnished with corn, beans, a scale, a bible, and the miner in bed; a Mormon's cabin; an *arrastre* (ore crusher); and a town that's almost disappeared. If you feel lucky, take your own gold pan and boots.

❖ Placer County Historical Museum
101 Maple Street, County Court House, Auburn 95603. (916) 889-6500. Tues.–Sun., 10–4. Free. Group tours by appt. **Ages 6 & up.** *W.*

This state-of-the art exhibit displays an overview of the history of Placer county. Highlights include a Native American habitat complete with a light and sound presentation, a holographic image of an early miner, and a 10-minute video on the history of the transcontinental highway. A restored sheriff's office, circa 1915, focuses on the early days of the courthouse.

The Pate Native American collection of more than 400 items includes artifacts from California, the Southwest, the Northwest Coast, Alaska, and the Eastern Tribes. The donor wished to show future children the lifestyle and culture of the Native American peoples.

❧ Gold Country Museum

1273 High Street, Gold Country Fairgrounds, Auburn 95603. (916) 889-4143; tours, (916) 889-6500. Tues.–Fri., 10–3:30; weekends, 11–4. Adults, $1, seniors and ages 6–16, 50 cents. Bags of gold and sand for panning are $1.25. **Ages 7 & up.**

Old mining equipment and pioneer mementos recall the early days of Placer County. Kids will like the 45-foot-long walk-through model mine, the operational stamp mill model, the hands-on gold panning stream, and the replica of an early tent saloon complete with faro table. The exhibits change regularly but center on the personality of the '49er.

❧ Bernhard Museum Complex

291 Auburn-Folsom Road, Auburn 95603. (916) 889-4156; tours: (916) 890-6500. Tues.–Fri., 11–3; weekends, 12–4. Adults, $1; ages 6–16 and seniors, 50 cents. Groups by appt. **Ages 8 & up.**

Benjamin Bernhard's restored home, built in 1851 as the Traveler's Rest Hotel, is one of the oldest wooden structures in Placer County. Bernhards have lived here from 1868 to 1957. The house is furnished in the style of the Late Victorian era. The winery houses the Placer Arts League Gallery on the top floor; the wine storage building features exhibits on early wine-growing. The carriage barn houses a variety of rolling stock.

❧ Whitewater Rafting

Beyond Limits Adventures, Inc., P.O. Box 215, Riverbank 95367. (800) 234-RAFT; (209) 869-6060. Call for brochure or reservations. Also Whitewater Voyages, P.O. Box 20400, El Sobrante 94820-0400. (800) 488-RAFT.

California's Gold Country is rich in history and gold. Much of that gold comes from rivers that range from mild to wild. Raft down the American River, where the gold rush began in 1848. The North Fork and Goodwin Canyon sections of the Stanislaus, the Yuba River, outside of Lake Tahoe, the Merced outside of Yosemite Valley, and the rugged Tuolumne rivers beckon for adventure.

Kayaking is also available on the Stanislaus.

❧ Griffith Quarry Park & Museum

Taylor and Rock Springs roads, Penryn 95663. (916) 663-1837. Weekends, 12–4. Free. Group tours: (916) 889-6500. **Ages 8 & up.**

The Quarry in Griffith Park, a relatively new Placer County museum, displays material on the granite works, the Griffith family, and the area.

The park offers three miles of nature trails, picnic places, and views of the old quarry sites.

❯ Forest Hill Divide Museum

24601 Harrison Street, Leroy Botts Memorial Park. Foresthill 95631. (916) 367-3988. Wed., Sat., Sun., 12–4, May–Oct. Free. Groups: (916) 889-6500. **Ages 8 & up.**

The history of the Foresthill and Iowa Hill divides is shown in exhibits featuring material on geology, prehistory, the Gold Rush, transportation, early business, recreation, and early firefighting. There's a scale model of the local logging mill. And special rotating exhibits keep kids coming back for more.

❯ Golden Drift Museum

32820 Main Street, Dutch Flat 95714. (916) 389-2126. Memorial Day–Labor Day; Wed. and weekends, 12–4. Free. Groups: (916) 889-6500. **Ages 8 & up.**

Exhibits explain methods of mining, especially hydraulic mining, and show how railroading, especially the Central Pacific, has affected the local communities, the "Golden Triangle" of Dutch Flat, Gold Run, Alta, and Towle.

❯ North Star Mine Powerhouse Museum

Lower Mill Street, at Empire, Grass Valley 95945. (916) 273-4255. Daily, May–Oct, 10–5. Donation. Picnic areas. **Ages 8 & up.** *W.*

Built by A. D. Foote in 1875, this is the first completely water-powered, compressed-air transmission plant of its kind. The compressed air, generated by 10-ton, 30-foot Pelton waterwheels, furnished power for the mine. The museum houses photos, ore specimens, safes, dioramas and models of the mines, an assaying laboratory, and a working Cornish pump. The star of the show is the 30-foot Pelton wheel itself.

❯ Grass Valley Museum

410 South Church at Chapel Street, Grass Valley 95945. (916) 273-1928. Tues.–Fri., 12–3; weekends, 10–3. Donation. **Ages 8 & up.** *W.*

The orphanage of the Holy Angels from 1865 to 1932 is now a quiet museum that displays antique clothing, an 1880s doctor's room, school rooms, and lace collection. The chapel is peaceful. There are lovely oil paintings in the Victorian era parlor. The rose garden in back is splendid.

To relive a bit of history, have a Cornish pasty at one of the bakeries in town. The miners called these meat and potato pies "letters from home." Grass Valley is a nicely preserved Gold Rush town. While browsing, you may want to see the homes of Lola Montez and Lotta Crabtree on Mill Street. Lola was a Bavarian singer, dancer, and king's favorite who fled to America in 1853 when her king fell from power. Lotta Crabtree was Lola's protégée and soon became famous, rich, and beloved by the American public. Lola's home is open to the public (daily in summer, 12–4. Free).

❧ Empire Mine State Historic Park
10791 East Empire Street, Grass Valley 95945. (916) 273-8522. Daily except Thanksgiving, Christmas, and New Year's Day, 10–5. Adults, $2; children, $1; under 6, free. Group tours. **Ages 7 & up.** *Partially W.*

Keeping alive the story of hard-rock gold mining and its significance in California's history, the Empire is the oldest, largest, and richest gold mine in the area. Some of the 20 stopping points along the mine's self-guided tour are in ruins, and the sites are being reconstructed. The William Bourn family "cottage" is furnished and also open for tours. Movies, tours, and Living History Days will help excite your imagination, so you'll think of the hundreds of Cornish miners who dug the 367 miles of tunnels, almost 11,000 feet deep (on an incline), and the mules that pulled the ore trains through the tunnels. Enterprising souls will want to know that there's still gold there to be gotten.

❧ Museum of Ancient and Modern Art
Wildwood Business Center, 11392 Pleasant Valley Road, 1 mile off Highway 20 West, P.O. Box 975, Penn Valley 95946. (916) 432-3080. Daily, 12–5; class for children, Saturday, 10–12. Tours by appt. Free. **Ages 6 & up.** *W.*

Kids love mummies, and they won't be disappointed in the one displayed here. The Museum of Ancient and Modern Art is a multifaceted museum tucked away in the Sierra foothills. Its prestigious art book collections contain etchings, engravings, and woodcuts printed as early as 1529 and illustrate the history of printing. The collection of African masks and statues represents over 20 different tribes from eight different countries. The large collection of 18th Dynasty Egypt is most intriguing to youngsters. Other notable artifacts, such as statues, pottery, masks, and objects of daily life, are from ancient Sumer, Ur, Assyria, Mesopotamia, Carthage, Alexandria, the Ottoman Empire, Persia, Phoenicia, and Byzantium.

The ancient jewelry collection, which spans thousands of years of gold-smithing techniques, dates from Neolithic to historical times.

There's also a beautiful diorama with real encased dinosaur bones as well as other dinosaur artifacts. Changing art exhibits can focus on anything from the work of local artists or beautiful butterflies and beastly bugs to an 11th-century illuminated manuscript.

Be sure to ask for directions to Penn Valley's covered bridges, a treat for all.

❥ Bridgeport Covered Bridge

Interstate 80 east to Highway 49, Highway 49 to State 20, 10 miles to Pleasant Valley Road, turn right and drive 9 miles to Bridgeport. For spring through fall schedules of bridge tours, gold panning expeditions, and trail maps, call (916) 432-2546. Free. **Ages 7 & up.**

California has 12 covered bridges and this, spanning the Yuba River, is the longest single-span covered bridge in the world today. Built in 1862, the 256-foot-long bridge allows no motor traffic, so it's a hidden oasis for walks, playing on the beach, picnicking, or walking along forest trails. The original builder, sawmill owner David Wood, collected tolls of $1 for a one-horse buggy and up to $6 for an eight-mule team.

❥ The Firehouse Museum

Firehouse No. 1, Nevada County Historical Society, Main and Commercial streets, Nevada City 95959. (916) 265-5468. Daily, 11–4 in summer; in winter: Mon., 1–2:30; Tues., 11–4; Thurs.–Sun., 11–4. Donation. **Ages 7 & up.**

Located in one of the quaint town's most photogenic buildings, the museum has been completely refurbished. Maidu Indian artifacts, relics of the Donner party, children's toys and books, a Chinese altar, showshoes for horses, a photograph of a miner with the image of himself as a 12-year-old appearing mysteriously on the film, and pioneer memories fill the space.

Nevada City, the best of the gold-mining towns, is a thriving community with the feel of turn-of-the-century Gold Country. Walking along the small streets is a pleasure. Visitors may want to stop at the **Orey Victorian Tour House** (401 North York Street. 916-265-9250), a pretty pink Victorian.

❥ Malakoff Diggins State Historic Park

23579 North Bloomfield Road, Nevada City 95959. North on Highway 49, 11 miles from Nevada City. Turn right on Tyler-Foote Road, travel 17 miles on the paved road and turn right on Derbec Road at the entrance sign. (916) 265-2740. Museum: daily, in summer, 10–5; winter weekends, 10–4.

Tours by appt. Campsites, $7 in winter; $10 in summer. Cabins, $15 in winter; $20 in summer. Day use: $5 per car. Picnicking. **Ages 7 & up.**

Many millions of dollars worth of gold poured from these huge "hydraulic diggins." A small sign tells visitors that there's still enough gold left here, and on other sites around the area, to mine $12 million annually for the next 50 years. This park is a silent monument to the hydraulic miners. The museum displays a model of the monitor used in gold mines and shows how hydraulic mining worked. Photos of the two-mile Bloomfield tunnel, the 12-foot-long miners' skis, a portable undertaker's table, mementos of the Chinese miners, and an old-time bar and poker room are some of the highlights. Visitors can also see a drugstore, a general store, and a livery filled with wagons. Films round out the experience.

❯❯ Kentucky Mine Museum & Sierra County Historical Park and Museum

Highway 49, P.O. Box 260, Sierra City 96125. North of Sierra City 1 mile. (916) 862-1310. Memorial Day–Sept. 30, Wed.–Sun., 10–5. Also weekends in Oct. Guided stamp-mill tour, $4; junior rate for tours, half price; 12 and under, free with parent. Museum: $1. **Ages 7 & up.**

Among the Northern Mines, the Kentucky Mine is one of the earliest of the hard-rock type mine, dating from 1854. The reconstructed stamp mill, based on sections built in the 1860s and 1880s, was completed in 1933. It is one of the only stamp mills in the area that is still operable with the original machinery intact. The informative guided tour begins at the opening of the mine and follows the gold milling process from beginning to end. The Pelton waterwheels still work, too! The museum constantly changes its displays on Sierra County's past, which include mining equipment, logging machinery, skis, clothing and household articles, local minerals, wildflowers, and other natural history items. There are also exhibits on the early Chinese and the Maidu Indians, and a school room. Picnic facilities are available. Concerts are held in the outdoor amphitheater in July and August.

❯❯ Alleghany Mining Museum

356 Main Street, P.O. Box 907, Alleghany 95910. (916) 287-3330. Weekends, Memorial Day to Labor Day. Tours intermittent in winter. **Ages 10 & up.**

The Alleghany Supply Company building, originally a livery stable and, recently, the town's general store, is being restored as a museum. A 3-D model of the Sixteen-to-One Mine is being completed. Until everything is in order, the museum will give tours to raise funds and serve the community. This is what backwoods mining life was really like. One tour ($25) covers the mine site, shop and mill buildings, dry room, and videos. The Underground Tour ($95) gets you down in a working underground gold mine, rubbing elbows with real gold miners who are proud to have links to the past.

❯❯ Forest City

Forest City. Up Ridge Road from Highway 49 in Yuba City, 15 miles. One mile on paved road on the left. Write: Forest City Historical Association, Alleghany 95910. (916) 287-3413/ 287-3207. Weekends, 12–4, Memorial Day to Labor Day & by Appt. Free. **Ages 9 & up.**

The tiny town of Forest City not only has a museum, it *is* a museum, since most of the buildings date from the 1800s. The museum itself is located in the 1883 Dance Hall. Artifacts from the barber shop, saloon, and billiard hall that occupied the first floor are on display, as well as other items of 19th-century mining town life, including a forge, a Pelton wheel, and the gold scales used by the Forest City Meat Market.

❯❯ Downieville Museum & Foundry

Main Street, on Highway 49 at mile marker SIE-17. The foundry is across the Downie River on Pearl Street. P.O. Box 484, Downieville 95936. (916) 289-3261. Daily, May–Oct., 10–5. Foundry tours, by reservation, include an audio tour of old Downieville, a meal, and a look into several historic structures. **Ages 12 & up.**

The Downieville museum building dates to 1832 and was originally a store and gambling hall for the Chinese who settled in the community. Its construction of mortarless schist rock saved it from the many catastrophic fires that periodically razed the town. For half a century, until the 1930s, it was a grocery store run by the Meroux family. Today it depicts life in the area from Gold Rush days to the present. Mining implements, Indian artifacts, household articles, and lodge regalia are exhibited, along with a one-sixth scale model stamp mill and an ore-grinding *arrastra*.

The Foundry, built in 1855, is a large wooden building that houses an incredibly detailed HO-scale model of turn-of-the-century Downieville, "Queen of the Northern Mother Lode." Logging and mining exhibits include slides, videos, photographs, and a replica of the furnace and operation of the foundry believed to be the oldest in the Mother Lode.

❯❯ Loyalton Museum

Highway 49, mile marker SIE-61 on Sierra County Route A24 north to edge of town. Loyalton Community Hall, just past Loyalton Elementary School.

(916) 993-6754. Wed.–Fri., 9–2; weekends, 11–4, later in summer. Free.
Ages 10 & up.

The Loyalton Catholic Church is a small museum that displays 19th-century clothing and housewares, wooden skis, and a collection of glass from the 1930s. Handmade farm implements from the late 1800s and a "donkey," or logging steam engine, represent the agriculture and timber industries. There are also Washoe baskets, arrowheads, and photographs.

❧ Plumas–Eureka State Park Museum

310 Johnsville Road, off county road A-14, Blairsden 96103. (916) 836-2380. Museum: daily, 8–4, in summer; weekends in winter when staff is available. Adults, $2; ages 6–12, $1. **Ages 7 & up.** *W.*

The site of hardrock gold mining, there are approximately 67 miles of mining shafts inside Eureka Peak. Birdwatchers see Caliope humming-birds as well as pileated woodpeckers in early summer. Museum displays include hard-rock mining equipment, an assay office, models of a stamp mill and an arrastre, natural history exhibits, and pioneer life remembrances. The out-buildings are fun, too.

❧ Plumas County Museum

500 Jackson, behind the Courthouse, Quincy 95971. (916) 283-6320. Mon.–Fri., 8–5, May–Sept.; Sat. & Sun. 10–4. Adults $1, ages 12–17, 50 cents. **Ages 7 & up.** *W.*

This "living museum" depicts local history with artifacts and displays about the lumbering, mining, and agricultural work that brought settlers to Plumas County. A large Maidu Indian basket collection centers the rotating exhibits. The three-story, 1878 Coburn-Variel home adjacent to the museum is restored and available for tour. Kayla wrote, "I liked the telephones a lot because they are different from the ones that we have right now. I also liked the Coburn House. There is lots of neat stuff in it. I liked how you cook waffles."

❧ Donner Memorial State Park

12593 Donner Pass Road, Donner Lake, Truckee 96161. (916) 582-7892. Daily, 10–4. Adults, $2; ages 6–12, $1. **Ages 8 & up.** *W.*

During the disastrous winter of 1846, a party of 81 people stranded in this area tried to make it through the mountains to California. Only 49 people survived, and some of the survivors allegedly resorted to cannibalism. The settling of the Sierra Nevada and the tragic story of the Donner party are told with relics, dioramas, pictures, and models that are combined with natural history and Emigrant Trail history in The Emigrant Trail Museum. The pedestal of the memorial to the Donner Party is 22 feet high—as high as the early snowfall that trapped them. Chinese railroad workers, the "Big Four" railroad tycoons, miners, and mountain men are also remembered here, as well as Native Americans. Picnic areas, camp sites, and guided hikes are available. My favorite memento: the replica of Patty Reed's doll.

❖ Sierra Nevada Children's Museum
11400 Donner Pass Road, Truckee 96161. (916) 587-KIDS. Wed.–Sat., 10–4. Parties & groups by reservation. $3. **Ages 7-13.** *W.*

Kids will enjoy the interactive hands-on activities in this engaging setting. There are rotating exhibits such as one called "Kids in Space." Children can don an engineer's cap and send the G gauge Truckee Model Railroad on its way across the mountain. They can learn how to listen to the sounds of the forest at night and study at the computer center.

❖ Lake Tahoe
Lake Tahoe Visitors Authority, 1156 Ski Run Boulevard, South Lake Tahoe 96150. (916) 544-5050/(800) AT-TAHOE. North Tahoe Visitors & Convention Bureau, P.O. Box 5578, Tahoe City 95730. (916) 583-3494. Road conditions: (800) 427-7623. Information: (916) 544-5050. Lake Tahoe magazine lists camping, dining, sporting, and lodging information, and other services. **All ages.**

Lake Tahoe is justifiably world famous for its crystal-clear water and beautiful setting. It was gouged from the crown of the Sierra during the Ice Age and named, in the language of the Washoe tribe, "Big Water." Visitors can ski, water ski, boat, bike, ride, swim (only in August unless you're a polar bear), surf, sun, golf, windsail, hike, and enjoy the forest wilderness and the invigorating clarity of the air and sunshine.

For an exhilarating overall picture, ride the **Scenic Aerial Tram** (800-2-HEAVEN/702-586-7000), a spectacular mile-long ride to the top of Heavenly, 2,000 feet high. From there you can hike the Tahoe Vista Trail by yourself or with a guided tour or have brunch, lunch, or dinner. To get there, ride the Nifty 50 Trolly from the South Shore (916-541-6328).

Naturalist programs are given on summer weekends in the D. L. Bliss and Emerald Bay state parks and at Camp Richardson. The U.S. Forest Service **Taylor Creek Stream Profile Chamber** near Camp Richardson is part of the El Dorado National Forest Visitors Center (daily, 10–5). You can take one of the self-guided nature walks through a mountain meadow and marsh and even down into the chamber for a fish-eye view of a mountain stream. Recorded messages help identify the fish and plants in front of you.

Vikingsholm Castle, a 38-room Nordic fortress (Emerald Bay State Park, P.O. Box 266, Tahoma 96142. 916-525-7277/541-3030. Daily, 10–4, mid-June–Labor Day) on Emerald Bay's southwest shore is open to the public.

The Ehrman Mansion (Sugar Pine Point, Highway 89, Tahoma 96142. Summer tours, 11–4. Fee), is an outstanding example of turn-of-the-century Lake Tahoe architecture.

The **Gatekeeper's Log Cabin Museum** (130 West Lake Boulevard, Tahoe City 95730. 916-583-1762. Daily, spring to fall) displays Washoe and Paiute artifacts, local minerals and fossils, and other Tahoe memorabilia.

On the lake, you can sightsee from the **Tahoe Queen**'s glass bottom boat (916-541-3364. Jun–Oct., 11 A.M., 1:30 and 3:55 P.M.; noon daily in winter. Adults, $13; ages 11 and under, $6) or take the **MS Dixie** (702-588-3508/882-0786), a Mississippi paddlewheeler that shows you another view of Emerald Bay. The *Dixie* also does a breakfast cruise to Glenbrook. Other boats cruise the blue waters as well.

In summer, you can also take a balloon ride with **Lake Tahoe Balloons** (800-872-9294/916-544-1221).

The **Lake Tahoe Historical Society Log Cabin Museum** (3058 U.S. 50/Lake Tahoe Boulevard, or P.O. Box 404, South Lake Tahoe 96150. 916-541-5458. Daily, 10–4 in summer) features artifacts from Tahoe's early days, including Washoe Indian basketry, photos, pioneer implements and a model of the historic SS *Tahoe* and the area's oldest building.

The Visitors Center in Truckee also offers information on dining, camping, sights, accomodations, skiing, transit, horseback riding, sleigh and hay rides, snowmobile rental, skating, wildlife scenic tours, four-wheel adventures, watersports, parasailing, and events. Pioneer belongings, railroad items, and historic photos decorate the renovated 1896 Southern Pacific Depot (916-587-2757).

The **Western America Ski Sports Museum** (Boreal Ski Area, Castle Peak exit on Interstate 80, P.O. Box 729, Soda Springs 95728. 916-426-3313. Tues.–Fri., 12–4; Sat–Sun., 11–5. Free) features ski exhibits from 1860 to the present, vintage ski movies, and artifacts of Snowshoe Thompson.

Venture to the Nevada side of the lake for a visit to the **Ponderosa Ranch** at Incline Village (100 Ponderosa Ranch Road, Incline Village, off Highway 28 on the North Shore, NV 89451. 702-831-0691. Daily,

9:30–5, late April through October, weather permitting) to see the Cartwright Ranch House, Hoss's Mystery Mine & Shootin' Gallery, an entire Frontier Town, an antique car and carriage museum, a petting zoo in the Ponderosa barnyard, and other attractions. There are breakfast haywagon rides through the tall timber.

The Fresno Area and Madera County

Some people think that Fresno exists only as a stopping-off place from San Francisco to Los Angeles, but it's a big, booming city. The trip to Fresno is four hours by car from San Francisco, but there are so many motels you can usually be assured of a room when you arrive. Surrounded by orchards and rich farmland, pretty lakes, and an impressive irrigation system, Fresno is also the gateway to Sierra National Forest and Sequoia, Kings Canyon, and Yosemite national parks. Hiking, skiing, spelunking, and wandering through groves of the largest living things on earth, the giant Sequoia redwoods, are all available within 40 minutes' drive. Closer to Fresno, seven lakes offer sailing, fishing, houseboating, waterskiing, and windsurfing.

➢ R. C. Baker Memorial Museum

297 West Elm, Coalinga 93210. (209) 935-1914. Mon.–Fri., 10–12 & 1–5; Sat., 11–5; Sun., 1–5. Donation. **Ages 7 & up.**

"I enjoyed going to your museum in Coalinga. I liked the photos of the earthquake, I loved those boxing cards that were $100 a card. I liked the old cameras, and that 1928 one dollar bill. I thought the car there was neat. I bet that would cost a lot of money. I liked all the different kinds of barbed wire. Speaking of barbed, I thought the barber or dentist chair was neat. And the big fossil was awesome. The uniforms and the guns were radical. The counting machines were weird, but I liked them too. One of the things that I liked the most was the telephone booth. I enjoyed the different rooms with dolls. But the thing I liked most about your museum was everything. Your museum was the best museum I have ever went to. Keep up the good work." This is the recommendation of Brandon, a visitor from Akers Elementary School.

The remodeled R. C. Baker Museum, named in honor of a Coalinga pioneer, oilman, and inventor, shows both the natural and man-made history of Coalinga. Visitors to Coalinga will enjoy a drive nine miles north on Highways 33 and 198 past the Grasshopper oil pumps—oil-field characters painted in many colors to look like clowns, birds, and animals.

➢ San Luis Reservoir

Romero Overlook, Highway 152, 15 miles west of Los Banos. (209) 826-1196. Daily, 9–5. Closed major holidays. Free. **Ages 10 & up.**

In the Romero Overlook on the reservoir, pictures, graphic wall displays, movies, and slide shows tell the story of the State Water Project and the Federal Central Valley Project, and how they work together at the San

Luis Complex. Telescopes at the center offer a spectacular view of the area. The State Water Resources guides who staff the Visitors Center love to explain things.

⇶ Tulare County Museum

27000 South Mooney Boulevard, Mooney Grove Park, Visalia 93277. (209) 733-6616. Fall and spring: Thurs.–Mon., 10–4. Winter weekends, 10–4. Summer: weekdays except Tues., 10–4; weekends, 12–6. Tours by reservation. Adults, $2; children, $1. **Ages 6 & up.** *W.*

"End of the Trail," the bronze sculpture by James Earl Fraser portraying a tired Indian on a pony—once the most copied piece of art in the world—is the star attraction at this lively museum spread throughout 11 buildings. That sculpture was first exhibited in San Francisco in 1915 at the Panama-Pacific Exposition. A one-room schoolhouse, newspaper and dental office, Yokuts Indian collection, and rooms from turn-of-the-century homes recreate the past. Furniture, clothes, cooking utensils, toys, baskets, World War I uniforms, and early farm machinery are also on exhibit.

The 143-acre park offers picnic arbors and oak trees, boating, skateboard tracks, and more.

⇶ Tulare Historical Museum

444 West Tulare Avenue, P.O. Box 248, Tulare 93275. (209) 686-2074. Thurs.–Sat., 10–4; Sun., 12:30–4. Donation. **Ages 8 & up.** *W.*

"Take a trip back in time" is the theme of this historic museum. You're greeted at the door by a life-size horse and doctor's buggy, then step back to a Yokuts village around Tulare Lake. Walk through the coming of the railroad, the lives of some of the early settlers, the three great fires that swept Tulare during its first 14 years, and the incorporation of the city. Mini-replicas of rooms in an early Tulare home and local businesses revivify a time gone by. Sports fans will like the statue of Olympian Bob Mathias.

⇶ Boyden Cavern

Kings Canyon National Park, Highway 180, 77 miles east of Fresno. (209) 736-2708. P.O. Box 78, Vallecito 95251. June–Sept., daily, 10–5; May & Oct., daily, 11–4. Adults, $6; children, 6–12, $3; seniors, $5.50. **Ages 6 & up.**

A 45-minute tour takes you into a wondrous world deep beneath the 2,000-foot-high marble walls of the famous Kings Gates. Massive stalagmites, delicate stalactites, and splendid arrays of crystalline formations defy description. Boyden Cavern is in the deepest canyon in the United States.

⇒ Clovis Big Creek Historical Museum

401 Pollasky Avenue, Clovis 93257. (209) 297-8033. Fri. & Sat, 11–3; in summer: Fri. 5–9 & by reservation. Free. **Ages 6 & up.**

This museum, in an old bank, is crammed with something for everyone. The bank is famous for being the first one in which nails were used in a robbery. The robbers threw nails out of their car (in the 1920s) to give every car in pursuit flat tires. Kids still get a thrill out of walking inside the bank vault. Joaquin Murietta's shotgun, baseball great Ty Cobb's letters, the boots Festus wore on the TV show *Gunsmoke*, Indian artifacts, a holocaust exhibit, a military exhibit, and more crowd the building. There are Clovis High School pictures from 1918 to 1964. Youngsters are particularly fascinated by the flume that swept lumber to Shaver Lake.

⇒ Wild Water Adventures

11413 E. Shaw Avenue, Clovis 93611-8859. Exit Highway 99 at Shaw Avenue in Fresno; park is 7 miles east of Clovis Avenue. (209) 299-WILD. All-day admission, $18.95; 3 years old to 48 inches high, $14.95; seniors, $16.95. After 4 P.M., $13.95 and $9.95. Free parking. Special barbecue days. Seasonal hours. **All ages.** *W.*

This 50-acre park has picnic spots with a great view of the Sierra mountains, a fishing lake, and a toddler's wading pool. There's a pool with waves and a wet bumper cars area, body surfing areas, speed slides, and a scary Black Hole.

⇒ Porterville Historical Museum

257 North D Street, Porterville 93257. (209) 784-2053. Thurs., Fri., & Sat., 10–4, and by appt. Free. **Ages 5 & up.** *W.*

The main room of the museum, a former Southern Pacific Railroad station waiting room, houses an interesting collection of Yokuts Indian baskets and other artifacts along with a collection of mounted birds and animals. Cattle industry memorabilia, including branding irons, barbed wire, and saddles and tack, are in the Wilcox Room. A graciously furnished turn-of-the-century bedroom, a lovely collection of glassware and china, and vignettes of a drugstore, dentist's office, and lawyer's office are in the arcade and baggage room areas of the museum. Outdoor exhibits include antique farm equipment, fire engines, a mill wagon, an oil wagon, a baggage wagon, a broom-making machine and a fully restored blacksmith shop.

Zalud House

393 North Morton, at Hockett, Porterville 93257. (209) 782-7548. Wed.–Sat., 10–4; Sun., 2–4. Adults, $1; children, 50 cents. Groups by appt. **Ages 8 & up.**

One of the state's unsung treasures is this remarkably preserved and lovingly cared for Victorian home. Pearle Zalud was born in 1884 and lived there until her death in 1970. Her world tour at age 19 was the first of many. The home bears the beautiful fruits of her worldwide souvenir hunting. The house is exactly as she left it—which is exactly as her father liked it in 1912, when her mother died. The art and furnishings, the hats, dolls, collars and laces, the framed antique valentines, and the family photos all create a house that is a home.

Since there was so much left in the closets, the curator changes the exhibits in the rooms with the seasons. The beautiful flower gardens outside are available for private parties and weddings. Kids love the story of Pearle's brother Edward, a cowboy who was killed while riding, and her brother-in-law William, who was shot to death by a woman in the Porterville Pioneer Hotel in 1917. The chair with the bullet hole is upstairs.

Third-grader Carrie wrote, "Thanks for taking us through the Zalud House. It was fun. Some people say that it is haunted but I don't think it is because it is beautiful. And I wish that I lived there."

Colonel Allensworth State Historic Park

Allensworth. On Highway 43, 20 miles north of Wasco; on Highway 99, 9 miles west of Earlimart. (805) 849-3433. Visitor center open daily, 10–4:30, except Thanksgiving, Christmas & New Year's Day. Parking fee, $3. Camping available. To schedule a tour, write: 4129 Palmer Avenue, P.O. Box 148, Allensworth-Earlimart 93219. **Ages 5 & up.**

The only California town to be founded, financed, and governed by and for African Americans is now perpetuated for the public's use and enjoyment. It is dedicated to the spirit of Colonel Allen Allensworth, who escaped slavery and served with the Union Army during the Civil War. When he retired in 1906, he held the rank of Lt. Colonel and was the highest ranking African-American officer in the U.S. military. A Visitors Center with exhibits and films, picnic area, and two museums, the colonel's residence, and the original schoolhouse are open to the public upon request, as is the 15-unit campground. The Mary Dickinson Memorial Library is open now, along with the Morris Smith House.

⇨ Pioneer Village Museum

Art Gonzales Parkway, adjoining Highway 99, Selma. (Mail: 1814 Tucker, 93662.) (209) 896-4929. Weekends, 9–4; weekdays, 8:30–5; also "seasonal hours." Adults, $2; seniors, $1.50; children, 50 cents. Groups by appt. **Ages 7 & up.** *W.*

Victorian homes and cherished buildings are being moved to, and restored in, this museum-in-progress. Visitors walk through a museum store and out on the grounds to a 1904 Victorian Queen Anne, the old barn built by a Civil War veteran, the Ungar Opera House, Selma's 1887 Southern Pacific Depot, and a 1901 Little Red School House, steepled church, doctor's office, barber shop, pottery shop, and newspaper office.

⇨ Fort Roosevelt Science Center

870 West Davis, P.O. Box 164, Hanford 93202. (209) 582-8970. By appt. only. Adults, $2; children, $1.25. Picnic areas, overnights, and birthday parties. **All ages.**

Local businesses and families have worked with the California Department of Fish and Game to set up this natural history museum and rehabilitation center. The museum itself is in the 1893 Hanford Railroad Freight Depot. There's an old two-story log cabin, covered wagons, a windmill, and a water wheel by the pond. There's an adopt-an-animal program, and on-site educators really get the youngsters involved with the world around them.

⇨ Kearney Mansion & Kearney Park

7160 West Kearney Boulevard, Fresno 93706. Kearney Park, 7 miles west of downtown Fresno. (209) 441-0862. Fri.–Sun., 1–4. Tours at 1, 2, and 3. Adults, $4; seniors, students & children, $2. Groups by appt. Gift shop. **Ages 8 & up.**

Built between 1900 and 1903, the home of M. Theo Kearney, pioneer Fresno land developer and raisin baron, has preserved many of the original furnishings, including European wallpapers, art nouveau light fixtures, and replicas of original carpets and wallpapers. The adjoining servants' quarters houses the ranch kitchen and museum store. A new educational center offers special programs for youngsters. The 225-acre park surrounding it features picnic and playground facilities.

❖ Discovery Center

1944 North Winery Avenue, Fresno 93703. Take Highway 9 to McKinley, then east to North Winery Avenue. (209) 251-5531. Tues.–Sat., 10–4; Sun, 12–4. Adults, $3; ages 3–16, $2. Group rates. Summer science camp and astronomy program. Picnic areas and playgrounds. Gift shop. **All ages.** *W.*

This hands-on science center helps children try things out for themselves. There's a bubble machine, a tree that lights up by sound, pipe phones, an electricity learning lab, a Gemini space capsule, and hands-on table stations. The Indian room has a Yokut hut and shows the many things that Indians have introduced to civilization. Dioramas of the animal and vegetable life of the valley and streams are also fun to look at. Outside, there's a little zoo of local animals, a desert tortoise colony, and a pond for exploring. Children have a great time here.

❖ Fresno Arts Museum

2233 North First Street, in Radio Park, between Clinton and McKinley Avenues, Fresno 93703. (209) 485-4810. Tues.–Fri., 10–5; weekends, 12–5. Adults, $2; students and seniors, $1. Tuesdays free. Tours by reservation. Gift shop. **Ages 8 & up.** *W.*

This forum for the arts of the 19th and 20th centuries, with revolving exhibits, classes, planned tours, and lectures, offers artists-in-residence and permanent collections of Mexican art and French Post-Impressionist graphics.

❖ Meux Home Museum

1007 R Street at Tulare, P.O. Box 70, Fresno 93707. (209) 233-8007. Fri.–Sun., 12–3:30. Adults, $3; ages 13–17, $2; ages 5–12, $1. Groups by appt: 209-431-1926. Story-telling afternoons. Gift shop. **Ages 5 & up.** *Partially W.*

The docents in this sweet blue-and-white Queen Anne enjoy talking about Victorian family life and explaining how things worked back then. Special events such as the Teddy Bears' picnic make this a class favorite. Indeed, Fresno schoolchildren were some of the many contributors to the refurbishment of this elegant family home. A plaque thanks them for the sponsorship of the breezeway in the kitchen area. Visitors enjoy Dr. Thomas R. Meux's Confederate uniform and surgical tools as well as his portrait in a Rhett Butler mustache, and the clothing, jewelry, wedding gowns, and photographs.

❯❯ Library Museum of Germans from Russia

*3233 North West Avenue, Fresno 93705. (209) 229-8287. Mon.–Fri.,
12–4; Sat., 9:30–12. Groups by appt. Free.* **Ages 10 & up.** *W.*

The Central California Chapter of the American Historical Society
of Germans from Russia offers genealogy workshops, a large assortment
of maps, and discussions about the folklore of their forefathers. The collection of art, literature, and folklore is housed in an old city firehouse. Exhibits include photographs and items brought from the Soviet Union as
well as artifacts of early Fresno immigrants.

The nearby **African-American Historical & Cultural Museum of
the San Joaquin Valley** (1857 Fulton Street. 209-268-7102) has started
its organization with special lectures and theatrical and musical events.

❯❯ Fresno Metropolitan Museum of Art, History and Science

*1555 Van Ness Avenue, Fresno 93721. (209) 441-1444. Wed., 11–7,
free; Thurs.–Sun., 11–5. Adults, $3; seniors $2; students, $1.50. Tours by
appt.* **Ages 5 & up.** *W.*

Explore art, history, and science in the San Joaquin Valley's largest
museum. Major multimedia exhibits change regularly. The Met features a
permanent hands-on center of science and art with 40 interactive exhibits.
In this "playground for the mind," children can weave a web of lightning
from their fingertips, walk away from their shadows, and become strong
enough to bend light. The museum also has a permanent exhibition devoted to the history of the early Armenians in the area. It stars Academy
Award-winning author William Saroyan, who wrote, "If you want to
behold a truly religious man in action, go to Fresno and watch a farmer
watering his trees, vines, and plants."

In a room full of Yosemite stagecoaches and wagons, you can
read eyewitness accounts such as this man's, from 1884: ". . . we tried
all possible devices to steady ourselves, and to avoid concussion of the
spine, which really appeared inevitable . . . at last we entered the true
forest belt and anything more beautiful you cannot conceive. We forgot
our bumps and bruises in sheer delight. Oh the loveliness of the pines
and cedars . . ."

❯❯ Fresno Zoo & Rotary Kids Country: Storyland and Playland

*894 West Belmont Avenue, Roeding Park, Fresno 93728. Freeway 99
between Olive and Belmont. (209) 492-2671. Zoo: ages 5–11, $2; ages 12–*

61, $4.50, over 62, $3. Daily, Nov.–Feb., 10–4; March–Oct, 9–5.
Groups: 264-2235. **All ages.** *W. Storyland: ages 3–12, $1.75; ages 12–*
61, $2.75; over 62, $2.25. Spring and fall weekends and holidays, 10–5.
Closed Dec. & Jan. May 1–Labor Day, 10–5. **Ages 2–11.** *Playland: 486-*
2124. Prices and hours vary depending on season; usually, 10–5 when school's
out. Boating costs also vary. **Ages 2–13.**

The Fresno Zoo is one of the most progressive in the country. In the
South American Tropical Rain Forest Exhibit, visitors walk through a
lush habitat of free-flying birds and small primates. A new favorite is the
Golden lion tamarin, a tiny, fluffy, fierce-looking monkey. The computerized state-of-the-art reptile house has been extremely successful in breed-
ing almost-extinct animals. The elephants thrive in the waterfall and deep
pool in their section. Winding paths and lush foliage add to the pleasure
of a stroll through the zoo, as does the "Ask Me!" cart program. Kids
especially like meeting hawks and owls face to face when the docent takes
them out of their cages for discussions with visitors. Enjoy birds from
Australia in the Australian aviary.

In Storyland, talking storybook keys ($1.50) persuade the blue cater-
pillar to tell eight classic fairy tales. Then when children have heard the
stories, they can go on to visit the heroes of the tales. They can play in
King Arthur's castle, Red Riding Hood's Grandmother's cottage, or Mr.
Toad's cart, or they can talk to Simple Simon's pie man, the knaves of
Alice's court, or Little Miss Muffet and Winnie the Pooh.

Children will find Playland irresistible. There's a roller coaster, a
Ferris wheel, a kiddie car ride, a scenic miniature train ride, and a merry-
go-round. Paddle boats, motor boats, and rowboats to rent by the hour on
Lake Washington attract the seaworthy, and there are concessions and
picnic areas.

Fort Millerton, also in the park (weekends, May 1–Sept. 30, 1–4.
Donation), houses a small exhibit of pioneer life, with antique toys, lumber tools, and the medical kit of Fresno's first doctor.

➤ San Joaquin Fish Hatchery

Friant 93626. Off Highway 41, 13 miles northeast of Fresno. (209) 822-
2374. Daily, 8–4:30; in summer, 7:30–4. Free. **All ages.**

There are more fish in this one spot than you'll ever see again: more
than two million trout in sizes that range from pinhead to fingerlings
ready to catch are raised in these trout-hatching ponds. Four times a day
the fish are fed high-protein dry pellets. When they're a year old and
10 inches long, they're taken in tanks by plane and truck to the heavily

fished lakes and streams of California. But while they're here, it's really
fun to walk along the 48 ponds and watch the fish leap over and slide
down the little dams between them. A photo exhibit explains about trout
habits and the trout-seeding program.

California's Fish Hatchery and Planting Program runs 22 hatcheries,
most open to the public. Call your local Fish and Game Department office
for information on the one nearest you.

⇨ Friant Dam & Millerton Lake State Recreational Area

*P.O. Box 267, Friant 93626. Off Highway 41, north of Fresno. (209)
822-2332. Daily, daylight hours. Park entry, $6 per car.*

Fed by Sierra snows, the waters of Millerton Lake are released into
the Friant-Kern and Madera irrigation canals to feed the rich croplands
of Fresno and Madera counties. The dam is 319 feet high and 3,488 feet
long, with a reservoir capacity of 520,000 acre feet. You can walk halfway
across the dam while guides tell you the history of the project.

⇨ Madera County Museum

*210 West Yosemite, P.O. Box 478, Madera 93637. (209) 673-0291. Off
Highway 99, 17 miles north of Fresno. Tues., 9–12 and weekends, 1–4:30
and by appt. Free.* **Ages 6 & up.**

This meticulous museum tells the story of Madera County and its
people. Third-grader Patrick wrote: "Thank you for letting us come. I saw
a lot of interesting rooms. I saw a lot of great ones. The best ones are mining, store, parlor, saloon, war and peace, Native Americans, and downtown." Three floors of displays in this 1900 granite courthouse emphasize
the county's mining, logging, and agricultural history. There's a miner's
cabin, a country store, a blacksmith shop, and an amazing section of flume
from the Madera Sugar Pine Lumber Company. The "downtown" room
shows what the city looked like in 1900 and even has a stagecoach in
which people rode to Yosemite Park.

⇨ Sierra Mono Museum

*P.O. Box 275, North Folk 93643. At the intersection of Roads 225 and
228, off Highway 41 from Fresno toward Bass Lake. (209) 877-2115.
Mon.–Sat., 9–4, and by appt. Adults, $2; high schoolers, $1; seniors, $1.50;
grade schoolers, 75 cents. Gift shop.* **Ages 3 & up.** *W.*

The only Indian museum in California owned and operated by an
Indian tribe without any outside help, the Sierra Mono Museum is a tri-
umph of care, hard work, and attention to detail. The dioramas of wildlife

in nature and vignettes portraying Indian foods and culture are well labeled and beautifully designed. Did you know that rattlesnakes are born alive, not hatched from eggs? You can see some unborn baby rattlesnakes if you look carefully. The museum offers classes and demonstrations on basketmaking, beadwork, acorn gathering, and other arts and crafts.

❯❯ Fresno Flats Historic Park

School Road, Oakhurst. School Road is Road 427, off Highway 41. (209) 683-6570/ 683-7766. Tues.–Sat., 1–3; Sun., 1–4. Costumed docents host groups. For appt., write to SHSA, P.O. Box 451, Oakhurst 93644. Free. Picnic Area. **Ages 5 & up.**

Designed to capture the flavor of family life in Central California's foothills and mountains a century ago, Fresno Flats is preserving buildings along with memories. The old Fresno Flats school is now a museum with interesting artifacts and revolving exhibits, but the Laramore-Lymon 1878 farmhouse and the 1869 Taylor log house are living museums. A jail, blacksmith shop, old barn, wagon-stage collection, and flume are also on the grounds. One side of the Taylor log house is furnished as a late-19th-century living room, and the other contains the re-creation of an early-day forest ranger's office, complete with maps, old tools, and a display on how the house was constructed.

One young visitor wrote, "I especially enjoyed the jail. I learned how they put their houses together and how they used horses and wagons to get around. Fresno Flats is an important part of Oakhurst's history. It's great to see how much our community has changed by visiting Fresno Flats."

If you're driving through Oakhurst, you must stop in the center of town, on Highway 41 and Road 426, and visit **The Talking Bear**. He'll give you and the kids a brief history of the now extinct California grizzly and ask for respect of the forest and its wildlife.

❯❯ Mariposa County History Center

P.O. Box 606, Mariposa 95338. At 12th and Jessie, off Highway 49. (209) 966-2924. Daily, Apr.–Oct., 10–4:30, until 4 in March; weekends, 10–4 in Feb, Nov., & Dec. Donation. **Ages 4 & up.**

In what proud Mariposans call "the finest small museum to be seen anywhere," you'll see a typical miner's one-room cabin with all his worldly possessions; the more comfortable home of the West's most famous explorer, John C. Fremont, and his wife, Jessie; a street of shops reminiscent of the 1850s; a one-room schoolhouse; a five-stamp mill used for crushing gold-bearing quartz; the Gazette Building, a newspaper office from 1860 to 1930; and art and artifacts showing how gold was formed and extracted. Of special interest are the "Dear Charlie" letters posted throughout: letters written by Horace Snow in 1852 through 1854 to Charlie, his boyhood friend in Cambridge, Massachusetts. They give a miner's-eye view of life in the mines more than a century ago. The Indian Village with bark houses, sweathouse, mining exhibits, and old wagons and buggies on the grounds are also worth seeing.

The Mariposa County Courthouse (10th and Bullion streets. 209-966-3222. In winter, Mon.–Fri., 9–5; Apr.–Oct., 10–4, on weekends; and by appt. Free) is the oldest courthouse still in use in California, and is also part of the History Center. The clock in its tower has been marking time since 1866.

❯❯ California's State Mining and Mineral Exhibit

P.O. Box 1192, Mariposa 95338. Mariposa County Fairgrounds, near Highways 140 and 49. (209) 742-7625. May 1–Sept. 30, Wed.–Mon., 10–6; Oct.1–Apr. 30, Wed.–Sun., 10–4. Adults, $3.50; seniors and students, $2.50; under 14, free. Group rates: 209-742-7625. Gift shop. **Ages 5 & up.**

The 20,000-piece collection flourishes on a hillside where '49ers once mined the gold-rich ore. There are Mother Lode gold specimens, including the fabulous 13-pound Fricot Nugget. Visitors can also see a turn-of-the-century assay office, model stamp mill, and historic mining equipment. Dramatic crystals and minerals from around the world are on display, as well as rare benitoite, the California State Gem. You can walk through a 200-foot mine tunnel and see underground mining tools from the early 1900s.

❯❯ Yosemite Mountain Sugar Pine Railroad

56001 Yosemite Highway 41, Fish Camp 93623. (209) 683-7273. Adults, $6.50–$9.75; children, $3.50–4.75. Gift & book shop. **All ages.**

Just four miles from Yosemite National Park's south entrance, this narrow-gauge steam railroad operates on a restored section of old logging rails for a four-mile narrated trip through magnificent forest scenery. Model A railcars operate daily, April through October; steam trains run May through October. Special winter runs are also available. Moonlight specials include a barbecue dinner and music around the campfire. An 1856 log cabin is the site of the Thornberry Museum with artifacts and photos of the logging era. Food service is available at the station. Call or write for complete schedule. Boarding assistance is offered for handicapped persons. Groups and parties are welcome.

⇝ Yosemite National Park

Enter through Fish Camp on Highway 41, at El Portal on Highway 140, or on Highway 120 (this road to Tioga Pass is closed during the winter, which can last until May). Visitors Center: (209) 372-0200. Center open daily: in summer, 8–6; in spring, fall, and winter, 9–5; Museums open daily. Cars, $5 for 7 days.

If you and your family had only one sight to see in California, your best choice would be Yosemite National Park. Yosemite is one of the world's wonders, a world within itself. Elevations range from less than 2,000 feet to over 13,000, and in these 11,000 feet, five different plant belts exist. Each sustains a part of the park's wildlife population of 220 bird and 75 mammal species. In this natural splendor, you can hike, swim, camp, fish, ski, ride horseback or mule, bicycle, or simply wander.

Your first stop should be the Visitors Center in Yosemite Valley, where you can learn about the park from the center's pamphlets, exhibits, audio-visual programs, lectures, and guided walks. The *Yosemite Guide,* free, at entrance stations, gives the latest schedules.

Where you go in Yosemite will, of course, depend on your time, interests, and the season. You can choose from mountains, giant sequoia groves, towering waterfalls like Bridal Veil, and sites with breathtaking vistas of Sentinel Rock and El Capitan.

There are also museums in Yosemite for rainy days or a change of pace. The **Indian Cultural Center** (Daily, 9:30–12, 1–4), near the Visitors Center, is of interest. Be sure to go through the self-guiding reconstruction of the **Ahwaneechee Indian Village,** which is open at all times. During the summer, there are cultural demonstrations in the Indian Village. At the **Pioneer Yosemite History Center** at Wawona, you can wander through a collection of horse-drawn vehicles, an old jail, a miner's hut, a working wagon shop, and a covered bridge. In the summer, you can talk to costumed historian-interpreters who portray the original occupants of the cabins, representing the different stages in the development of Yosemite National Park.

The **Wassama Roundhouse** (Daily, 11–4. Adults, 75 cents. Tours by appt. Write: The Wassama Roundhouse Assoc., P.O. Box 328, Ahwahnee 93601, or call 209-683-3631) is a rare authentic ceremonial Indian roundhouse open to the public. Its oak-shaded grounds include picnic areas, old Native American grinding stones, and other Native American artifacts. By the way, *Ahwahnee* is the Miwok Awani name for "deep grass valley."

The **Yosemite Travel Museum** in the administration area near the Arch Rock entrance, tells the story of early-day railroad and auto transportation in the region. It has a caboose, a locomotive, and a couple of cars on the grounds. The **Geology Museum** at the Visitors Center in Yosemite Valley shows how the mountains, waterfalls, and gorges were formed. The natural history of the area is also explored at the **Happy Isles Nature Center,** which is youth oriented, with summer Junior Ranger programs, dioramas, and interactive displays.

Yosemite By Air is one way to see it all. One-and-one-half-hour tours leave from Fresno Air Terminal (Adults, $109; ages 2–12, $69). Call or write, but be sure to reserve in advance (800-622-8687/ 209-251-7501. 4885 East Shields Avenue, Suite 201, Fresno 93727).

Yosemite is overcrowded in summer, so aim for other times, if possible. For information about the park, write to Superintendent, Yosemite National Park, CA 95389, or telephone (209) 372-0200. Camp reservations may be made through Destinet, 1-800-436-7275. Hotel reservations are a must. Call (209) 252-4848 or contact Yosemite Park & Curry Co., Yosemite National Park 95389. For road and weather information, call (209) 372-0200. For recorded general information, call (209) 372-0265; live, 372-0265 (weekdays, 9–12, 1–5). Yosemite Valley/Big Trees Tour will give you an overall picture of the park (209-658-TOUR). For a brochure on access for disabled visitors, including special programs, parking, free shuttle bus service, guides, restrooms, and more, call (209) 372-0200 or write to Yosemite National Park, P.O. Box 577, Yosemite National Park 95389. All facilities and services are listed in the free quarterly *Yosemite Guide,* (209) 683-4636.

⤜• Bodie State Historic Park

Bodie is 13 miles east of Highway 395; take Highway 270, 7 miles south of Bridgeport. The road is paved for 10 miles, rough dirt the final 3 miles. (Mail: Friends of Bodie, P.O. Box 575, Bridgeport 93517.) Museum open May–Sept. 30, at least, usually 10–5. Park open daily, year round, weather permitting. Roads do close in winter. Call for current conditions and park hours: (619) 647-6445. There are no facilities. Admission, $5 per passenger vehicle, $40 per bus. Smoking in parking lot only. **Ages 6 & up.**

Nestled high in sagebrush country, Bodie, the largest ghost town in the West, has escaped the commercialism often found in ghost towns. The 170 original buildings that still stand are maintained in a state of arrested decay—neither restored nor allowed to decay further. You walk through the townsite, passing the 1882 Methodist church, the old jail, a frame schoolhouse, a small home that once belonged to President Herbert Hoover's brother, the morgue with caskets still on view, and the brick vault of the bank. The Boone Store at Main and Green streets looks as if

Harvey Boone, a direct descendent of Daniel, has just locked the door and walked away—the shelves are still full of merchandise and the window displays are still in place. Information comes from a self-guiding tour pamphlet ($1), sold, in summer, at the entrance station. The only commerce here is in the park's museum and visitor center, housed in the Miner's Union Hall built in 1878. Just wander through this quiet, ramshackle town and imagine all the high adventures that occurred here, more than a century ago. As Mark Twain wrote, "The smoke of battle almost never clears away completely in Bodie."

✳ North Central California

The north-central to northeastern area of California is the most rugged,
remote section of the state, offering many unique and extraordinary
sights. Lassen Volcanic National Park, Lava Beds National Monument,
and Modoc National Forest are snowed-in in winter and blazingly hot in
summer. Distances between towns are long, so be sure to arrange overnight camping or lodging before you set out. Take picnics, sweaters, and
wetnaps. Nature lovers will enjoy the Whiskeytown-Lake Shasta-Trinity
area and McArthur Burney Falls Memorial State Park—and all the
wonderful open spaces whose inaccessibility leaves them unspoiled. These
"Fun Places" are laid out going north from Sacramento to the Oregon
border, down again and east to Susanville and up to the most northeastern
point in California.

❖ Community Memorial Museum
Butte House Road, Yuba City 95991. From Sacramento take Highway 99
north, turn left in Yuba City at the Highway 99/20 intersection, then turn
right at Civic Center Boulevard and right onto Butte House Road. (916)
741-7141. Tues.–Fri., 9–5; Sat. & Sun., 12–4. Free. **Ages 6 & up.** *W.*

This small community museum uses local artifacts—from baskets
and grinding pots to antique pianos and dishes—to celebrate and explain
the life and times of Sutter County. Experience life in Sutter County
from the first Maidu Indian inhabitants and the settlement of John Sutter
at Hock Farm to the "civilization" of the county and its agricultural development. Changing exhibits reflect the diverse interests of Sutter
County today. Eight-year-old Tasha's "favorite thing was Lola Montez's
dressing table," and her schoolmate, Anay, liked the player piano and
blacksmith's tools.

❖ Mary Aaron Memorial Museum
704 D Street at 7th Street, Marysville 95901. (916) 743-1004. Call for
times and prices, since the museum is being remodeled.

Warren P. Miller built his crowned gray and white Gothic family
home for $5,000 in 1857. Today, it is a museum with period furniture
and clothing and an interesting display of dolls, documents, and photos.
Our favorite: the 1860s wedding cake that was discovered perfectly intact
and petrified in a wooden Wells Fargo storage box. The bricked garden
has Victorian wrought-iron furniture and plantings.

On the levee of the river, the **Bok Kai Temple** (on D Street; 916-742-
ARTS; by appointment), an 1879 Chinese temple for the River God of
good fortune, houses many cultural artifacts.

❧ Museum of the Forgotten Warriors

5865 A. Road off North Beale Road, Marysville 95901. (916) 742-3090. Open the first Saturday of each month, Veterans & Memorial Days, 10–4 and Thurs., 7 P.M.–10 P.M. Groups by reservation. Free. **Ages 9 & up.** *W.*

Dedicated to veterans of the Vietnam War, this museum houses artifacts, photographs, and personal histories collected from veterans across the United States. There are uniforms and patches, including the black garb of the Viet Cong, nurse uniforms, and a mannequin of a Navy Seal, complete with camouflage and paint. Other exhibits highlight World War II, the Korean War, and the Persian Gulf War. You know you've found it when you see the light observation helicopter, a Marine Corps tank, and an equipment trailer.

❧ Sacramento Valley Museum

1495 E Street, Highway 20 at Interstate 5, P.O. Box 1437, Williams 95987. (916) 473-2978. Apr.–Oct., Thurs.–Sat., 10–4; in winter, Fri. & Sat., 10–4, and by appt. $1. Picnic area. **Ages 6 & up.** *Partially W.*

This 21-room museum captures the past with a fully stocked general store, a blacksmith shop and saddlery, an apothecary shop, a barbershop, and restored early-California rooms filled with memories. The double cradle from the 1700s is special. The fashion doll collection is a history of civilization from ancient Greek times to the 1930s. In the document room, there's an 1800 newspaper reporting George Washington's death. Lacey wrote, "I like the big bell, the buggy, and the old quilts." Her friend Liliana said, "I like the dresses the best and I liked the store the best. I liked the hats the best of all. I found out that women couldn't ride boy saddles so that was what I didn't know. Thank you."

❧ Oroville Chinese Temple Complex

1500 Broderick at Elma Street, Oroville 95965. (916) 538-2496. Mon.–Thurs., 11–4:30; Tues. & Wed., 1–4. Ages 12 and over, $2. In groups, by appt., $1.50. **Ages 10 & up.**

This complex of Buddhist, Taoist, and Confucian temples houses one of the finest collections of Chinese artifacts, art, and folk art in the United States. At the door of one building stands a two-ton, cast-iron urn given to the temple by Emperor Quong She. Carved teakwood altars, old tapestries, gods and goddesses, dragons, rare lanterns, and shrines decorate the buildings.

The Moon Temple, used for Buddhist worship, is entered through a circular doorway, which symbolizes the circle of life. The arts and lives of the thousands of Chinese who migrated to the gold fields are reflected in this peaceful spot. One young visitor wrote, "I enjoyed when the dragon was playing with the Moon. And the room where I saw the big guardians at the door and the big swords."

❧ Judge C. F. Lott Historic Home in Sank Park

1607 Montgomery Street, Oroville 95965. (916) 538-2497. Fri., Sun., & Mon., 12–4. Over 12, $2. In groups by appt., $1.50. **Ages 6 & up.**

"I like the courting chair because I think it was neat that the father got to know the daughter's fiance. I also liked the kitchen and the bride's room and the guest room." A fourth grader from the Camptonville Elementary School wrote this in her thank-you note. This sweet Victorian has a lot of love in it—from the plaque in the front trellis that says, "In commemoration of a kiss and a promise given between these columns," to the semiprecious stones from the local riverbed spelling out "Love" in the front parlor. Visitors of all ages will walk through authentically furnished rooms and learn what it was like to live in the late 19th and early 20th centuries.

❧ Butte County Pioneer Memorial Museum

2332 Montgomery Street, P.O. Box 1743, Oroville 95965. (916) 534-0198. Sun., 1–4 and by appt. Closed July & August, December & January. Donation. **Ages 6 & up.**

This grand collection of pioneer memorabilia is housed in a replica of a miner's cabin that has been expanded to include rooms furnished in Victorian style. Visitors will see, among other things, early typewriters, a doll collection, kitchenware, an old fire engine, and pictures of the Oroville floods.

The **Butte County Historical Society** has opened **The Ehmann Home** (1480 Lincoln Street, Oroville 95965. 916-533-5316. Sat., 11–3; Sun., 12–4 and by appt. Donation. W). This furnished Colonial Revival home features displays from the society's collection of historical artifacts and a gift store specializing in Ehmann-brand olives.

❧ Feather River Fish Hatchery & Oroville Dam

5 Table Mountain Boulevard, Oroville 95965. (916) 538-2222. Hatchery, daily, 8–6. Dam overlook (538-2219): daily, except major holidays, 9–6. Tours, (916) 534-2306. Free. **All ages.**

A large window in one of the world's largest chinook salmon and steelhead trout hatcheries enables visitors to see the salmon climb the fish ladder to spawn, usually in September through November. Tours of the nursery reveal the artificial spawning process in action. Over 10,000 salmon and steelhead make their homes here. Ten miles up the road, you can get a good view of the 770-foot dam across the Feather River.

❧ Sacramento National Wildlife Refuge

752 County Road 99 W, 7 miles south of Willows on the east side of Interstate 5, Willows 95988. (916) 934-2801. Weekdays, 7:30–4. Free. **All ages.**

The Visitor Center of this wildlife refuge has a diorama featuring three dozen bird species and a helpful staff that will send you on a two-mile trail where you'll see ponds and marshes, vernal pools, blue herons, great egrets, and other migratory wildbirds.

❧ Yuba Feather Historical Museum

19096 New York Flat and Forbestown Roads, Forbestown 95941. (916) 675-1025/675-0194. Weekends & holidays, Memorial Day through Labor Day, 10–4, and by appt. Free. **Ages 6 & up.**

Visitors can step back in time at this historical museum and park. Museum exhibits highlight the region's history with logging and blacksmith artifacts, photographs, and, in the Junior Museum, exhibits by local schoolchildren. Step up to a miner's cabin, a saloon, a doctor's office, a harness shop, mercantile, or a Wells Fargo Office and pretend. The one-room schoolhouse has a teacher in authentic period garb and a bell to call children to class.

❧ Gold Nugget Museum

502 Pearson Road, at Mallan Lane, Paradise 95969. (916) 872-8722. Wed.–Sun., 12–4, Free. **Ages 8 & up.**

This local history museum is named for the Willard Nugget, a 54-pound gold nugget discovered in nearby Magalia Canyon in 1859. Kids will enjoy the doll collection, mining tools, a gun collection, antique furniture, and the exhibit about Yellowstone Kelley, the famous Indian guide.

❧ Bidwell Mansion

525 The Esplanade, Chico 95926. (916) 895-6144. Mon.–Fri., 12–5; Sat. & Sun., 10–5. 45-minute tours on the hour. Adults, $1. **Ages 8 & up.**

Rancho del Arroyo Chico, covering 26,000 acres, was purchased in 1849 by agriculturalist and politician John Bidwell. His large Victorian home soon became the social and cultural center of the upper Sacramento Valley. Bidwell's is a California success story. He arrived in California in 1841, worked as a clerk for John Sutter, rose to the rank of general in the Mexican War, and then on July Fourth, 1848, struck it rich at Bidwell Bar. He set himself up at Chico and built a model farm. He raised corn, oats, barley, peaches, pears, apples, figs, quince, almonds, walnuts, wheat, olives, and casaba melons. He was elected state senator and congressman, and even ran for president. Visitors may walk through the graciously furnished rooms. Children will like the cabinet of stuffed birds in the general's office, Annie Bidwell's telescoping organ in the attic, and the intricate Victorian hair wreaths in the parlor. Bidwell Park, the fourth largest municipal park in the nation, is also part of the Bidwell estate. There are picnic and barbecue areas.

The **Stansbury Home** (916-895-3848/343-0442. Weekends, 1–4, and by appt. Donation), an 1883 Italianate Victorian nearby at 305 West 5th Street, at Salem, is filled with period furnishings. It's remarkable because only Stansburys have lived in it and it has never been remodeled or modernized.

❧ Chico Museum

141 Salem Street, Chico 95926. (916) 891-4336. Wed.–Sun., 12–4, Adults, $1; children, 50 cents. **Ages 8 & up.** *W.*

Household items, clothing, and photographs show what Chico was like in yesteryear in this sweet museum. Youngsters will be fascinated by the 19th-century musical instruments and the altars, ceremonial pieces, and other memorabilia from Chico's Taoist temple. In another section, history and art exhibits rotate with children's interactive science exhibits.

❧ South Shasta Lines

G. A. Humann Ranch, 8620 Holmes Road, Gerber 96036. Holmes Road is 2 miles south of Gerber. (916) 385-1389. Open Sun. in Apr. and May, 12– 4. Adults, $4; under 12, $3. **Ages 5 & up.**

A quarter-inch scale model railroad based on the Southern Pacific, Gerber to Dunsmuir, under construction for 42 years, is now finished. There are 16 steam-type locomotives and 100 freight and passenger cars on 900 feet of track. There are 1,500 miniature trees, 1,000 people, and hundreds of animals on this detailed miniature system. In addition, a real steam locomotive takes visitors for a mile-long ride. A steam and gas antique farm machinery museum is also on hand.

❧ William B. Ide Adobe State Historic Park

21659 Adobe Road, Red Bluff 96080. Off Interstate 5, north of town 1 mile. (916) 529-8599. Park open 8 to sunset for picnics and fishing. Adobe open 12–4 or whenever the ranger is on hand, and by appt. Craft and Living History demonstrations most weekends in May and most days from June 15 through Labor Day. Parking fee, $3. **Ages 6 & up.** *W.*

"He hereby invites all good and patriotic citizens in California to assist him—to establish and perpetuate a liberal, a just and honorable government, which shall secure to all civil, religious and personal liberty." So wrote William B. Ide to introduce the Bear Flag Republic to California. As first president of the Bear Flag Republic, he brought California into the Union. But when the Republic failed, Ide went to the gold fields.

This adobe, which served as a ferry station between Sacramento and Shasta's northern gold mines, is one of the state's earliest and best-preserved examples of an American pioneer homestead. It has been restored and refurnished to its full 1852 glory by volunteers. The house is small and unassuming, with family photos, cradle and high chair, a furnished kitchen, and an unusual sleeping platform under the eaves. A smokehouse and a carriage house, with covered wagons, buggies, and Ide's branding equipment are also open to the public. Two 300-year-old oaks mark the way to another small museum that includes gold-mining tools, an old button collection, and a well-used cribbage board. The simple timber-framed period workshop has been crafted by volunteers using tools and methods used in 1852. The Visitors Center display panels help explain the exhibits. The garden and chickens—and the cantankerous donkey named Lucy—will be the kids' favorites.

❖ Kelly–Griggs House Museum

311 Washington Street, Red Bluff 96080. (916) 527-1129. Thurs.–Sun., 1–4. Donation. **Ages 8 & up.**

Visitors walk into the past in this early 1880s classical Victorian house, which is furnished and "peopled" with costumed mannequins depicting life in the Victorian era. Our favorite item is the minutely detailed Victorian dollhouse in the master bedroom. It was built by Bob Grootveld, who also handcarves and paints carousel horses. The fence around the house is made from bars of the old jail. Ben, a third-grader, wrote, "I like the Indian room and dress room, the pictures of Mt. Lassen and the steamboat. I wonder how it was like back then with all those great clothes and neat hidden places in the dressers. Getting to see all that was nice!"

❖ Salmon Viewing Plaza

Lake Red Bluff Recreation Area, North Central Valley Fish & Wildlife Office, 10950 Tyler Road, Red Bluff 96080. Exit Interstate 5 at Antelope Boulevard and follow Antelope Boulevard west to first stoplight, which is Sale Lane. Continue on Sale Lane 2¹/₃ miles to the plaza. (916) 527-3043. Daily, 6 A.M.–10 P.M., May–Sept. 15. Free. **Ages 7 & up.**

Visitors may see, on TV monitors, king salmon on their way past fish ladders to upstream spawning grounds at the Salmon Viewing Plaza near the Diversion Dam in the Red Bluff Recreation Area. They can also see fish trapping from an elevated walkway. The site is self-guided with several interpretive displays. The best time to visit is September and October.

The U.S. Fish & Wildlife Service also operates the **Coleman National Fish Hatchery** 20 miles away, next to the Battle Creek Wildlife Area on the boundary between Shasta and Tehama counties. From Interstate 5 take the Balls Ferry Road exit in Cottonwood and go east on Balls Ferry Road (Route 1, Box 2105, Anderson 96007. 916-365-8781. Oct. 1–Dec. 1, 8–4. Free). Here chinook salmon eggs are spawned daily in October, less frequently in November, December, and January.

❯❯ Yreka Western Railroad

P.O. Box 660, Yreka 96097. 300 East Miner Street, just east of Interstate 5 via the Central Yreka exit. (916) 842-4146. Three-hour-long summer excursions depart at 10 A.M., Wed.–Sun.; on weekends only in September and October. Adults, $9; children, $4.50. Reservations required. **Ages 5 & up.**

Established by the local citizenry in 1889 to link Yreka with the Southern Pacific tracks, the local short-line railroad has been in continuous operation ever since. The Blue Goose excursion train now takes new pioneers brave enough to be carried by Ol' No. 19, a boot-shined black 1915 Baldwin steam locomotive, through the Shasta Valley into Montague, with a one-hour stop in a quaint 1887 Southern Pacific depot/museum. Bandits have been known to attack the train to snatch bags of "gold" away from the kids—and replace them with candy.

❯❯ Carter House Natural Science Museum

Caldwell Park, 48 Quartz Hill Road, Redding 96003. (916) 243-5457/ 225-4125. Tues.–Sun., 10–5. Adults, $1; children, 50 cents. **Ages 5 & up.**

Did you know that tarantulas enjoy walking along your arm? In the animal discovery section of this lively science museum, you can pet a tarantula, or an opossum, or ground squirrel. Native animals that are injured—sparrow hawks, screech owls, California king snakes—and domestic animals are cared for here. Programs such as hikes and science classes keep the place busy. Annie wrote, "Dear Carter House Museum. Thank you for telling us about animals. I liked learning about birds best. I learned that birds have beaks and bunnies don't."

❯❯ Redding Museum and Art Center

Caldwell Park, 56 Quartz Hill Road, Redding 96003. (916) 225-4155. Tues.–Sun., 10–5. Closed holidays. Tours by appt. Over 13; $1. **Ages 6 & up.** *W.*

The excellent collection of Pomo and Wintu Indian basketry, from cradles to pots, dresses, and luggage, houses and gifts for the funeral pyre, provides rotating exhibits in this constantly changing museum. The history section always focuses on the Shasta County area. The art galleries offer changing exhibits of contemporary artists and collections. There are always one or two hands-on exhibits, such as a puzzle that shows how the Shasta Dam works, for the youngest.

⇝ Waterworks Park

*151 North Boulder Drive, Redding 96003. (916) 246-9550. Memorial Day to Labor Day; call for times and prices. Group rates and team and barbecue nights. Gift & food shop. **All ages.***

Beat the heat and cure those summertime blues with the wildest, wettest time of your life. Three giant, twisting, turning, serpentine water slides, an awesome "Flash Flood," a 400-foot wild white-water innertube river ride, a children's aquatic playground with fountains, pool, and slides, and beach volleyball, picnic grounds, and games add up to a great vacation day.

⇝ Fort Crook Museum

*Fall River Mills 96028. (916) 336-5110. Northeast of Redding 75 miles on Highway 299 East. Daily, 12–4. Closed Nov.1–May 1. Free. **Ages 6 & up.***

There are six little buildings, including an 1884 one-room schoolhouse, in this historical museum, where artifacts reflect the history of the area. Old farm machinery, buggies, an old fire hose, baskets, a dugout canoe, and dolls all attract youngsters.

⇝ Shasta State Historic Park

*P.O. Box 2430, Old Shasta 96087. Highway 299, west of Redding. (916) 243-8194. Wed.–Sun., 10–5. Adults, $2; children, $1. Picnic areas near the stagecoach and pioneer barn. **Ages 7 & up.***

Once the center of the rich northern gold mines, Shasta is a quiet almost-ghost town now restored. The old county courthouse contains a remarkable collection of California art along with displays of photographs and relics of the Indians, Chinese, gold miners, and pioneers who once lived here. Modoc handicrafts, Chinese wooden pillows and money, an 1879 *Godey's Ladies Book*, and the pistol John Brown used in his raid at Harper's Ferry are among the highlights. The courtroom is furnished as it was when in use, and the jail is still equipped with chains, leg irons, and a gallows. The Litsch General Store, open Sundays in summer, looks just as it did in the 1880s, with barrels of meat and wine, old hats, and picks and shovels for sale. Within the park are the ruins of what was once the longest row of brick business buildings north of San Francisco, the town's Catholic cemetery, and other sites that are fun and safe to explore.

❥ J. J. (Jake) Jackson Memorial Museum and Trinity County Historical Park

508 Main Street, Highway 299 West, P.O. Box 333, Weaverville 96093-0333. (916) 623-5211. Daily, May–Oct., 10–5; Apr. & Nov., 12–4; Dec.–Mar., Tues. & Sat., 12–4. Donation. **Ages 10 & up.** *W.*

Clear displays trace Trinity County's history from the days of the Indians through the gold-mining years. Ray Jackson's collection of antique firearms, Chinese tong-war weapons, and a reconstructed miner's cabin, 1904 steam-powered stamp mill, and blacksmith shop help to recall this bygone era. One popular item is the boots worn by a man who tried to poison the entire town of Weaverville during the Tong War of 1854.

❥ Weaverville Chinese Joss House

P.O. Box 1217, Weaverville 96093. Main Street, Highway 299 West. (916) 623-5284. Wed.–Sun., 10–4, except holidays. Adults, $2, children $1. **Ages 9 & up.**

The Temple of the Forest Beneath the Clouds is open for worship now, as it has been since 1874. A small museum offers Chinese art, mining tools, weapons used in the tong wars, and photos of Chinese laborers building the railroads. A Lion Dance headdress, an abacus, opium pipes, and a huge gong are also shown. Inside the temple, you see the paper money that is burned for the gods and the drum and bell that wake the gods so they'll hear your prayers. In the rear of the temple, the attendant's quarters are furnished as they were a hundred years ago, with bunk beds and wooden pillows. Colorful altars, temple saints, celebration drums and flags, and the mirror-covered king's umbrella that guarded him against evil spirits create a vivid picture of what to many is another world.

❥ Ironside Museum

Hawkins Bar, on Highway 299 West near Burnt Ranch. (Mail: HCR #34, Hawkins Bar 95527.) (916) 629-2396. By appt. Donation. **Ages 7 & up.**

Ray Narchand shares his personal collection "whenever anyone wants to see it—if we're home." Pioneer artifacts include butter churns, doctors' instruments, a collection of 200 padlocks, a glass insulator collection, Mrs. Narchand's carnival glass collection, and high-button shoes. Assaying equipment, a stamp mill, a 10-foot waterwheel and a Little Pelton waterwheel, mining equipment, and a blacksmith shop share the bill with a complete dentist's outfit. If you call before your visit, Mr. Narchand will bring out his gun and gold collections, too. Kids are especially fascinated by the shoe horn and key collections.

⇾ Shasta Dam

Highway 15 off Interstate 5, 10 miles north of Redding. (Mail: 16349 Shasta Dam Boulevard, Shasta Lake 96019.) (916) 275-1554/275-4463. Daily, 8–4. Visitors can drive or walk on the dam at any time. Information center, 9–5 daily. Tours on the hour from 9–4 in summer; at 10, 12, & 2 in winter. Videos on request. Free. **Ages 8 & up.**

It's said that once you see Shasta Dam you'll never forget it. Completed in 1945, Shasta is the second largest concrete structure ever built in the U.S. (Grand Coulee dam is the largest). Its spillway is three times the height of Niagara Falls. The Bureau of Reclamation offers one-hour tours of the dam and powerplant, including an elevator ride up to the top to view both the construction and the lake side of the same. There are picnic areas near the Visitor Center.

Snow-capped Mount Shasta (which the athletic can climb) looms in the distance, accentuating the differences between natural and man-made wonders. Jet-boat tours, camping, houseboating, and every kind of water sport are popular in this Shasta-Whiskeytown-Trinity National Recreation Area.

⇾ Lake Shasta Caverns

P.O. Box 801, O'Brien 96070. Off Interstate 5 on Shasta Caverns Road. 20 minutes north of Redding. (916) 238-2341/(800) 795-CAVE. Tours every half hour in summer; hourly, 9–3 in April, May & Sept.; at 10, 12, and 2, Oct.–March. Closed Thanksgiving & Christmas. Reservations suggested. Adults, $14; ages 4–12, $7. Group rates. Gift shop. **Ages 7 & up.**

Discovered in 1878 by J. A. Richardson (you can still see his inscription), the Lake Shasta Caverns are a natural wonder. Stalactite and stalagmite formations range from eight inches to, in the Cathedral Room, 60-foot columns of stalactite draperies that are studded with crystals.

Multicolored formations unfold before you during your tour, as you hear geological facts and Wintu Indian legends from a knowledgeable guide. The two-hour tour consists of a boat ride and bus ride, as well as the one-hour guided tour of the caverns.

⇾ Sisson Hatchery Museum

1 North Old Stage Road at Hatchery Lane, Mt. Shasta 96087. (916) 926-5508. Mon.–Sat., 10–4; Sun., 1–4. Free. **Ages 7 & up.** *W.*

Early life in a mountain town is portrayed in this little museum in the Old Fish Hatchery Building. The history of Mount Shasta City and the hatchery is on display, with wildflower displays, antique cameras and photographs, and an exhibit of the geology of Mount Shasta.

❖ Heritage Junction of McCloud

320 Main Street, Box 607, McCloud 96057. (916) 964-2604. Mon–Sat., 11–3; Sun., 1–3. Donation. **Ages 8 & up.**

McCloud has been put on the National Register of Historic Places as an early logging center. This museum celebrates the logging industry with memorabilia of the people and their tools, such as saws of all kinds, measuring sticks, mill office equipment, and clothing and accessories from the mid-1800s to the early 1900s. The big equipment is on the grounds: firefighting equipment, the Corliss engine from a 1903 McCloud Steam Log Mill, and there's even a replica of an old church.

❖ McCloud Railway Company

Reservations: (800) 733-2141. Three-hour dinner train: $70 for adults; $35 for those under 12. Saturdays, mid-May through Sept., 5:30 P.M. One-hour excursions in open air rail cars depart every Saturday at 4. Adults, $8; children under 12, $5. **Ages 6 & up.**

Dine in 1916 splendor in two beautifully restored dining cars. The four-course dinner is served on tables covered with white linen table-cloths, fine china and sterling silver. Lace curtains frame the outstanding views as the train winds its way through the forest.

❖ Siskiyou County Museum

910 South Main Street, Yreka 96097. (916) 842-3836. Tues.–Sat., 9–5. Free. **Ages 7 & up.**

In this reproduction of the Callahan Ranch Hotel, one of the first stage stops in Siskiyou County in the 1850s, visitors learn the story of Siskiyou County from prehistoric days to the present. On the mezzanine, you'll find a parlor, bedroom, children's room, and office complete with an antique switchboard. A schoolhouse, blacksmith shop, church, 1856 pioneer log cabin, ore car, and logging skid shack are situated in the $2\frac{1}{2}$-acre Outdoor Museum. Among the buildings is a replica of the Denny Bar Mercantile Company, the first chain store in California. Period merchandise is sold during summer months.

In town, the foyer of the **Siskiyou County Courthouse** (311 4th Street. Weekdays, 9–4. Free) shows off raw, natural gold nuggets taken from Siskiyou County placer mines during the Gold Rush in one of the largest displays of gold south of Alaska.

➤ Weed Lumber Town Museum

303 Gilman, Weed 96094. (916) 938-5050. Daily, 10–5, May 30–Sept. 30 & by appt. Free. **Ages 8 & up.**

Memories of the logging industry in its early days attract visitors. Inside are photographs and personal mementos of Weed, including an old movie projector. Outside you'll find logging equipment, including a stagecoach, a D-8 Cat, a snag pusher, and rail cars for hauling lumber.

➤ Lava Beds National Monument

P.O. Box 867, Tule Lake 96134. Off Highway 139. (916) 667-2282. Camping: $10 in summer, $6 in winter (800-326-6944 for information on lodging and dining). Monument visitor center: in summer, 8–6; in winter, 8– 5. Tours and maps for independent exploring. Closed Thanksgiving and Christmas. **Ages 8 & up.**

"Thank you for letting us go to the Lava Beds. I really enjoyed it. The reason skull ice cave was my favorite cave is because of the ice at the end. My second favorite was Hopkins Chocolate. That's because it's long and narrow." So wrote Michelle about her visit.

Natural and Indian history vie for visitors' attention in this monumental landscape of lava formations. The area abounds with natural wonders, including cinder cones that reach up to 500 feet. Most of the sights at this 70-square-mile "monument" are underground. There are more than 300 lava tube caves that can be explored with care. Some caves hold Modoc drawings that date back centuries. Captain Jack's Stronghold, formed of natural lava fortifications, is a grim reminder of later history: In 1872, Captain Jack led a band of Modoc Indians in an unsuccessful revolt against the U.S. Cavalry. A short visit to the monument's visitor center will help you understand the geology, natural history, and past events of the area.

➤ Lassen County Historical Museum

75 North Weatherfowl Street, P.O. Box 321, Susanville 96130. (916) 257-3292. Daily, May 1–Oct. 31, 10–4. Free. **Ages 8 & up.** *W.*

Lassen County memorabilia, farming and lumbering machinery, artifacts of the Native Americans, and remembrances of the first settlers fill this interesting museum. Many wagon trains stopped here at Roop's Fort, which is undergoing restoration. Susanville is named after the daughter of Isaac Roop, one of the founders of the Provisional Territory of Nevada and Nataqua. Peter Lassen, one of the Danish pioneers of the area, was shot in Black Rock Desert, a murder that remains unsolved to this day. Historic murals are being painted all over town, including one of Susan and her father on Lassen Street.

≫ Lassen Volcanic National Park

Highway 36, Mineral 96063. (916) 595-4444. Information centers at Manzanita Lake and Sulphur Works are open 8–4 daily from June to late September. Road closed in winter. Call for road, park, trail, camping, accomodations, education, and interpretation information. **Ages 8 & up.**

Among the attractions in this rugged area are hot springs, boiling pools, mud pots, sparkling lakes, and the cinder cone that erupted in 1851. An Indian lore program at Manzanita Lake Visitor Information Center presents the story and customs of the Native Americans who once lived here. Other programs are scheduled irregularly. During the pioneer programs, naturalists use covered wagons to show how people lived when they were on the Nobles Immigrant Trail. Subway Cave, north of Manzanita Lake on old Highway 44 toward North Burney, just outside the park, is also worth a trip.

One note of warning: The grounds and thermal areas are treacherous, so keep hold of your children at all times. Lassen Peak erupted for seven years beginning in 1915, and it's still considered active. Remember, the hydrothermal caves are named Devil's Kitchen, Sulphur Works, and Bumpass Hell for good reason. With the smell of sulphur in the air and fenced boardwalks over land that changes from cracked mud to hissing steam as you walk, you'll think you're on another planet.

≫ Alturas Modoc County Historical Museum

600 South Main Street, P.O. Box 1689, Alturas 96101. (916) 233-6328. Tues.–Sat., May 1–Oct. 31, 10–4. Donation. **Ages 6 & up.** *W.*

To learn more about Captain Jack, who earned his fame in the Modoc Indian Wars in the Lava Beds, and see pictures of him, go to this pleasant museum in the far corner of the state. There are beads, baskets, arrowheads, and other artifacts of the Pit River, Paiute, and Modoc tribes, along with pioneer memorabilia. The collections of mounted animals and birds and antique guns are popular with visitors. Becky wrote, "I liked the old dolls. They were beautiful. Thank you." Tom said, "Way cool dude. I like the old guns." Rebecca, "I like the swords because they are nice to look at." And Jose, "I like the knives. They are cool." Janie wrote, "I'm bringing my friends tomorrow!"

Special Annual Events

THE FOLLOWING LISTING of special annual events in Northern California is arranged in order of the estimated time of the month the event will take place, from the first weekend to the last. Some celebrations, such as July Fourth and Halloween, inspire events in most major towns. So, if something sounds intriguing but it's listed in a city that's far away, call around to see if you can't find something similar, but much handier for you.

For exact dates and prices, please call the local chamber of commerce. The California Trade and Commerce Agency (801 K Street, Suite 1700, Sacramento 95814-3520. http://gocalif.ca.gov) offers a free calendar of 1,000 special events and insider tips. *Motorland*, the magazine of the California State Automobile Association of America, also lists events in California in each monthly issue.

❖ January
Teddy Bear Exhibit, Lakeport
San Francisco Sports and Boat Show, Cow Palace
San Mateo Auto Show, Fairgrounds
Winter's Eve at Chaw-Se State Historic Park, Jackson
Golden Gate Kennel Club All Breed Dog Show, San Francisco
Four-Dog Sled Races, Prosser Lake and Donner Lake
Gold Rush Discovery Day Festival, Coloma (Jan. 24)
Whale Watching begins, Point Reyes National Seashore
Fiddlers Contest and Crab Cioppino Feed, Cloverdale
Crab, Wine & Art Festival, Eureka
Sealabration, Año Nuevo State Reserve, Big Sur

❖ February
Sutter Creek Doll, Toy, & Miniature Show
Chinese New Year's Celebration, San Francisco

National Roadster Show, Oakland Coliseum
Crab Festival, Crescent City
Crab Feast, Bodega Bay
Redwood Region Logging Conference, Eureka
Chinese Bomb Day, Bok Kai Festival, Marysville
Cloverdale Citrus Fair
Monarch Migration Festival, Santa Cruz
Black History Month, Col. Allensworth State Historic Park
Clam Beach Run, Trinidad
Carnival and Spring Fair, Lakeport
California Special Olympics Water Games, Sonora

❖❖ March

St. Patrick's Day Parades & Celebrations take place almost everywhere.
Irish Days, Murphy
Celtic Music & Arts Festival, San Francisco and Sonora
Daffodil Hill Blooms, Volcano
Snowfest, Lake Tahoe
Hot Dog Skiing Festival, Alpine Meadows, Tahoe
Annual Winter Round-Up, Red Bluff
Camellia Show, Santa Rosa, Fresno, and Modesto
Crab Feed, Ukiah
Draggin' Wagons Dance Festival, Sonora
Sierra Dog Sled Races, Sierra City, Truckee, and Ebbetts Pass
Candlefishing at Night, Klamath River
Junior Grand National Livestock Expo, Cow Palace, San Francisco
Jackass Mail Run, Porterville
Whale Festival, Mendocino and Fort Bragg
Back Country Horsemen Annual Rendezvous, Anderson

❖❖ April

Ducky Derby, Santa Cruz
Teddy Bear Convention, Nevada City
Log Race, Petaluma River
Fisherman's Festival, Bodega Bay
Annual Trinidad Crab Feed
Gem & Mineral Show, Cow Palace, San Francisco
Yacht Parade, Redwood City
Annual Trail Days, Bothe-Napa Valley State Historic Park
Clovis Rodeo and Big Hat Days Festival
Cherry Blossom Festival, Lodi and San Francisco

Earth Day celebrations in San Francisco and many other towns
Easter Egg Hunt, Casa de Fruita, Hollister, Lakeport, and Monterey
Great Duck Race, Sutter Creek
Carmel Kite Festival
Gold Nugget Days, Paradise
Children's Lawn Festival, Redding
Tuolumne County Cowboy & Cowgirl Days, Sonora
Scottish Games & Gatherings, Roseville
Red Bluff Romp and Rodeo Roundup
Tea and Musicale, Vintage Cars Display, Anderson Marsh State Historic Park
Pebble Beach Concours D'Elegance
Stockton Asparagus Festival
Coalinga Water Festival
Nikkei Matsuri Festival, San Jose
Apple Blossom Festival, Sebastopol
Fresno Folk Festival
Rhododendron Festival, Eureka
Boonville Buck-a-Roo Days
Motherlode Dixieland Jazz Festival, Sonora
Auburn Wild West Stampede
Butter & Eggs Day Parade, Petaluma

❖ May

Laguna Seca Races, Monterey
Cinco de Mayo Festivals, San Francisco and San Jose
Opening Day Yacht Parade, San Francisco
Ione Homecoming Picnic, Parade, & Carnival
Avenue of the Giants Marathon, Garberville
Bay to Breakers Race, San Francisco
Luther Burbank Rose Parade and Festival, Santa Rosa
Living History Days, Petalume Adobe State Historic Park
Native American Cultural Day, Anderson Marsh State Historic Park
Mt. Folk Festival, Potter Valley
West Coast National Antique Fly-In, Watsonville Airport
Bok Kai Festival and Parade, Marysville
Salinas Valley Fair, King City
Lilly Langtry Day, Middletown (May 11)
Sacramento Jazz Jubilee
Silver Dollar Fair, Chico
Shasta Art Fair & Fiddle Jamboree
Native American Pow Wow, Hollister

Dixieland Monterey Jazz Festival
Calaveras County Fair and Frog Jumping Jubilee, Angels Camp
West Coast Relays, Fresno
Roaring Camp Mining Company Gold Prospecting Days
Chamarita Festival and Parade, Half Moon Bay, Sausalito, and Pescadero
  (Pentecost Sunday)
Feather Fiesta Days, Oroville
Old Settler's Day, Campbell
Fireman's Muster, Columbia
Lamb Derby Days, Willow
Miniature Horse Show, Amador County Fairgrounds
Russian River Wine Festival, Healdsburg
Stump Town Days and Rodeo, Guerneville
Coarsegold Rodeo, Madera County
Fiddletown Gold Country Hoedown
Prospector's Daze, Willow Creek
Carnival, San Francisco
Oakdale Chocolate Festival

❖ June

Black Bart Celebration, Redwood Valley and Cloverdale
Sonoma/Marin Fair, Petaluma
Upper Grant Avenue Street Fair, San Francisco
Fly-In and Moonlight Flight, Porterville
Alameda County Fair, Pleasanton
Merienda, Monterey's birthday party
Scottish Highland Games, Modesto
Gualala Whale Festival
Valhalla Renaissance Festival, South Lake Tahoe
San Antonio Mission Fiesta, Jolon
Springfest, San Mateo Fairgrounds
Old Auburn Flea Market
Italian Picnic and Parade, Sutter Creek
Klamath Salmon Barbecue
Carvevela, Weed
Street Painting Festival, San Rafael
California Railroad Festival, Sacramento
Shasta Bridge Jamboree, Redding
Malakoff Homecoming, Nevada City
Solano County Fair, Vallejo
Novato County Fair

Pony Express Days, McKinleyville
Garberville Rodeo and Western Celebration
Father's Day Kite Festival, San Francisco
Bear Flag Day and Ox Roast, Sonoma
Tuolumne Jubilee, Tuolumne City
Kit Carson Days, Jackson
Butterfly Days, Mariposa
Cornish Miner's Picnic, Grass Valley
Fiddler's Jamboree, Railroad Flat
Bonanza Days, Gilroy
Redwood Acres Fair, Eureka
Western Daze, Fairfield
Western Weekend, Novato
Vaquero Days, Hollister
Scandinavian Midsummer Festival, Ferndale
Rice Festival, Gridley
San Juan Bautista Peddler's Fair
Midsummer Music Festival, Stern Grove, San Francisco
Highway 50 Wagon Train, Placerville
Secession Day, Rough and Ready (June 27)
San Francisco's Birthday Celebration
Russian River Rodeo and Sumptown Days, Guerneville
Truckee-Tahoe Air Show
Trinidad Fish Festival
Middletown Days, Middletown
California High School Rodeo Finals, Red Bluff
Oakland Festival at the Lake

❖ July

San Francisco Waterfront Festival
Old Time Fourth of July Celebration, Columbia
Old-Fashioned Fourth, Mt. Shasta, Modesto, Arcata, Redding, Clovis,
  Martinez, Truckee, Nevada City, Mt. Shasta, Crescent City
San Jose America Festival
Napa County Fair, Calistoga
Willits Frontier Days
Hoopa Fourth of July Celebration, Hoopa
Salmon B-B-Q, Noyo
Sonoma County Fair, Santa Rosa
C.B. Radio Convention, Eureka
Bach Festival, Carmel

California Rodeo, Salinas
Obon Festival, San Jose, Monterey, and Fresno
Clearlake Worm Races
Indian Gathering, Ahwahnee
Annual Antique and Arts & Crafts Show, Oakdale
Asian Festival, Oakland Museum
Christmas in July Jazz Band Festival, Sutter Hill
Pony Express Celebration, Pollack Pines
Arcata Salmon Festival
Mendota Sugar Festival
Garberville Rodeo
Folsom Rodeo
San Mateo County Fair
Woodminster Music Series, Oakland (through September)
San Francisco Fair and Exposition
Hangtown Festival, Placerville
Sacramento Water Festival
Dune Daze, Samoa
Fortuna Rodeo
Water Carnival, Monte Rio
Jeepers Jamboree, Georgetown to Lake Tahoe
Fiesta Rodeo de San Juan Bautista
Holy Ghost Celebration, Benicia
Gilroy Garlic Festival
Lassen County Fair, Susanville
Placerville County Fair, Roseville
Captain Weber Days, Stockton
Scotts Valley Days
Gold Rush Jubilee, Callahan, Siskiyou County
Feast of Lanterns, Pacific Grove
Orick Rodeo
Roaring Camp '49er Day (July 22)
Gasket Raft Races
Turtle Races, Cloverdale
Nightboat Parade, Lakeport and Clearlake Highlands
Marin County Fair, San Rafael
Amador County Fair

 August

Old Adobe Days, Petaluma Adobe State Historic Park
Monterey County Fair

Humboldt County Fair, Ferndale
Dipsea Race, Mill Valley
Nihonmachi Street Fair, Japantown, San Francisco
California State Horseman's American Horse Show, Sonoma
"Annie and Mary Day," Blue Lake
Santa Clara County Fair, San Jose
Indian Fair Days, Sierra Mono Museum, North Fork
El Dorado County Fair, Placerville
San Mateo County Fair
Stanislaus County Fair, Turlock
Japanese Culture Bazaar, Sacramento
California State Fair, Sacramento
Oakland Chinatown Streetfest
Petaluma River Festival
Wildwood Days and Peddlers' Fair, Rio Dell
Siskiyou County Fair and Paul Bunyan Jubilee
Calamari Festival, Santa Cruz
Jamestown Pioneer Days
El Dorado Days at Mt. Ranch, San Andreas
Mother Lode Fair and Loggers' Contest, Sonora
Plumas County Fair, Quincy
Pony Express Day, McKinleyville (August 22)
Children's Fairytale Birthday Week, Oakland
Air Round-Up, Red Bluff
Willow Creek Bigfoot Days
Adobe Day, Ide Adobe, Red Bluff
Del Norte County Fair, Crescent City
Gravenstein Apple Fair, Sebastopol
Lake County Fair, Lakeport
Renaissance Pleasure Faire, Novato
Sonoma County Fair, Santa Rosa
Paul Bunyan Days, Fort Bragg
Nevada County Fair, Grass Valley

❖ September

Renaissance Pleasure Faire, Novato
Sausalito Art Festival
Begonia Festival and Sand Castle Contest, Capitola
Monterey Jazz Festival
Mendocino County Fair and Apple Show, Boonville
A la Carte, a la Park, Golden Gate Park, San Francisco

San Francisco Art Festival
Redwood Empire Logging Festival, McKinleyville
Constitution Days, Nevada City
Vintage Festival, Hall of Flowers, Golden Gate Park, San Francisco
Festival of Viewing of the Moon, Japantown, San Francisco
Scottish Games, Santa Rosa
Shasta County InterMountain Fair, McArthur
Gold Country Fair, Auburn
Valley of the Moon Vintage Festival, Sonoma
Pleasanton Pasta Festival
Columbia Admission Day
Blue Grass Festival, Amador County Fairgrounds
Pageant of Fire Mountain, Guerneville
Vintage Car Fair, Fremont
Moon Festival with Chinese Dragon, Chinatown, San Francisco
Opera in the Park, Golden Gate Park, San Francisco
National Indian Observance Day, Crescent City
American Indian Pow Wow, Volcano
Paul Bunyan Days, Fort Bragg
Black Bart Day, San Andreas (Sept. 14)
Atwater Fall Festival
Cedar Grove Pow Wow, Chico
MiWuk Indian Acorn Festival, Tuolumne City
California Prune Festival, Yuba City
Concord Jazz Festival
Indian "Big Time" Days, Amador County
Santa Cruz County Fair, Watsonville
Vintage Festival, Sonoma
LEAP Sand Castle Contest for Architects, Aquatic Park, San Francisco
San Francisco Blues Festival, Justin Herman Plaza and Fort Mason, San
   Francisco
KQED Ice Cream Social, San Francisco
Blessing of the Fishing Fleet, Fisherman's Wharf, San Francisco
Northcountry Fair, Arcata
Carmel Mission Fiesta
Fiesta del Pueblo, San Jose
Porterville Pow Wow
Redwood Invitational Regatta, Big Lagoon, Humboldt County
Oktoberfest, San Mateo Fairgrounds
Oktoberfest, San Jose
Lodi Grape Festival

Fiesta Patrias, Woodland
Castroville Artichoke Festival
Walnut Festival, Walnut Creek
Worldfest, Live Oak Park, Berkeley
Sourdough Days, Sutter Hill
Weaverville Bigfoot Daze
Bridge to Bridge Run, Bay Bridge to Golden Gate Bridge, San Francisco

❖ October

Laguna Seca Grand Prix, Monterey
Fortuna Arts Festival
Sonoma Country Harvest Festival, Santa Rosa
U.S. National Gold Panning Championship, Coloma
Fresno Fair
National Livestock Expo, Cow Palace, San Francisco
Marin Grape Festival, San Rafael
Pumpkin Festival, Half Moon Bay
Spanishtown Art and Pumpkin Festival
Columbia Fiddle and Banjo Contest
Candle Lighter Ghost House, Fremont
Pro-Am Surfing International, Santa Cruz
Old Mill Days, Bale Grist Mill State Historic Park
Redding Children's Art Festival
Fall Festival, Clearlake Oaks
Selma Parade and Band Festival
Johnny Appleseed Day, Paradise
Lumberjack Day, West Point
Harvest Festival, Pacific Grove
Great Sandcastle Building Contest, Carmel
Great Snail Race, Folsom
Oktoberfest, Tahoe City
Old Timers' Day, King City
Columbus Day Festival, San Francisco
Reedley Festival
Chinese Double Ten Celebration, San Francisco
San Francisco International Film Festival
Discovery Day, Bodega Bay
Harvest Hoedown, Healdsburg
Victorian Village Octoberfest, Ferndale

❖ November

North California Boat and Sports Show, Oakland
Christmas Balloon Parade, San Jose (day after Thanksgiving)
Thanksgiving Art Fair, Mendocino
Santa's Steamboat Arrival and Antique Wagon Procession, Petaluma
Teddy Bear Exhibit opens, Lakeport

❖ December

Grandma's Christmas Open House, Anderson Marsh State Historic Park
Dixieland Christmas, Jamestown
Pioneer Christmas, Bale Grist Mill State Historic Park
Christmas at the Mission, Sonoma Mission State Historic Park
Christmas Art and Music Festival, Eureka
Great Dickens Faire, San Francisco
Nutcracker Suite, San Francisco Ballet and Oakland Ballet
Native American Christmas Fair, Sacramento
Los Posada Nativity Procession, Columbia State Historic Park
Currier & Ives Christmas Open House, Sutter Creek
Festival of the Trees, Monterey and San Rafael
Pioneer Christmas, Roaring Camp, Felton
Oakland Temple Christmas Pageant, Oakland
Children's International Craft & Food Fair, Santa Cruz
Lighting of the Tree of Lebanon, Santa Rosa
Native Christmas Tree Ceremony, Sequoia National Park
Christmas Tree Lane, Fresno
Christmas Boat Parade, Eureka
Pioneer Christmas Party, Ide Adobe, Red Bluff
Rice-Pounding Ceremony, Japantown, San Francisco
Miner's Christmas, Columbia
Amador Calico Christmas
San Juan Bautista da Posada Fiesta
Adobe Luminaria Fiesta, Petaluma
Victorian Christmas, Nevada City
Festival of Lights, Volcano, Yountville and Auburn
New Year's Eve Fireman's Ball, Cloverdale
Claim Jumper's New Year's Eve Square Dance, Plymouth

Index

Index by Age Group

6 up

6–14

7 up

Alphabetical Index

FUN PLACES TO GO WITH CHILDREN IN NORTHERN CALIFORNIA

An Appreciation

I'd like to close with a note of special thanks to people who have written with suggestions for this edition of *Fun Places to Go with Children in Northern California.*

Thanks to the Bailey family, Concord; Adina Klein, Jerusalem and Washington, D.C.; Deane Fae, San Mateo; Alexandra Pappas, Stockton; Jeff Hudson, Freedom; Ron Baca, Oakdale; Anna Sherlock, Davis; and Rebecca Honekar, Piedmont.

Thanks, too, to Linda Mathre, Fremont; Lily Liang, Los Altos; Karyn Ruth Cheng, Citrus Heights; Margaret Lukens, Burlingame; Hilary Clayson Lock, Atherton; and Henry Darius, Los Altos, for their suggestions.